SHELBY'S EXPEDITION TO MEXICO

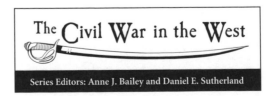

The Civil War in the West

Series Editors: Anne J. Bailey and Daniel E. Sutherland

SHELBY'S
EXPEDITION TO MEXICO

An Unwritten Leaf of the War

By John N. Edwards

Edited and with an introduction by Conger Beasley Jr.

The University of Arkansas Press
Fayetteville
2002

06   05   04   03   02   5   4   3   2   1

Designer: John Coghlan

⊚ The paper used in this publication meets the minimum requirements of the American
National Standard for Permanence of Paper for Printed Library Materials Z39.48-1984.

Library of Congress Cataloging-in-Publication Data

Edwards, John N. (John Newman), 1838–1889.
Shelby's expedition to Mexico : an unwritten leaf of the war / by John N. Edwards ;
edited and with an introduction by Conger Beasley Jr.
p. cm. — (Civil War in the West)
Originally published: Kansas City, Mo. : Kansas City Times Steam Book
and Job Printing House, 1872. With new introd.
Includes bibliographical references (p.) and index.
ISBN 1-55728-732-5 (cloth : alk. paper)
1. Shelby's Expedition to Mexico, 1865. 2. Shelby, Joseph Orville,
1830–1897. I. Beasley, Conger. II. Title. III. Series.
F1233 .E27 2002
917.204'7—dc21
2002007386

In memory of John Shelby Masterman
1928–1999

CONTENTS

SERIES EDITORS' PREFACE

The Civil War in the West has a single goal: to promote historical writing about the war in the western states and territories. It focuses most particularly on the Trans-Mississippi theater, which consisted of Missouri, Arkansas, Texas, most of Louisiana (west of the Mississippi River), Indian Territory (modern-day Oklahoma), and Arizona Territory (two-fifths of modern-day Arizona and New Mexico), but it also encompasses adjacent states, such as Kansas, Tennessee, and Mississippi, that directly influenced the Trans-Mississippi war. It is a wide swath, to be sure, but one too often ignored by historians and, consequently, too little understood and appreciated.

Topically, the series embraces all aspects of the wartime story. Military history in its many guises, from the strategies of generals to the daily lives of common soldiers, forms an important part of that story, but so, too, do the numerous and complex political, economic, social, and diplomatic dimensions of the war. The series also provides a variety of perspectives on these topics. Most importantly, it offers the best in modern scholarship, with thoughtful, challenging monographs. Secondly, it presents new editions of important books that have gone out of print. And thirdly, it premieres expertly edited correspondence, diaries, reminiscences, and other writings by witnesses to the war.

It is a formidable undertaking, but we believe that the Civil War in the West, by focusing on some of the least familiar dimensions of the conflict, significantly broadens understanding of that dramatic story.

The names of Joseph O. Shelby and John N. Edwards are familiar to anyone who has studied the war in the Trans-Mississippi. Some participants in the war as well as some historians believe Jo Shelby was the greatest cavalry commander of the war, North or South. Shelby has also been praised as a master of irregular warfare, and to that extent has been favorably compared to John S. Mosby. But whatever the modern judgments of

Shelby, what he was or seemed to be was crafted to a large extent by John Edwards. Edwards served as Shelby's adjutant during the war and as his chronicler after the conflict. He wrote two books about Shelby, *Shelby and His Men* (1867) and *Shelby's Expedition to Mexico* (1872), that record the wartime and immediate postwar history of the intrepid commander and his Iron Brigade. Most scholars regard the latter volume as the more reliable and valuable of the two.

As the reality of Confederate defeat slowly set in during the spring of 1865, not a few Rebels announced that they would never live under Yankee rule. Instead of returning to their homes, as did the vast majority of soldiers, public officials, and civilian refugees, they fled the South. They scattered in every direction, to the American West, to Canada, to Europe, to South America. Hundreds of "undefeated" Rebels, including Shelby, Edwards, and many men from the Iron Brigade, crossed the Rio Grande into Mexico. Much of what we know about the lives of the Confederates in Mexico comes from Edwards, and the story of their self-imposed exile, which lasted two years for Shelby and most of his band, is as much a part of the war in the West as are the battles and campaigns they waged between 1861 and 1865. First published in 1872 and reissued in 1889, *Shelby's Expedition to Mexico* has been out of print for more than a century. Its republication in this series makes an important document in the history of the Civil War available once more to a wide audience.

This edition of Edwards' book is also better than the original, insofar as it has been skillfully edited and annotated by Conger Beasley Jr. Beasley has identified people, places, and events that Edwards failed to describe in adequate detail, and he has provided background information that puts sometimes puzzling episodes in historical context. Most importantly, Beasley has written an eloquent introduction that tells us about the author of this riveting book, John Edwards. No biography exists for Edwards, and that is unfortunate. Edwards was as fascinating a character who led just as adventurous a life as his hero, Shelby. Someday, Edwards will doubtless have his story told, but until then, Beasley's excellent sketch may serve to introduce him to the world and to reintroduce one of the most fascinating odysseys in American history.

Anne J. Bailey
Daniel E. Sutherland
Series Co-editors

EDITOR'S NOTE

An editor's hand hopefully remains transparent, even in the midst of the most arcane and garbled texts. It is not his or her job to rework the original, but to function as a kind of harmonium through which the spirit and authenticity of the original can pour forth, unaltered and unimpaired. John N. Edwards wrote in a prose style emblematic of the times in which he lived; he tended, with irrepressible enthusiasm, to rhetorical flights that sound contrived and sentimental compared to the austere, hard-boiled renderings we are accustomed to today. He gushed and swooned over matters, such as women, warfare, and the knightly qualities of Confederate warriors, that we have come to regard, in the twenty-first century, with a far more steely eye. And yet, for all his showy flashes, there is something deeply appealing about the story he has to tell. Maybe it has to do with the tumultuous events pertaining to the Civil War in the West, events of which he was an integral part; whatever, he spins a vivid tale, epical in scope, packed with scores of memorable characters, and we cannot fault him too much if the manner in which he tells it seems a bit strained and outmoded to our jaded ears and sensibilities.

Shelby's Expedition to Mexico was first published in 1872; it was then reprinted in 1889 by his widow, Jennie Plattenburg Edwards, shortly after his death that same year. Edwards was a newspaper man, accustomed to deadlines, and he wrote in haste, sloppily at times, eager to get it all down, hell-bent on filling out his allotted word-count. The text of this new edition remains as originally published, except where I have corrected obvious misspellings, inserted missing words, and compensated for typesetting errors. In the end notes, I have identified people, terms, and references germane to the story. A few of the references, such as poetry quotes and popular figures of the era, proved impossible to track down, and I have left them unannotated, which, for any editor, is always a source of frustration.

I first ran across a copy of *Shelby's Expedition to Mexico* some thirty years ago in a used bookstore in downtown Kansas City, Missouri. A first reading piqued my curiosity about the author, the subject, and the book that evolved between them. I remember thinking to myself how incredible the story was, how grandiose and spectacular, and how much it needed to be disseminated to a wider audience. That wish has now come true, and I am grateful to the University of Arkansas Press for making it so.

My heartfelt thanks go to Kevin Brock, formerly of the University of Arkansas Press, for initially entertaining the idea; to Daniel Sutherland, co-editor of the Civil War in the West series, for his superb editorial input; to press director Larry Malley for steering the project through to completion; to Sheridan Logan, one of the revered elders of my hometown, St. Joseph, Missouri, for whetting my curiosity about all things pertaining to John Edwards and Jo Shelby; to Marshall White of St. Joseph, regional historian extraordinaire, who generously opened his private library and archives to me; to Al Kinsall, of Eagle Pass, Texas, director of the Centro de Estudios e Investigaciones Documentados de la Historia de Coahuila y Texas, who plugged so many gaps about Shelby's Rio Grande crossing; and to Betsy Beasley, whose interest and enthusiasm for matters concerning the Border Wars have for so many years sustained and inspired me.

Conger Beasley Jr.
St. Joseph, Missouri
February, 2002

INTRODUCTION

THE SPLENDID PALADIN

THE LIFE AND TIMES OF JOHN N. EDWARDS

1

John Newman Edwards—to give his full name—was born in Front Royal, Virginia, on January 4, 1838. His parents were John and Mary A. (Newman) Edwards, both from Virginia, both from sturdy Anglo-Scots lineage. Background details regarding that lineage are sparse. We know the Edwards family immigrated to Virginia in the eighteenth century. We know, too, that the family's hot-blooded temperament was displayed by the aptly named Colonel Conquest Wyatt, who, at the age of ninety, avenged an insult by pinning his adversary to a door with a knife thrust through the ear.[1]

After a common school education in Warren County, young John Edwards studied Latin and Greek in Washington, D.C. His mother, a woman of strong intellect, encouraged his earliest writing efforts; at age fourteen, he composed his first story.

At the urging of Thomas J. Yerby, an older relative, the family moved to Lexington, Missouri, in the mid-1850s. Young John was first a printer, then editor, of the *Lexington Expositor,* a weekly newspaper owned by a local planter-manufacturer named Oliver Anderson. While still in his teens, during the Missouri-Kansas border dispute, John Edwards wrote inflammatory editorials castigating Yankee squatters working to establish Kansas as a free state. Unfortunately, the few remaining copies of these issues were destroyed in a raid on Lexington by Union guerrillas early in the war.[2]

The young John Edwards did not resemble a fire-breathing secessionist. He was short, slight, soft-spoken, with sandy hair and a quiet demeanor.

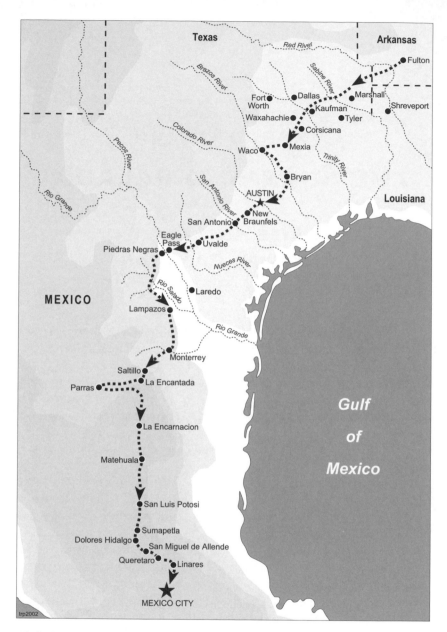

Shelby's expedition from Arkansas to Mexico City.

The mustache he grew to make himself look older drooped delicately from his upper lip. He was inhibited around women and consigned them to a lofty pedestal, thus divesting them of any humanizing qualities. "In his writings," says historian Dan Saults, "no woman sweats, swears, or swills—she only swoons."[3]

Around 1855, after moving to Missouri, Edwards met Joseph Orville Shelby, originally from Kentucky, cousin to future cavalry terror John Hunt Morgan, cousin to future Missouri governor B. Gratz Brown, cousin to future advisor and confidant of Abraham Lincoln, Francis Preston Blair. Short, slim, intense, eight years Edwards's elder—a nervous, edgy man with a piercing stare and clipped manner of speaking—Shelby, nicknamed "Jo" for the initials of his first and middle names, was a blue-chip member of the gentry of entrepreneurs and hemp planters who controlled the economic and social fortunes of the central Missouri River valley. "Jo Shelby was wealthy, John Edwards was poor," says Dan Saults, "but they liked the same things: drinking, fishing, hunting, talking, planning for a time of troubles that lay not far ahead."[4]

Edwards doted on the fierce, intractable Shelby. Early on, he appeared more than willing to sacrifice his own ego to elevate the image of the Confederate leader into a paragon of military and manly virtue. Or perhaps Edwards projected upon the older man all the salient virtues he deemed requisite in a chivalric Southern warrior. Whatever, he followed him into the Kansas border skirmishes, downplaying his own remarkable courage while establishing a solid foundation for the early Shelby legend. What had been a local conflict between Yankee abolitionists and pro-slavery sympathizers for nearly seven years (1854–1861) was about to erupt on a national scale. Shortly after South Carolina troops shelled Union-held Fort Sumter in Charleston harbor in April of 1861, Jo Shelby formed a company of horse-mounted volunteers in the river town of Waverly—the heart of the heart of "secesh" Missouri, settled by planters from Kentucky, Tennessee, and Virginia. Under his energetic leadership, the outfit distinguished itself at the battle of Wilson's Creek in August of 1861, and later that same year at the first battle of Newtonia. In both these encounters, Shelby, according to John Edwards, displayed "an almost infallible divination of his enemy's designs, and a rare analysis which enabled him, step by step, to fathom movements and unravel demonstrations as if he held the printed programme in his hand."[5]

We do not know for sure, but it is likely that Edwards linked up with Shelby in the spring of 1862, when Shelby rode through the Waverly-Lexington area on a recruiting expedition. The intricacies of that symbiotic relationship took shape almost immediately. So completely did Edwards subsume his personality in the glittering image he created for the gifted Shelby that we know a great deal about the latter and very little about the former. Edwards's reticence to speak about his own exploits leaves huge gaps in the record that can only be filled by guesswork and inference. He and Shelby were friends, but to what degree we do not know. Despite the difference in their social stations, Edwards was present at Shelby's wedding in 1858. Obviously, Shelby was a man whose qualities of character touched a responsive chord in the feelings of the younger man.

By all objective standards, Jo Shelby was gifted with every good thing that mattered to the male psyche in the 1860s: good looks, buoyant health, boundless optimism, personal magnetism; plus, at age twenty-one, his father left him an $80,000 trust fund. "He was the finest looking man I ever saw, black hair and handsome features," an Arkansas foot soldier wrote after the war. "He looked like somebody."[6]

Shy, sensitive, impressionable, thoroughly imbued with the code of the *bayard chevalier*, John Edwards went to work for the man, not just as an adjutant, but as a hagiographer of sorts. The terse, plain-spoken Shelby was reluctant to write the obligatory accounts expected of a field commander; Edwards, a natural chronicler, took over this function. What better way to put the best possible spin on his hero's exploits than to write his own version of the official records, which future historians would consult? Edwards's account of the battle of Lone Jack in eastern Jackson County in August of 1862 marks his debut as Shelby's adjutant and amanuensis. Thereafter, Shelby's reports of major and minor conflicts possess a verve, zest, and wealth of literary allusions that could only have flowed from the fecund literary brain of the former *Lexington Expositor* editorialist.

John Edwards may have been something of a fabulist when it came to factual objectivity in his delineation of Shelby's efforts on behalf of the Confederate cause west of the Mississippi, but there is no denying his own personal bravery. He had more horses shot out from under him than anybody in Shelby's command, including Shelby himself. By all accounts he was fearless in battle, always present where the action was hottest. "He was only a boy but he soon became the hero of Shelby's brigade," Major J. F. Stonestreet wrote after the war. "It was a grand sight to see him in battle. He was always where the fight was thickest. He was absolutely devoid of fear."[7]

We would know nothing about his conduct were it not for testimonies such as these. Throughout the war, Edwards steadfastly refused to put anything of himself into his narratives; they were always about others. Why this was we can only speculate. A natural modesty, an ingrained sense of reticence, a troubling fear that even the slightest mention of his own exploits might detract from the ongoing enshrinement of his idol—whatever, there are times when Edwards's aversion to personal utterance seems pathologically disturbing.

In April of 1863, during a raid on the southeast Missouri town of Cape Girardeau, a shell fragment tore away the inside of his leg, and Edwards lay all night on the field without medical care. He was found by federal soldiers and was personally cared for by General John McNeil. He languished in a prison camp near St. Louis for several weeks before being exchanged, in time to rejoin Shelby's brigade for the disastrous assault on Helena, Arkansas, on July 4, 1863.

There is no mention of this ordeal in Edwards's magnum opus about Shelby's wartime exploits, *Shelby and His Men* (1867). All kudos and accounts, gripes and accusations, are attributed to other people. How Edwards felt about anything, we are hard-pressed to discover. Instead of speaking to the reader in a personal voice, he conceals his innermost thoughts by parroting nineteenth-century rhetorical clichés in a flashy stage whisper. "Edwards had a gift for exaggeration, and no ear for contemporary conversations," says Daniel O'Flaherty, Jo Shelby's biographer. "His characters spoke a language never heard on land or sea outside the pages of Sir Walter Scott, his literary model."[8]

He also distorted the facts. Not content with the impressive statistics of Shelby's 1863 raid into central Missouri, Edwards skewed the figures to make Shelby look even better. During forty-one days and fifteen hundred miles of riding, Edwards says, the raiders killed and wounded 600 Federals, captured and paroled as many more. They destroyed ten forts and nearly eight hundred thousand dollars' worth of property, plus a million dollars' worth of supplies. They seized three hundred wagons, forty stands of colors, twelve hundred rifles and revolvers, six thousand horses and mules. All this in a thirty-four-day period between September 22 and October 26, by a cavalry force of 1,200 men, at a cost, says Edwards, of only 150 killed and wounded.[9]

The raid was successful, though in all likelihood not as successful as Edwards claims. Federal commanders reported far fewer casualties. Total Federal losses, says historian Stephen B. Oates, were about 240 killed, wounded, missing, and captured.[10]

Eighteen sixty-four was a grueling year for Shelby's Brigade—the Fourth Missouri Cavalry Brigade, better known by this time as the "Iron Brigade." In March, Union general Nathaniel Banks with some 27,000 men, plus a fleet of gunboats, moved up the Red River to destroy the lucrative cotton supply centers in northwest Louisiana and East Texas. On March 23, a second Federal army under General Frederick Steele marched south out of

Little Rock to rendezvous with Banks at Shreveport. Opposing Banks was a small force under General Richard Taylor. Steele's column, slogging through Arkansas, clashed with several Confederate units, one of which, led by John S. Marmaduke, included Shelby's Brigade. The Rebels inflicted heavy losses on Steele's troops at Camden and Jenkins' Ferry. In Louisiana, Taylor's army of about 13,000 met Banks at Sabine Crossroads (April 8) and Pleasant Hill (April 9) and threw his forces back against the Red River. By the first of June, 1864, the Union campaign was in shambles.

In September there was Price's Raid, the last major effort by a Confederate field command to entice Missouri into the southern fold. Ostensibly for political reasons, Edmund Kirby Smith, commander of the Trans-Mississippi Department, selected General Sterling Price to lead the expedition, when it was obvious to everyone that Jo Shelby, despite his inexperience with large bodies of men, would have been a better choice. The raid called for speed, audacity, and discipline—precisely the qualities that Price lacked. True to form, the Confederate commander—gouty and obese, topping out at three hundred pounds—squandered whatever hope he might have had of dealing the Yankees a major blow with a costly assault on a fortified federal position at Pilot Knob in southeast Missouri. Instead of attacking St. Louis and possibly causing General William T. Sherman to divert troops from his Georgia campaign to defend the vital Missouri metropolis, Price turned west to Jefferson City. Cowed by the defenses ringing the capital, he bypassed it and trundled west like a tortoise, bogged down by a huge wagon train swollen with booty stolen from the very people he was trying to attract to the Confederate cause.

Two Yankee armies, one pursuing west from St. Louis, the other east from Kansas, converged on the sluggish invaders. The climax came on October 23, 1864, at the battle of Westport, in the heart of present-day Kansas City, Missouri, when the Confederates were routed by a flank attack. Amidst the chaos of his retreating army, Price, riding in a carriage driven by a black servant, sent a note to Shelby saying he was the only person who could save the army from annihilation. And save it Shelby did, more than once, during the long, harrowing retreat to the Arkansas line, as he fought against staggering odds at places such as Mine Creek and Newtonia. "Every hill-top was a battlefield, and every bottom stretch drank the blood of some of his soldiers," Edwards wrote of those awful days, with little exaggeration or bravado.[11] An outbreak of smallpox further decimated the ranks; at this bleak time, the heroism of John Edwards shone forth like a beacon. "When the dark days came," wrote Major J. F. Stonestreet, "it was John Edwards who, more than anybody else, inspired hope in the hearts of the men, cheered and encouraged them, and spurred them on to renewed exertions."[12]

The spring of 1865 found the remnants of Shelby's Brigade bivouacked in southwest Arkansas. Word of Robert E. Lee's capitulation at Appomattox was greeted with dismay by many members of the Trans-Mississippi army. The prevailing sentiment, at least initially, was to prolong the fight. After fleeing Richmond in early April, Jefferson Davis was rumored to be making his way west to link up with the fifty thousand troops still under the command of Edmund Kirby Smith. Diehards such as Edwards envisioned a strategic retreat into Mexico, where the troops could regroup. Just when this thought occurred to anyone is difficult to determine. Edwards says, in *Shelby and His Men,* that the idea was first seriously discussed at a conference of Southern governors and Trans-Mississippi generals held in Marshall, Texas, at the end of April.[13] News of Joe Johnston's surrender to Sherman in North Carolina had just trickled in, triggering mass defections. Jefferson Davis seemed to have disappeared off the map. Kirby Smith— pious, soft-spoken, sporting a patriarchal beard—appeared to be wavering in his resolve to continue the struggle. Spurred on by John Edwards, Shelby proposed that Kirby Smith relinquish command; the remnants of the Trans-Mississippi army would then assemble along the line of the Brazos River, where, in Edwards's words, they were "to fight step by step to the Rio Grande, when, in the event of everything else failing [they] would take service with one or the other of the contending parties in Mexico and establish either an Empire or a Republic."[14]

Instead, on June 3, 1865, in an act of perfidy excoriated by Edwards, Kirby Smith surrendered all Confederate troops west of the Mississippi. The Civil War was officially over. Those Confederates still remaining in the field were instructed to proceed to the nearest U.S. Army depot, lay down their arms, and secure paroles. Despite a few defections, the Iron Brigade remained intact. Shelby called the troop to order and asked for volunteers to enter Mexico under the aegis of establishing a Confederate presence south of the Rio Grande. Such a move raised a host of international issues regarding sovereignty and the spectre of imperialist aggression. A cadre of battle-tested troops, well-equipped and superbly led, at loose in a country already torn by factional strife, could significantly alter the balance of power.

But the official government message regarding a possible exodus to Mexico was ambivalent. Early in 1865, Shelby had received a curious message from his cousin, General Francis Preston Blair, confidant of Lincoln, saying that the U.S. government would not be averse to having a force of ex-Confederates cross into Mexico and join forces with Benito Juarez, then fighting against a joint Franco-Austrian effort to establish a European monarchy on Mexican soil, in violation of the Monroe Doctrine. Upon entering Mexico, would the men of the Iron Brigade be regarded as saviors or renegades? Whichever, they were riding into a cauldron of international conflict that would take all of their skill and experience to survive.

As they rode through Texas, Shelby's force, acting independently or upon request, put down outbreaks of civil strife in towns such as Tyler, Waxahachie, and Houston. In Austin, his command fought a vicious gun battle with thugs attempting to rob the state treasury. During the long march from northeast Texas to the Rio Grande, the brigade maintained regular military discipline, riding in columns during the daylight hours, with scouts out ahead and flankers trailing alongside. The men abided by Shelby's strict orders not to forage off the local population; at night, pickets and sentries patrolled the outer perimeter of their camp. From Austin, the men moved through San Marcos and New Braunfels to San Antonio, where they arrived on June 16, 1865.

San Antonio was packed with Confederate personalities fleeing from Federal forces. Louisiana governor Henry Watkins Allen, Missouri governor Thomas C. Reynolds, Judge John Perkins, Commodore Matthew Fontaine Maury, General John Magruder, and General Edmund Kirby Smith were all in town weighing their options regarding exile in Latin America. Word had arrived that Federal authorities were arresting politicos back in the former Confederate states and jailing them without writ of habeas corpus; the mood in San Antonio was defiant and uncompromising.

Shelby used his stay in San Antonio to rearm and reprovision his command. New enlistees joined the ranks, swelling their numbers to several hundred. Just how many troopers rode with the Iron Brigade at any given time between San Antonio and Mexico City is a matter of conjecture. John Edwards cites 1,000, then reduces the tally to 400. Historian Roy Bird puts the number at the end of the march at exactly 813.[15] Robert L. Kerby, author of *Kirby Smith's Confederacy,* says the total amounted to no more than 300 soldiers, plus 200 civilians.[16] A few days later the brigade moved out, headed for El Paso del Aguila, Eagle Pass, on the Rio Grande, so named because of an eagle that flew back and forth across the river to its nest in a cottonwood on the Mexican bank. Across the river from Eagle Pass lay the Mexican village of Piedras Negras, "the place of black stones." Between the two flowed a milky brown stream, wide and deep, which Mexicans called the Rio Bravo del Norte and gringos the Rio Grande.

In charge at Piedras Negras was Governor Andres Viesca, Juarista governor of the Mexican state of Coahuila. He had two thousand men under his command, at least twice as many as Shelby, but he must have had a few misgivings as he watched the Confederates go into camp on a bluff above the river, with their artillery pointed in the direction of the Mexican town. The politics of the situation were complex. The men across from him were ex-Confederates, reportedly in favor of the imperial usurper, Archduke Maximilian of the Austro-Hungarian empire, who, with the connivance of Napoleon III and units of the French army, had toppled the popularly elected Benito Juarez and sent him into exile to the desert provinces of the north.

Viesca was elegant and polished, eager to make a deal. After a two-day palaver, he made an offer he did not think Shelby could possibly refuse. In return for Shelby throwing in with Juarez, Viesca offered him military control of the provinces of Coahuila, Nuevo Leon, and Tamaulipas—practically all of northeast Mexico—with Viesca retaining civilian authority. That night, in camp on the Texas side of the river, Shelby put the proposal to a vote of the entire brigade. To a man, they voted against joining Juarez, opting for Maximilian instead.

Ponder for a moment what might have happened had the men of the Iron Brigade cast their vote for Juarez. It is pure speculation, but the course of North American history might have turned out differently. Confederates had long envisioned a refuge in northern Mexico where they could reestablish their traditional way of life. French troops to the south would have welcomed a buffer between them and the Yankee nation. Shelby's troops could very well have policed the area, purging it of outlaws and brigands; whether the Union would finally have sent troops across the river to unseat Shelby is impossible to say. General Philip H. Sheridan, in charge of the occupying forces in Texas, revealed many years later at a dinner attended by Shelby in Washington, D.C., that he was eager to match his skills against the legendary Rebel.[17] The Monroe Doctrine, formulated early in the country's history, decades before the country possessed the muscle to enforce it, was one of the sacred cows of U.S. foreign policy; with a hundred thousand men still in uniform at the close of the Civil War, it is quite plausible that Sheridan would have been sent across the river to uproot a neo-Confederate fiefdom.

Shelby would have been virtual dictator of three Mexican provinces, something that went against the grain of his character. Granted, he was a martinet; granted, he drove his men unmercifully, but they in turn revered him and did what he told them. Even discounting the possibility of a Philip Sheridan intervention, the odds were stacked against a successful Shelby rule in northeast Mexico. Once he had neutralized the French threat in the south, Benito Juarez would have turned his attention to the newcomers in the north. Moreover, Shelby's men, no matter how comfortable their life in these desert states, would have wanted to return home. They were

Protestants in a Catholic land, Anglos in an Hispanic environment, agriculturalists from the fertile valleys and broad rivers of the Middle Border.

Instead of throwing in with Juarez, who was backed by the U.S. government and destined to emerge triumphant in the struggle with the foreign power, Shelby's men voted to enlist in yet another Lost Cause. This doughty band of *beau sabreurs,* so fulsomely celebrated by John Edwards, was also racist, scornful of dark-skinned people; when put to the test, they demonstrated that they were patently unwilling to support a Mexican leader of Indian descent. Instead, they were swayed by the sham chivalries of the European interlopers, presided over by a weak-chinned prince and his mentally disturbed wife, daughter of the king of Belgium, who stirred reveries of knightly fealty in tough, pragmatic men who should have known better. They were imperialists, the vanguard of a new breed of American pioneers, eager to extend their influence into foreign places. Of Shelby, says Edwards, "His ideas were all of conquest. If he dreamed at all, his dreams were of Cortez."[18] In one bold stroke then, Shelby set the diplomatic tone of the new postwar America—expansionist, confrontational, fortune-seeking, acquisitive—and all this a good thirty years before the blatant land grab of the 1898 Spanish-American War.

Historian Edwin Adams Davis puts this pivotal moment on the banks of the Rio Grande into perspective: "So when the vote was taken at Eagle Pass, the men who had been living in a heroic, though bloody fantasy were willing to gamble on a bloody, unrealistic future rather than on a more realistic opportunity, in order to continue their supposed heroics by marching into a foreign country, not in the cause of democracy, but in the cause of kings and queens. . . . It was heroic, magnificent, but it was not sound, considered judgment."[19]

The exact date that Jo Shelby led his men across the Rio Grande into Mexican territory is not known. John Edwards does not say; Edwin Davis claims it was the Fourth of July;[20] historian Robert Kerby thinks it was June 26, 1865.[21] Whatever, the date was memorialized with a touching ceremony. The brigade drew up in dress parade along the north bank of the Rio Grande (though not even the location is known for certain; it could very well have been on the Mexican side). Out front of the first rank floated the Stars and Bars, the last flag to fly over an organized Confederate force; the flag, tattered and rent, had been presented to the brigade two years earlier by the women of a small Arkansas town. Each of the five colonels— Ben Elliott, D. A. Williams, George Gordon, Alonzo Slayback, and Yandell Blackwell—took hold of a corner or edge of the banner and splashed on foot into the river. At the last moment, Jo Shelby, overcome with emotion, placed the black ostrich plume that had decorated his campaign hat onto the flag. Weighted with a rock, the flag was then lowered into the water.

2

How long the brigade remained in Piedras Negras after crossing the Rio Grande is not known. Edwards is fuzzy about dates at times. A lot happened during their stay in the border town, including a nasty shoot-out over an accusation that some of Shelby's men had stolen horses in Texas and ridden them over the border. Once he recovered from the shock of Shelby's refusal to become Benito Juarez's northern military commander, Viesca tried to cut several more deals, including the purchase of Shelby's entire battery of ten cannon. Shelby knew that on the long march to Mexico City he could take only what could be carried in saddle bags or on pack animals. He decided to divest himself of his battery, most of his supplies, and many of his rifles. When questioned in later life by reporter George Creel about the wisdom of selling off his artillery to the Mexicans, who vastly outnumbered him and who could turn on him at any moment and annihilate his command, Shelby replied with typical aplomb, "You seem to forget, sir, that we still had our side arms."[22]

Shelby's command rode south over a grassless plain, dotted with mesquite and chaparral, fissured with arroyos that wound back across the dry ground in the direction of the Rio Grande. Buzzards glided in sluggish circles. The sun blazed like a molten orb. The vast emptiness of this forbidding land was intimidating to these men from Missouri and Arkansas, accustomed to green fields and generous rivers. Camp time provided the only respite from the grueling monotony of the march. Once they had rested and watered their horses, Shelby ordered them to drill, which never failed to provoke an outburst of complaints. "Throughout the march to the City of Mexico, Shelby never relaxed this old habit," says Edwin Davis. "They were in dangerous country, and a trained company would survive where an untrained troop would be shot to pieces."[23]

Many miles into that hot, wretched country, they encountered a trio of deserters from the French Foreign Legion, a precursor of what was to come as enthusiasm for Napoleon III's venture in the New World began to wane among the rank and file shipped out to serve him. At a crossing of the Sabinas River, some eighty miles south of Piedras Negras, they fought a savage engagement against a combined force of Indians and Juaristas. Two hundred enemy dead were later counted. Shelby's losses were severe: twenty-seven killed and thirty-seven wounded. The brigade rested at the Sabinas crossing for nearly a week before pushing on for Mexico City.

Monterrey was a burgeoning metropolis of several thousand people, located on a plateau shaded with fragrant orange and lemon groves. When Shelby arrived sometime in July, he found the town full of ex-Confederates; several state governors were present, as well as former field generals such as John Magruder, Sterling Price, and Thomas Hindman. The town was under the military command of Colonel Pierre Jean Joseph Jeanningros, who held it with a mixed force of five thousand French regulars and loyal Mexican troops.

Shelby proposed that he be granted the use of a seaport on the Pacific or the Gulf of California as a conduit through which to funnel the thousands of enlistees from the United States clamoring to enter Mexico to establish a Confederate kingdom. Jeanningros told Shelby that Marshal Achille Bazaine, supreme commander of European forces in Mexico, had forbade him to march to the Pacific, and ordered him instead to proceed to Mexico City.

On September 3, 1865, the troop rode into Mexico City, the most fabulous city in the Western Hemisphere, with a quarter million people, located on a high plateau, ringed by snow-capped volcanoes. Two days later, Shelby and Edwards were received by the emperor and Marshal Bazaine. The emperor was in his early thirties, over six feet tall, with a high forehead, blond hair, creamy complexion, and a yellow beard which fell in a billowing wave to his chest. After a brief exchange of pleasantries, Shelby offered the services of his men to spearhead a fighting force which he was confident would soon swell to forty thousand exiles. Much to his amazement, the emperor turned him down, saying that he did not wish to jeopardize any future relationship with the United States by employing ex-Confederates.

A few minutes before noon on September 5, 1865, the last fighting unit of the Confederacy, the invincible Iron Brigade, disbanded in Mexico City. The Fourth Missouri Cavalry, to give it its official designation, had never been defeated, whether by Union armies or Juarista rebels or the French in the service of Emperor Maximilian. That day at high noon in the Mexican capital, Brigadier General Joseph Orville Shelby faced his men, who had loyally followed him through countless battles and skirmishes, for the last time, the guidon bearer at his side. The plaza was jammed with thousands of Mexicans, the streets thronged with peons, the balconies packed with elegant Creoles and French military personnel. The day was pleasant, cloudless, cool for early September. Shelby spoke briefly, less than ten minutes. Then, at a signal, the guidon bearer set fire to the pennant, and in strained, sorrowful silence the men of the Iron Brigade watched their tattered symbol of honor and bravery disappear in a curl of smoke. As the final shred of the pennant fell flaming to the ground, the bugler rang out a blast and the men snapped to attention next to their mounts. Shelby then walked along the lines, shaking hands with each man, patting them on the shoulder, calling them by their first names, recalling half-forgotten incidents, straightening a collar or buttoning a button with trembling hands. Many of the men wept openly. The bugle call sounded again, and Shelby swung onto his horse. The order ran down the line, "Prepare to mount." The men stood to horse. "Mount!" The men swung up in a smart, synchronized move, their right legs snapping across their saddles. Shelby took his position at the head of the line, and the brigade passed in full review to the huge audience, first at a walk, then at a canter, finally at a gallop, which quickly intensified into a wild battle charge as the troopers screeched the high-pitched Rebel yell for the last time.[24]

"Mexico City under the Empire was another Paris," says Daniel O'Flaherty, "although with the advent of Shelby's borderers the paseos and boulevards began to take on some of the overtones of the Wild West, the American Civil War, and Election Day in Missouri."[25] The citizens, dressed in Parisian finery or Indian blankets, were either very rich or very poor. With monarchial largesse, to the sound of military bands playing French and Mexican songs, Maximilian and Carlota clattered around the plazas every evening in a topless carriage, where they were bowed to by dandified Creoles and their dark-eyed ladies.

Edwards went to work for the *Mexican Times,* funded by Maximilian, who saw the need for an expatriate newspaper and underwrote it for ten thousand dollars. Henry Watkins Allen, former newspaperman and governor of Louisiana, was appointed editor, with Edwards as his assistant. The first issue rolled off the press on September 16, 1865. Edwards was thoroughly enamored of his new job. He loved Mexico City; he loved the climate and the swirl of life in the streets. A bachelor with no home ties tugging at his heartstrings, he was free to sample any aspect of the city that piqued his fancy.

Predictably, too, he fell under the spell of Their Majesties, Maximilian and Carlota, and wrote about them with the slavish devotion of a courtier. He was to mourn the empress all his days; when she was confined to a madhouse in Europe, he wrote the famous editorial "Poor Carlota," originally published in the *Kansas City Times,* May 29, 1870, which was reprinted all over the English-speaking world. Says Daniel O'Flaherty, "It was such an editorial as Galahad might have written of Guinevere."[26]

Four letters to his family in Virginia and Missouri survive from that period. Shortly after arriving in Mexico City, he wrote to his two sisters, Edmonia and Fanny, that Maximilian and Carlota were "very favorably disposed to Confederates, and ere long our party of exiles hopes to be well settled."[27]

On April 6, 1866, he wrote them again, saying he had had no word from them in many months. A note of anxiety and loneliness pervades the letter. "I would be willing to shorten my life by ten years to be with you tonight."[28] He confessed to working sixteen hours a day, but was still confident of success. He had purchased half a farm at Carlota, a region midway between Mexico City and Vera Cruz, which had been set aside by the empress for Confederate exiles.

The next letter, to sister Fanny in Leesburg, Virginia, is dated September 18, 1866. Henry Watkins Allen had died, and as the surviving partner in the newspaper venture, Edwards had to pay all the expenses. Maximilian had chosen not to renew his subsidy, and Edwards, beset with bills and creditors, had to suspend publication of the *Mexican Times* for several weeks. Despite this setback, his optimism was unquenchable. "I will succeed," he wrote Fanny, adding, "until I win gold I cannot come back."[29]

That same day, Edwards wrote to his brother Tom and asked him to come to Mexico, offering to send him money for the voyage and to set him up in business once he got settled. Ever the courtly brother, Edwards closed by saying, "I want above all things for us to be again united and to go to work bravely and manfully for a home and an independence for our sisters."[30]

By November the *Mexican Times* was in serious trouble. Edwards was no businessman; he did not understand how to market his enterprise; when December rolled around, he had to put the paper on the block. The *Times* was sold at an undisclosed price to an American named B. C. Barksdale, who ran a successful sewing-machine agency in Mexico City.

Edwards left the *Times* on December 5, 1866. Earlier that summer, as the newspaper began to falter, as his fellow exiles commenced to bicker and fight, as the dream of a tropical empire began to sputter and fade, Edwards penned a passage which aptly summed up his personal creed: "Life is very brief and commonplace, but crest it with a crown, deck it with the glory and grandeur of royalty illumined by great and heroic deeds, and it floats away in an eternal sea of history and renown."[31]

3

John Edwards arrived back in Missouri in April of 1867. His stint as editor and chief writer at the *Mexican Times* had deepened his commitment to journalism, and once he returned to Missouri he sought employment at the *St. Louis Republican*. The climate in his adopted state was precarious. Victorious Unionists had rammed through the state legislature a vindictive reprisal against pro-Southerners known as the Drake Constitution. Former Confederates were not only disenfranchised in Missouri, they were forbidden to teach, preach, practice law, perform marriage ceremonies, or engage in corporate business.[32]

These severe measures did not prevent Edwards from forming an alliance with Colonel John C. Moore, another Confederate veteran, who, with the backing of the R. B. Drury Company, launched the *Kansas City Times* in 1868. Edwards remained with the *Times* until 1873 as chief editorial writer, tweaking the noses of the Unionists at every opportunity. On May 12, 1872, he wrote a panegyric to the memory of William Clarke Quantrill, which must have stirred the hackles of those ex-bluecoats who had chased the wily guerrilla through the dense woods of western Missouri.

The battle to resurrect and preserve in nostalgic amber the reputations of the Southern border warriors had begun in earnest. This battle was part of a movement that eventually engulfed the entire South. "Lost Cause literature" it has been called, and instead of on the battlefield, it was played out in magazines, memoirs, speeches, and veterans' reunions over the next thirty years. At the root of it was the "better man" concept, which posited the view that the war was a grand epic fought by genuine heroes such as Robert E. Lee, Jeb Stuart, and Stonewall Jackson against the "churlish Saxons" of Yankeedom, with their heretical ideas of industrialism, mongrelization of the white race, and Jacobin theories of excessive democracy. "The down-fall of empire is always the epoch of romance,"[33] wrote Albion Tourgee, and that spirit not only permeated the pages of Edwards's two books about the Iron Brigade, it fueled his effusive reappraisal of psychopathic bushwhackers such as Quantrill, "Bloody" Bill Anderson, and Archie Clements. "It was a war of races," Edwards declared in *Shelby and His Men*. "It was Puritan against Cavalier; Patrician against Proletarian; grim fanatics, who, like Cromwell's followers, carried bibles in their belts and iron pots on their heads, against the descendants of those men who died for Charles the First, and shed blood like water rather than forgo a rollicking song or sing psalms through their nostrils."[34]

Edwards's personal life underwent an important change at this time. On March 3, 1871, he married his cousin, Mary Virginia "Jennie" Plattenburg of Dover, Missouri, in a ceremony performed at Jo Shelby's residence, outside Aullville, Lafayette County, Missouri. Jennie's parents objected to the union on the grounds of the proximity of their bloodlines, but Edwards, with typical élan, ignored their objections and eloped with his bride. Three children were born of the marriage.

In 1873 Edwards moved back to St. Louis to become an editorial and feature writer, first for the *Dispatch,* then for the *Times.* It was while at work on the *Times* that he fought a bloodless duel with Colonel Emory S. Foster, editor of the *St. Louis Journal,* a rival newspaper. The origin of the affair grew out of an invitation to former Confederate president Jefferson Davis to address the Winnebago County Fair, in Illinois. On August 25, 1875, Edwards penned an article in the *Times* objecting to the intolerant spirit of those who opposed Davis's appearance. The *Journal* took exception to the tone of Edwards's piece and accused him of blatant falsification of the facts concerning the matter.

Edwards demanded a retraction of what he deemed offensive language. Colonel Foster disavowed any personal allusion to Edwards but declined to retract the language. A bristling correspondence ensued, to which Edwards issued a challenge. The assignation was set for the fourth day of September, 1875, between the hours of 6 and 7 P.M., in a grassy meadow north of the town of Rockford, Illinois. At a prearranged signal, both men fired their pistols and missed. Edwards, excitable as always, demanded to fire another round. Foster put an end to the lunacy by declining another chance to discharge his weapon. He was the challenged party, and, as he felt no personal animosity toward his antagonist, he wasn't particularly anxious to draw blood.[35]

Following the war, as a powerful and influential editor-writer for several major Missouri newspapers, Edwards sought to defend the reputations of former guerrilla fighters such as Frank and Jesse James, who experienced difficulty adjusting to peacetime life.

The vindictive retribution against ex-Confederates as embodied in the 1865 Drake Constitution made going straight for some former bushwhackers a difficult task. The economic conditions in the state were appalling. Land was worth no more than ten dollars an acre; railroads controlled by eastern consortiums charged outrageous fees to local farmers to haul their crops to market; money in general was largely manipulated by banks whose creditors resided out of state.[36] Four years of war—actually eleven years, counting the seven years of Kansas-Missouri border strife preceding the firing on Fort Sumter in 1861—had ravaged the landscape of western Missouri, leaving it barren and unproductive.

On December 7, 1869, the Daviess County Savings Association in Gallatin, Missouri, was robbed in broad daylight by a party of gunmen who entered town firing their six-shooters in the air. While Frank James and others stood guard outside, Jesse and a companion entered the bank on the public square and looted it of eighty thousand dollars. During the robbery, Jesse, irritated by the cashier's reluctance to hand over the goods, gunned him down in cold blood. John W. Sheets, the slain cashier, may have been mistaken for a man named S. P. Cox, who was known to have collaborated in the killing of Confederate guerrilla Bill Anderson in 1864.

In the flurry of accusations following the heist, Jesse James, displaying the instincts of a budding media star, was anxious to clear his name of any wrongdoing. He enlisted the aid of John Edwards, then editor of the newly formed *Kansas City Times*. In June of 1870, the *Times* published an open letter to Missouri governor Joseph McClurg, signed by Jesse James, heavily doctored by Edwards, that stated, "I deny the charge [of having robbed the Gallatin bank]. There is not a word of truth in it."[37]

The letter regarding the Gallatin affair was the first of many missives sent by Jesse James in his bid to put a positive spin upon the perception that he was a common outlaw. Edwards would prove to be not only Jesse's greatest ally, but an astute public relations mentor. During their long association, which lasted until Jesse's death in 1882, the two men discovered that they could mutually benefit from one another while remaining true to the Rebel cause.

Not content with the occasional article, Edwards in 1877 published a book entitled *Noted Guerrillas,* which presents die-hard bushwhackers such as Quantrill, Bill Anderson, and Archie Clements as mythic figures shrouded in a phony cloak of nobility and brotherhood borrowed from Sir Walter Scott's renditions of the Anglo-Scots border wars. The book is Edwards's worst and presents him at his most egregious. In Edwards's eyes, Quantrill and company were little more than ordinary farm boys, stirred to action by unprovoked outrages from Yankee demons who rode over from Kansas to burn, loot, and kill.

Little wonder that pariahs such as Jesse and Frank James were eternally grateful for Edwards's efforts to rehabilitate their reputations. Jesse showed his gratitude by presenting the glib penman with a gold watch (which Edwards claims he did not accept) and by naming his firstborn child, a son, Jesse Edwards James.

Jesse James was assassinated by Bob Ford on the morning of April 3, 1882, in the living room of a rented house overlooking downtown St. Joseph, Missouri, where he was staying incognito with his wife and two small children.

With Jesse gone, there was little left for Frank James to do but give himself up. Like Jesse, Frank was weary of outlaw life, the chronic stress and secretiveness, skulking about under the guise of multiple identities. Like Jesse, Frank had a young family and devoted wife, whom he wished to reward for years of unwavering loyalty with a safer, more comfortable life. Shortly after Jesse's death, he began a clandestine correspondence with Edwards to discover what might result were he to turn himself in.

The full story of the behind-the-scenes negotiations for the surrender of Frank James has never been revealed, but it is safe to say that John Edwards, meeting behind closed doors with Governor Thomas T. Crittenden, played a pivotal role. He most likely wrote the long letter Frank sent to the governor on September 30, 1882, confessing his disenchantment with the fugitive life and asking the governor if there was any hope of amnesty. The letter was signed, "Yours contritely and hopefully, Frank James."[38]

On the night of October 4, 1882, Edwards and Frank James arrived in the Missouri state capital of Jefferson City on a creaky, eastbound train. They registered at the fashionable McCarty House as "Jno. Edwards, Sedalia," and "B. F. Winfrey, Marshall, Mo." Around five the next afternoon, they emerged from the hotel. They walked over the capitol grounds, up the hill, through the door of the governor's mansion, and down the hall to the private offices of Governor Crittenden.

Several officials invited to witness the event were busy caucusing among themselves and took little notice of Major Edwards and his companion. It was not until Frank James pulled back his coat and unbuckled his pistol belt and handed it over to the governor that the room grew impressively quiet. "Governor, I am Frank James," the stranger declared. "I surrender my arms to you. . . . They have not been out of my possession since 1864. . . . I now give them to you personally."[39]

It is perhaps not too much of an exaggeration to say that with this gesture the civil war in Missouri, a bitter conflict lasting twenty-eight years, from the opening salvo in 1854 between abolitionists and slaveholders until this final moment in the Missouri governor's mansion in the fall of 1882, came to a peaceful, dignified close.

Edwards attended the trial, remaining discretely in the background. The trial convened in Gallatin, Missouri, on August 20, 1883, at ten o'clock sharp, inside a packed courthouse. A few days later the venue was changed to the opera house to accommodate the throngs of spectators. As if sensing the end of an era, reporters from every newspaper in the state flocked to the little town to listen attentively as the prosecution and defense presented their cases. At four o'clock on the afternoon of September 6, 1883, the jury returned a verdict of not guilty. Enthusiastic applause erupted in the room, which the presiding judge had to gavel into silence. Frank James remained stonily unmoved by the news. His wife, unable to contain her joy, rose from her seat and bowed to the jury.

In January of 1887, at the prodding of his close friend Morrison Munford, John Edwards left the *St. Joseph Gazette* and took up employment again at the *Kansas City Times*. During the past fifteen years, he had bounced around from newspaper to newspaper, and Munford was convinced that the *Times* offered the most congenial place for Edwards to showcase his diverse talents. Newspapers had grown enormously in prestige and influence in post–Civil War America; they were the medium by which the majority of literate Americans received not only the bulk of their information, but a steady stream of learned opinions on an endless variety of topics. In his new job at the *Times*, Edwards was pretty much free to write about whatever he wanted: religion, literature, politics, science. It was an era when a man, even a self-educated man of Edwards's talents, could know a little about a lot of different subjects. If he could write about those subjects with lucidity and enthusiasm, he was liable to find himself lionized by a public hungry for news about the outside world. "What he did in these last years of his life . . . is known to the world," Morrison Munford said in a eulogy to his friend after his death in 1889, "but how much of effort and endeavor, of strife and contention he had to endure, and the fierce contest he waged against his only enemy day and night, no one can know, except those who knew him."[40]

We have a photo of Edwards taken around this time. His face is round and cherubic, the skin soft and pale. The forehead is high, the hair receding to a clipped thatch crowning his oval skull. He wears a light-colored suit with a vest and a white shirt tabbed at the collar by some kind of stud or stick pin. His nose is long, fleshy at the tip. His eyes radiate a kind of tender sorrow; they appear light-colored, laced with wistful melancholy. His lips are completely veiled by a wispy mustache that dribbles to a pudgy chin. He looks nothing like a fearsome bushwhacker or a veteran of the Iron Brigade. There is something soft and mild about him, meek perhaps. He looks like a clerk, or an aging choirboy. It is hard to imagine him challenging anyone to a duel, or writing a vitriolic editorial in support of the James boys, or riding a horse through a hail of bullets.

Edwards's "only enemy" was the demon of drink, which tormented him all his adult life. Over the next seven years, he struggled to kick the habit. He tried various cures, including checking himself into a sanitarium in Illinois. Nothing worked. Partway through yet another series of treatments, he wrote Munford a glowing letter, claiming that he now had "no more desire to drink than if whiskey were prussic acid."[41] After a few weeks of sobriety, he slipped back into his old habits.

Death came with comparative ease to John Newman Edwards. The immediate cause, in the words of the Reverend George Plattenburg, who delivered the eulogy at his funeral, was "inanition of the cardiac nerves,"[42] heart failure of some sort, no doubt fostered by his prolonged debauches, the stress resulting therefrom, plus the medical consequences of the various cures he had tried. He expired at approximately 9:40 A.M.,

Saturday, May 4, 1889, in a room at the McCarty House in Jefferson City, where he and Frank James had spent the night together seven years before. He was fifty-one years old.

News of his death spread quickly. Edwards had been a frequent visitor to the capital, attending all the sessions of the Missouri state legislature for the past eighteen years. He was well known to a majority of the members of the general assembly, as well as to state officials and people in the street. His reputation as a journalist and editor transcended the boundaries of Missouri. "For twenty years he was recognized and acknowledged as the most gifted writer in the West," said the Reverend Plattenburg at the funeral services.[43]

The Missouri Senate passed a resolution at their afternoon session expressing profound regret. In the House, a similar resolution was unanimously adopted. That evening a number of senators and representatives visited the McCarty House to pay their respects to the famed journalist.

The following day a special car provided by the Missouri Pacific was placed at the disposal of the family to convey the body to its final resting place in the hamlet of Dover, Lafayette County, Missouri. Tributes poured in from all over the country, from newspapers as far away as New York City and Pueblo, Colorado. Personal tributes poured in as well, from public figures and total strangers who knew him only by name and reputation. Jo Shelby, who had fallen out of favor with former Confederates for having been appointed U.S. marshal of western Missouri by a Republican president (Chester A. Arthur), remained spotless and without sin in Edwards's pantheon of heroes. The admiration was mutual; upon hearing of the death of his former adjutant and comrade-in-arms, Shelby said, "God never created a more noble, magnanimous, and truer man than John N. Edwards."[44]

4

John Edwards belongs to a special category, the warrior-writer, men of action who, in addition to experiencing combat, write about the experience with insight and flair. They are usually not professional military men, and the books they write are not dry accounts of their maneuvers in the face of enemy fire and why they behaved as they did. For the most part they are passionate amateurs, attracted to war for complex personal reasons, eager to define their identities in the context of an experience in which all is revealed, or eclipsed, by the hum of a bullet. Leo Tolstoy, Stephen Crane, and T. E. Lawrence belong to this group; war—the experience of war—endowed them with an authenticity, a sense of self, that no other endeavor could possibly match.

To experience war is one thing, to write about it another. Many combatants compose a memoir about their experiences as a way of coming to terms with the desolation and horror; the book is usually a one-time effort, an act of purgation, an effort at accommodation, before getting on with their lives. For John Edwards, writing was his lifeblood; there was nothing else, other than a soldier, that he ever wanted to be.

The image of the soldier dying young in knightly splendor, a literary convention since the Middle Ages, haunted the imagination of John Edwards. Noble, brave, true, a paragon of virtues and manly values, such a figure embodied the promise of a meaningful death, the death that resonates down through the ages and provides a fitting example for future generations to emulate. The literary models for such a death abound in the Arthurian legends and medieval epics such as *El Cid* and *The Song of Roland*.

Edwards was one of the last propagandists of the willful glorification of war. That kind of writing touched all the right buttons, and he embraced it with an enthusiasm that belied the depth of his experience and the keenness of his intelligence. He uncritically accepted the conventions of war handed down to him by an older generation of writers and reveled in the heraldic figures that cropped up in his consciousness like so many cardboard cutouts. He was incapable of distancing himself ironically from the chivalric figures that stirred his imagination; in his world, there were only two kinds of combatants, heroes and lesser folk, and naturally the people he knew and fought with belonged to the former category.

Consider his account of the wounding of Colonel David Shanks, a battalion commander of the Iron Brigade, during the 1864 raid into Missouri. "There he [Shanks] lay bleeding fearfully upon the cold damp ground, the red sun of autumn shining fitfully upon his upturned face, pale and drawn with agony. . . . Very soon General Shelby came to the fatal spot, and all of Shanks' features, wan and worn with pain, were lighted up with a tenderness and joy inexpressible, as his loved leader bent over him with a heart too sick for words. . . . The parting was solemn and deeply sad. A few words of hope he did not feel; a few tears hot and scalding from eyes unused to weep—a long, lingering, fond good-bye, and Shelby rode swiftly away, not daring to look back upon the spot where he had left his flower of chivalry."[45]

Contemporaneous with this idealization, a new kind of writing about war was being formulated on American battlefields in the 1860s. John W. DeForest and Ambrose Bierce, veterans of the same war, encountered a different reality, which they wrote about in a fresh and compelling fashion. Consider this description of a badly wounded man in Bierce's story, "What I Saw of Shiloh:"

He lay face upward, taking in his breath in convulsive, rattling snorts, and blowing it out in sputters of froth which crawled creamily down his cheeks, piling itself alongside his neck and ears. A bullet had clipped a groove in his skull, above the temple; from this the brain protruded in bosses, dropping off in flakes and strings. I had not previously known one could get on, even in this unsatisfactory fashion, with so little brain. One of my men whom I knew for a womanish fellow, asked if he should put his bayonet through him. Inexpressibly shocked by the cold-blooded proposal, I told him I thought not; it was unusual, and too many were looking.[46]

The difference in tone and detail between the two passages is so extreme as to make one question whether the two writers actually witnessed the same war. With Edwards we have stock stuff, a figurative conceit, stiff and predictable. With Bierce we have a tone that modern readers can instantly identify—arch, wry, ironic, sarcastic, self-mocking—encapsulating a raft of complex emotions, from the horrific to the humorous.

Edwards wrote a hyper-inflated prose spun off from older literary models such as Sir Walter Scott and Alexander Dumas. A decade earlier, Leo Tolstoy, in the *Sebastopol Sketches* (1860), was just beginning to invent a language capable of parsing the experience of war into a credible narrative. And while that language would not reach its apotheosis until the generation of World War I writers (Ernest Hemingway, Robert Graves, Henri Barbusse), other Civil War soldier-writers such as Bierce and DeForest endeavored to give uninflected accounts of what they saw and experienced. By temperament, such an effort was alien to Edwards. He was too steeped in the mock-heroic tradition of the worst Romantic hacks. What he observed and felt, he distanced himself from through a facile use of allusion and euphemism. Instead of provoking outrage and disgust, the sight of blood inspired a rapturous litany of ornamental symbols that spangled his sentences like shiny medallions, detracting from the very figures he wished to exalt.

Edwards is firmly grounded in the belles-lettres tradition of Southern literature. Sidney Lanier, Albion Tourgee, and John Esten Cooke, to name but three, exude a refined and rarefied air in their postwar works that obscures the realities brooding under the languid surface of their aspirated prose. Add to this the tradition of public oratory, long a staple of Southern (male) self-expression. Missouri artist George Caleb Bingham painted a genre picture, entitled *Stump Speaking* (1854), which features a politico addressing a crowd of rapt admirers. The man leans out over a plank pulpit, hands extended, as if exhorting his listeners to pay close attention to what he has to say. To hold such an audience spellbound with a torrent of words, larded with classical allusions, was to exercise a unique personal power; it was one of the primary forms of entertainment in the mid-nineteenth century, a kind of precursor to today's performance art. It meant you were somebody, an important figure, educated and distinctive, an oracle of sorts, a genuine character, the embodiment of the Southern beau ideal.

Following the war, the onslaught of industrialism and the depredations of the Gilded Age cast a gloomy pall over the nation. With the influx of factories and immigrants, cities became harsher and uglier. The spiritual optimism of the prewar transcendentalists and the plein-air enthusiasm of the painters of the Hudson River School soured into the gritty realism of Stephen Crane's *Maggie, A Girl of the Streets*. Newspaper writing cultivated brevity and precision, spelling the death knell to the tangled rhythms of "stump" prose stylists such as John Edwards. His long, looping sentences, bolstered by a succession of dependent clauses, strung out in biblical cadences, reinforce the urgency of its fundamental purpose, which is to create a mythos that his reader-listeners can submit to without reservation or doubt. And while Edwards was largely preaching to the choir, that audience could never get enough of what he had to say. Speaking of Edward Everett, the great orator who delivered the keynote address at the Gettysburg commemoration services in November of 1863, critic Garry Wills says that he "aspired to more than mere accuracy. Along with [George] Bancroft and other romantic historians of his time, he meant to create a tradition that would inspire as well as inform. Like the [Ancient Greek] orators—and dramatists—he knew the power of symbols to create a people's political identity."[47]

5

Shelby's Expedition to Mexico: An Unwritten Leaf of the War was first published in 1872 by the *Kansas City Times* Steam Book and Job Printing House. Few copies of the original edition survive today. In 1889 the book was republished by his widow, Jennie Edwards, along with a festschrift of tributes and eulogies to her recently deceased husband. Between 1919 and 1923, the *Missouri Historical Review* reprinted the book in nine separate installments. In 1964, the Steck Company of Austin, Texas, reprinted a facsimile version of the 1889 edition.

It is believed that the book was mostly composed around 1866, when Edwards was living in Mexico. Presumably, as Shelby's adjutant, Edwards kept some kind of journal during the long journey from Eagle Pass, Texas, to the City of Mexico. Trained as a journalist, he was accustomed to writing for deadlines; he played loose with the facts, and what he could not verify he frequently made up. Unlike *Shelby and His Men*—a history of the war west of the Mississippi from the perspective of the Iron Brigade—we have precious few accounts of the Mexico City march with which to compare it. Two journals survive, kept by men who accompanied Shelby—one by Thomas Westlake, the other by Alexander Watkins Terrell.

Shelby's Expedition to Mexico is the briefest of Edwards's books, 196 pages in its 1889 edition. In many ways it is also his best. The story is enthralling, a military anabasis deep into the heart of unknown territory by a cadre of light cavalry about whom Edwards could justifiably say, "Surrounded, it never surrendered; surprised, it never scattered; overwhelmed, it never wavered; decimated, it bled in silence; and victorious, it was always merciful and just."[48]

Not enough credit has been given to the exploits of this superb mounted brigade and its quixotic final march in search of a place where it could continue to defy the will of the United States government. Edwards's telling of the story contains some of his finest writing. Superb action scenes alternate with vivid portraits of the people and places they encountered along the way. Who can forget the bloody shoot-out at Piedras Negras, the eccentric Englishman who dreams of dying in a train wreck, the rescue of the mysterious *gringa* held captive in a hacienda by a jealous hidalgo, the last-minute relief of a French force on the verge of annihilation at Matahuela? After four years of bloody combat on Trans-Mississippi soil, the brigade clawed its way mile by mile to Mexico City, a distance of fifteen hundred miles, fighting Juaristas, Indians, desperadoes, and disgruntled gringos.

For all his faults, John Edwards deserves to be recognized by a wider audience. He was a rattling good storyteller who wrote with great sweep and power. He flourished best when he had a big canvas to fill, like those grandiose paintings of nineteenth-century battles; he was adept at depicting the dash of brave men in the throes of bloody conflict.

Shelby's expedition is unique in the military annals of the Western Hemisphere. It deserves to be ranked with Pizarro's march from the Peruvian coast to Cuzco, Alexander Doniphan's trek through Mexico and the American Southwest, Chief Joseph's attempt to pilot his Nez Perce people through a gauntlet of bluecoats to the sanctuary of Canada. We have to go back all the way to Xenophon and his heroic tale of a Greek unit that fought its way across Asia Minor in 401 B.C. to find a story of comparable valor. Like those legendary Greeks, Shelby and his men, cut off from all sources of supply, were forced to march across hostile terrain, through hordes of enemies hell-bent on destroying them, toward a rendezvous, with the Austrian pretender to an illusory Mexican throne, that culminated in a bitterly disappointing end. No matter; thanks to Edwards's

unabashed enthusiasm, their honor remains intact, their glory undimin-
ished. Even shorn of the author's embellishments, the story of this
neglected saga is stunning and epical, set against the backdrop of a pun-
ishing desert, lofty plateaus, and dusty adobe villages, charged with
romance, intrigue, and high adventure. Oh, that David Lean, the great
British director, were still alive to film it!

SHELBY'S EXPEDITION TO MEXICO; AN UNWRITTEN LEAF OF THE WAR

BY JOHN N. EDWARDS

CHAPTER I.

"They rode a troop of bearded men.
Rode two and two out from the town,
And some were blonde and some were brown,
And all as brave as Sioux; but when
From San Bennetto south the line
That bound them to the haunts of men
Was passed, and peace stood mute behind
And streamed a banner to the wind
The world knew not, there was a sign
Of awe, of silence, rear and van.
Men thought who never thought before;
I heard the clang and clash of steel,
From sword at hand or spur at heel,
And iron feet, but nothing more.
Some thought of Texas, some of Maine,
But more of rugged Tennessee—
Of scenes in Southern vales of wine,
And scenes in Northern hills of pine,
As scenes they might not meet again;
And one of Avon thought, and one
Thought of an isle beneath the sun,
And one of Rowley, one the Rhine,
And one turned sadly to the Spree."
Joaquin Miller[1]

What follows may read like a romance; it was the saddest reality this life could offer to many a poor fellow who now sleeps in a foreign and forgotten grave somewhere in the tropics—somewhere between the waters of the Rio Grande and the Pacific Ocean.

The American has ever been a wayward and a truant race. There are passions which seem to belong to them by some strange fatality of birth or blood. In every port, under all flags, upon every island, shipwrecked and stranded upon the barren or golden shores of adventure, Americans can be found, taking fate as it comes—a devil-may-care, reckless, good-natured, thrifty and yet thriftless race, loving nothing so well as their country except an enterprise full of wonder and peril. Board a merchant vessel in mid-ocean and there is an American at the wheel. Steer clear of a lean, lank, rakish-looking craft beating up from the windward toward Yucatan, and overboard as a greeting comes the full roll of an Anglo-Saxon voice, half-familiar and half-piratical. The angular features peer out from under *sombreros,* bronzed and brown though they may be, telling of faces seen somewhere about the cities—eager, questioning faces, a little sad at times, yet always stern enough for broil or battle. They cruise in the foreign rivers and rob on the foreign shores. Whatever is uppermost finds ready hands. No guerrillas are more daring than American guerrillas; the church has no more remorseless despoilers; the women no more ardent and faithless lovers; the *haciendas* no more sturdy defenders; the wine cup no more devoted proselytes; the stranger armies no more heroic soldiers; and the stormy waves of restless emigration no more sinister waifs, tossed hither and thither, swearing in all tongues—rude, boisterous, dangerous in drink, ugly at cards, learning revolver-craft quickest and surest, and dying as they love to die, game to the last.

Of such a race came all who had preceded the one thousand Confederates led by Shelby into Mexico.[2] He found many of them there. Some he hung and some he recruited, the last possibly not the best.

The war in the Trans-Mississippi Department had been a holiday parade for some; a ceaseless battle and raid for others. Shelby's division of Missourians was the flower of his army. He had formed and fashioned it upon an ideal of his own. He had a maxim, borrowed from Napoleon without knowing it, which was: "Young men for war." Hence all that long list of boy heroes who died before maturity from Pocahontas, Arkansas, to Newtonia, Missouri, died in that last march of 1864, the stupidest, wildest, wantonest, wickedest march ever made by a general who had a voice like a lion and a spring like a guinea pig.[3] Shelby did the fighting, or rather, what he could of it. After Westport, eight hundred of these Missourians were buried in a night. The sun that set at Mine Creek set as well upon a torn and decimated division, bleeding at every step, but resolute and undaunted.[4] That night the dead were not buried.

Newtonia came after—the last battle west of the Mississippi River.[5] It was a prairie fight, stern, unforgiving, bloody beyond all comparison for the stakes at issue, fought far into the night, and won by him who had won so many before that he had forgotten to count them. General Blunt is rich, alive and a brave man and a happy man over in Kansas.[6] He will bear testimony again, as he has often done before, that Shelby's fighting at Newtonia surpassed any he had ever seen. Blunt was a grim fighter himself, be it remembered, surpassed by none who ever held the border for the Union.

The retreat southward from Newtonia was a famine. The flour first gave out, then the meal, then the meat, then the medicines. The recruits suffered more in spirit than in flesh, and fell out by the wayside to die. The old soldiers cheered them all they could and tightened their own saber belts. Hunger was a part of their rations. The third day beyond the Arkansas river, hunger found an ally—*small pox*. In cities and among civilized beings this is fearful. Among soldiers, and, therefore, machines, it is but another name for death. They faced it as they would a line of battle, waiting for the word. That came in this wise: Shelby took every wagon he could lay his hands upon, took every blanket the dead men left, and improvised a hospital. While life lasted in him, a soldier was never abandoned. There was no shrinking; each detachment in detail mounted guard over the terrible *cortege*—protected it, camped with it, waited upon it, took its chances as it took its rest. Discipline and humanity fraternized. The weak hands of the one were intertwined with the bronzed hands of the other. Even amid the pestilence there was poetry.

The gaps made in the ranks were ghastly. Many whom the bullets had scarred and spared were buried far from soldierly bivouacs or battle-fields. War has these species of attacks, all the more overwhelming because of their inglorious tactics. Fever can not be fought, nor that hideous leprosy which kills after it has defaced.

One day the end came, after much suffering and heroism and devotion. A picture like this, however, is only painted that one may understand the superb organization of that division which was soon to be a tradition, a memory, a grim war spirit, a thing of gray and glory forevermore.

After the ill-starred expedition made to Missouri in 1864, the Trans-Mississippi army went to sleep. It numbered about fifty thousand soldiers, rank and file, and had French muskets, French cannon, French medicines, French ammunition and French gold. Matamoras, Mexico, was a port the Government could not or did not blockade, and from one side of the river there came to it all manner of supplies, and from the other side all kinds and grades of cotton. This dethroned king had transferred its empire from the Carolinas to the Gulf, from the Tombigbee to the Rio Grande. It was a fugitive king, however, with a broken sceptre and a meretricious crown. Afterward, it was guillotined.[7]

Gen. E. Kirby Smith[8] was the Commander-in-Chief of this department, who had under him as lieutenants, Generals John B. Magruder[9] and Simon B. Buckner.[10] Smith was a soldier turned exhorter. It is not known that he preached; he prayed, however, and his prayers, like the prayers of the wicked, availed nothing. Other generals in other parts of the army prayed, too, notably Stonewall Jackson, but between the two there was this difference: The first trusted to his prayers alone; the last to his prayers and his battalions. Faith is a fine thing in the parlor, but it never yet put grape-shot in an empty caisson, and pontoon bridges over a full-fed river.

As I have said, while the last act in the terrible drama was being performed east of the Mississippi river, all west of the Mississippi was asleep. Lee's surrender at Appomattox Court House awoke them. Months, however, before the last march Price had made into Missouri, Shelby had an interview with Smith. They talked of many things, but chiefly of the war. Said Smith:

"What would you do in this emergency, Shelby?"

"I would," was the quiet reply, "march every single soldier of my command into Missouri—infantry, artillery, cavalry, all; I would fight there and stay there. Do not deceive yourself. Lee is overpowered; Johnston is giving up county after county full of our corn and wheat fields; Atlanta is in danger, and Atlanta furnishes the powder; the end approaches; a supreme effort is necessary; the eyes of the East are upon the West, and with fifty thousand soldiers such as yours you can seize St. Louis, hold it, fortify it, and cross over into Illinois. It would be a diversion, expanding into a campaign—a blow that had destiny in it."

Smith listened, smiled, felt a momentary enthusiasm, ended the interview, and, later, sent eight thousand cavalry under a leader who marched twelve miles a day and had a wagon train as long as the tail of Plantamour's comet.

With the news of Lee's surrender there came a great paralysis. What had before been only indifference was now death. The army was scattered throughout Texas, Arkansas and Louisiana, but in the presence of such a calamity it concentrated as if by intuition. Men have this feeling in common with animals that imminent danger brings the first into masses, the last into herds. Buffalo fight in a circle, soldiers form squares. Smith came up from Shreveport, Louisiana, to Marshall, Texas. Shelby went from Fulton, Arkansas, to the same place. Hither came also other generals of note, such as Hawthorne, Buckner, Preston and Walker. Magruder tarried at Galveston, watching with quiet eyes a Federal fleet beating in from the Gulf. In addition to this fleet there were also transports blue with uniforms and black with soldiers. A wave of negro troops was about to inundate the department.

Some little reaction had begun to be manifested since the news of Appomattox. The soldiers, breaking away from the iron bands of a rigid discipline, had held meetings pleading against surrender. They knew Jefferson Davis was a fugitive, westward bound, and they knew Texas was filled to overflowing with all kinds of supplies and war munitions. In their simple hero faith they believed that the struggle could still be maintained. Thomas C. Reynolds was Governor of Missouri, and a truer and braver one never followed the funeral of a dead nation his commonwealth had revered and respected.[11]

This Marshall conference had a two-fold object: first to ascertain the imminence of the danger, and second to provide against it.[12] Strange things were done there. The old heads came to the young one; the infantry yielded its precedence to the cavalry; the major-general asked the advice of the brigadier. There was no rank beyond that of daring and genius. A meeting was held, at which all were present except General Smith. The night was a Southern one, full of balm, starlight and flower odor. The bronzed men were gathered quietly and sat awhile, as Indians do who wish to smoke and go upon the war-path. The most chivalrous scalp-lock that night was worn by Buckner. He seemed a real Red Jacket in his war-paint and feathers.[13] Alas! why was his tomahawk dug up at all? Before the ashes were cold about the embers of the council-fire, *it was buried.*

Shelby was called on to speak first, and if his speech astonished his audience, they made no sign:

"The army has no confidence in General Smith," he said, slowly and deliberately, "and for the movements proposed there must be chosen a leader whom they adore. We should concentrate everything upon the Brazos river. We must fight more and make fewer speeches. Fugitives from Lee and Johnston will join us by the thousands. Mr. Davis is on his way here; he alone has the right to treat for surrender. Our intercourse with the French is perfect, and fifty thousand men with arms in their hands have overthrown, ere now, a dynasty, and established a kingdom. Every step to the Rio Grande must be fought over, and when the last blow has been struck that can be struck, we will march into Mexico and re-instate Juarez[14] or espouse Maximilian. General Preston[15] should go at once to Marshal Bazaine[16] and learn from him whether it is peace or war. Surrender is a word neither myself nor my division understand."

This bold speech had its effect.

"Who will lead us?" the listeners demanded.

"Who else but Buckner," answered Shelby. "He has rank, reputation, the confidence of the army, ambition, is a soldier of fortune, and will take his chances like the rest of us. Which one of us can read the future and tell the kind of an empire our swords may carve out?"

Buckner assented to the plan, so did Hawthorne, Walker, Preston and Reynolds. The compact was sealed with soldierly alacrity, each general answering for his command. But who was to inform General Smith of this sudden resolution—this semi-mutiny in the very whirl of the vortex?

Again it was Shelby, the daring and the impetuous.

"Since there is some sorrow about this thing, gentlemen," he asked, "and since men who mean business must have boldness, I will ask the honor of presenting this ultimatum to General Smith. It is some good leagues to the Brazos, and we must needs make haste. I shall march to-morrow to the nearest enemy and attack him. Have no fear. If I do not overthrow him I will keep him long enough at bay to give time for the movement southward."

Immediately after the separation, General Shelby called upon General Smith. There were scant words between them.

"The army has lost confidence in you, General Smith."

"I know it."

"They do not wish to surrender."

"Nor do I. What would the army have?"

"Your withdrawal as its direct commander, the appointment of General Buckner as its chief, its concentration upon the Brazos river, and war to the knife, General Smith."

The astonished man rested his head upon his hands in mute surprise. A shadow of pain passed rapidly over his face, and he gazed out through the night as one who was seeking a star or beacon for guidance. Then he arose as if in pain and came some steps nearer the young conspirator, whose cold, calm eyes had never wavered through it all.

"What do you advise, General Shelby?"

"Instant acquiescence."

The order was written, the command of the army was given to Buckner, and the first act in the revolution had been finished. The next was played before a different audience and in another theater.

CHAPTER II.

Gen. Simon Bolivar Buckner was a soldier handsome enough to have been Murat.[1] His uniform was resplendent. Silver stars glittered upon his coat, his gold lace shone as if it had been washed by the dew and wiped with the sunshine, his sword was equaled only in brightness by the brightness of its scabbard, and when upon the streets women turned to look at him, saying, "That is a hero with a form like a war-god." General Buckner also wrote poetry. Some of his sonnets were set to music in scanty Confederate fashion, and when the red June roses were all ablow and the night at peace with bloom and blossom, they would float out from open casements as the songs of minstrel or troubadour. Sir Philip Sidney was also a poet who saved the English army at Gravelines, and though mortally wounded and dying of thirst, he bade his esquire give to a suffering comrade the water brought to cool his own parched lips.[2] From all of which it was argued that the march to the Brazos would be but as the calm before the hurricane—that in the crisis the American poet would have devotion equal to the English poet. From the Marshall conference to the present time, however, the sky has been without a war cloud, the lazy cattle have multiplied by all the water-courses, and from pink to white the cotton has bloomed and blown and been harvested.

Before Shelby reached his division, away up on the prairies about Kaufman, news came that Smith had resumed command of the army, and that a flag-of-truce boat was ascending the Red river to Shreveport. This meant surrender. Men whose *rendezvous* has been agreed upon, and whose campaigns have been marked out, had no business with flags of truce. By the end of the next day's march Smith's order of surrender came. It was very brief and very comprehensive. The soldiers were to be concentrated at Shreveport, were to surrender their arms and munitions of war, were to take paroles and transportation wherever the good Federal deity in command happened to think appropriate.

What of Buckner with his solemn promises, his recently conferred authority, his elegant new uniform, his burnished sword with its burnished scabbard, his sweet little sonnets, luscious as strawberries, his swart, soldierly face, handsome enough again for Murat? Thinking of his Chicago property,[3] and contemplating the mournful fact of having been chosen to surrender the first and the last army of the Confederacy.

Smith's heart failed him when the crisis came. Buckner's heart was never fired at all. All their hearts failed them except the Missouri Governor's and the Missouri General's,[4] and so the Brazos ran on to the sea without having watered a cavalry steed or reflected the gleam of a burnished bayonet. In the meantime, however, Preston was well on his way to Mexico. Later, it will be seen how Bazaine received him, and what manner of a conversation he had with the Emperor Maximilian touching Shelby's scheme at the Marshall conference.

Two plans presented themselves to Shelby the instant the news came of Smith's surrender. The first was to throw his division upon Shreveport by forced marches, seize the government, appeal to the army, and then carry out the original order of concentration. The second was to make all surrender impossible by attacking the Federal forces, wherever and whenever he could find them. To resolve with him was to execute. He wrote a proclamation destined for the soldiers, and for want of better material had it printed upon wall paper. It was a variegated thing, all blue and black and red, and unique as a circus advertisement:

"Soldiers, you have been betrayed. The generals whom you have trusted have refused to lead you. Let us begin the battle again by a revolution. Lift up the flag that has been cast down dishonored. Unsheath the sword that it may remain unsullied and victorious. If you desire it, I will lead; if you demand it, I will follow. We are the army and the cause. To talk of surrender is to be a traitor. Let us seize the traitors and attack the enemy. Forward, for the South and Liberty!"

Man proposes and God disposes. A rain came out of the sky that was an inundation even for Texas. All the bridges in the West were swept away in a night. The swamps that had been dry land rose against the saddle girths. There were no roads, nor any spot of earth for miles and miles dry enough for a bivouac. Sleepless and undismayed, the brown-bearded, bronzed Missourian toiled on, his restless eyes fixed on Shreveport. There the drama was being enacted he had struggled like a giant to prevent; there division after division marched in, stacked their arms, took their paroles, and were disbanded. When, by superhuman exertions, his command had forced itself through from Kaufman to Corsicana, the fugitives began to arrive. Smith had again surrendered to Buckner, and Buckner in turn had surrendered to the United States. It was useless to go forward. If you attack the Federals, they pleaded, you will imperil our unarmed soldiers. It was not their fault. Do not hold them responsible for the sins of their officers. They were faithful to the last, and even in their betrayal they were true to their colors.

Against such appeals there was no answer. The hour for a *coup d'etat* had passed, and from a revolutionist Shelby was about to become an exile. Even in the bitterness of his overthrow he was grand. He had been talking to uniformed things, full of glitter and varnish and gold lace and measured intonations of speech that sounded like the talk stately heroes have, but they were all clay and carpet-knights. Smith faltered, Buckner faltered, other generals, not so gay and gaudy, faltered, they all faltered. If war had been a woman, winning as Cleopatra, with kingdoms for caresses, the lips that sang sonnets would never have kissed her. After the smoke cleared away only Shelby and Reynolds stood still in the desert—the past a Dead Sea behind them, the future, what—the dark?

One more duty remained to be done. The sun shone, the waters had subsided, the grasses were green and undulating, and Shelby's Missouri Cavalry Division came forth from its bivouac for the last time. A call ran down its ranks for volunteers for Mexico. One thousand bronzed soldiers rode fair to the front, over them the old barred banner, worn now, and torn, and well-nigh abandoned. Two and two they ranged themselves behind their leader, waiting.

The good-byes and the partings followed. There is no need to record them here. Peace and war have no road in common. Along the pathway of one there are roses and thorns; along the pathway of the other there are many thorns, with a sprig or two of laurel when all is done. Shelby chose the last and marched away with his one thousand men behind him. That night he camped over beyond Corsicana, for some certain preparations had to be made, and some valuable war munitions had to be gathered in.

Texas was a vast arsenal. Magnificent batteries of French artillery stood abandoned upon the prairies. Those who surrendered them took the horses but left the guns. Imported muskets were in all the towns, and to fixed ammunition there was no limit. Ten beautiful Napoleon guns were brought into camp and appropriated. Each gun had six magnificent horses and six hundred rounds of shell and canister. Those who were about to encounter the unknown began by preparing for giants. A complete organization was next affected. An election was held in due and formal manner, and Shelby was chosen colonel with a shout. He had received every vote in the regiment except his own. Misfortunes at least make men unanimous. The election of the companies came next. Some who had been majors came down to corporals, and more who had been lieutenants went up to majors. Rank had only this rivalry there, the rivalry of self-sacrifice. From the colonel to the rearmost men in the rearmost file it was a forest of Sharp's carbines. Each carbine had, in addition to the forty rounds the soldiers carried, three hundred more in the wagon train. Four Colt's pistols each, dragoon size, and a heavy regulation saber, completed the equipment. For the revolvers there were ten thousand rounds apiece. Nor was this all. In the wagons there were powder, lead, bullet molds, and six thousand elegant new Enfields just landed from England, with the brand of the Queen's arms still upon them. Recruits were expected, and nothing pleases a recruit so well as a bright new musket, good for a thousand yards.

For all these heavy war materials much transportation was necessary. It could be had for the asking. General Smith's dissolving army, under the terms of the surrender, was to give up everything. And so they did, right willingly. Shelby took it back again, or at least what was needed. The march would be long, and he meant to make it honorable, and therefore, in addition to the horses, the mules, the cannon, the wagons, the fixed ammunition, and the muskets, Shelby took flour and bacon. The quantities were limited entirely by the anticipated demand, and for the first time in its history the Confederacy was lavish of its commissary stores.

When all these things were done and well done—these preparations, these tearings down and buildings up, these re-organizations and re-habilitations, this last supreme restoration of the equilibrium of rank and position, a council of war was called. The old ardor for battle was not yet subdued in the breast of the leader. Playfully calling his soldiers young recruits, he wanted as a kind of purifying process to carry them into battle.

The council fire was no larger than an Indian's, and around it were grouped Elliot, Gordon, Slayback, Williams, Collins, Langhorne, Crisp, Jackman, Blackwell and a host of others[5] who had discussed weighty questions before upon the eve of battle—questions that had men's lives in them as thick as sentences in a school book.

"Before we march southward," said Shelby, "I thought we might try the range of our new Napoleons."

No answer, save that quiet look one soldier gives to another when the firing begins on the skirmish line.

"There is a great gathering of Federals at Shreveport, and a good blow in that direction might clear up the military horizon amazingly."

No answer yet. They all knew what was coming, however.

"We might find hands, too," and here his voice was wistful and pleading; "we might find hands for our six thousand bright new Enfields. What do you say, comrades?"

They consulted some little time together and then took a vote upon the proposition whether, in view of the fact that there was a large number of unarmed Confederates at Shreveport awaiting transportation, it would be better to attack or not to attack. It was decided against the proposition, and without further discussion the enterprise was abandoned. These last days of the division were its best. For a week it remained preparing for the long and perilous march, a week full of the last generous rites brave men would pay to a dead cause. Some returning and disbanded soldiers were tempted at times to levy contributions upon the country through which they passed, and at times to do some cowardly work under cover of darkness and drink. Shelby's stern orders arrested them in the act, and his swift punishment left a shield over the neighborhood that needed only its shadow to ensure safety. The women blessed him for his many good deeds done in those last dark days, deeds that shine out yet from the black wreck of things, a star.

This kind of occupation ended at last, however, and the column marched away southward. One man alone knew French, and they were going to a land filled full of Frenchmen. One man alone knew Spanish, and they were going to the land of the Spaniards.[6] The first only knew the French of the schools which was no French, and the last had been bitten by a tawny tarantula of a senorita somewhere up in Sonora, and was worthless and valueless when most needed in the ranks that had guarded and protected him.

Before reaching Austin a terrible tragedy was enacted—one of those sudden and bloody things so thoroughly in keeping with the desperate nature of the men who witnessed it. Two officers—one a captain and one a lieutenant—quarreled about a woman, a fair young thing enough, lissome and light of love. She was the Captain's by right of discovery, the Lieutenant's by right of conquest. At the night encampment she abandoned the old love for the new, and in the struggle for possession the Captain struck the Lieutenant fair in the face.

"You have done a serious thing," some comrade said to him.

"It will be more serious in the morning," was the quiet reply.

"But you are in the wrong and you should apologize."

He tapped the handle of the revolver significantly, and made answer:

"This must finish what the blow has commenced. A woman worth kissing is worth fighting for."

I do not mention names. There are those to-day living in Marion County whose sleep in eternity will be lighter and sweeter if they are left in ignorance of how one fair-haired boy died who went forth to fight the battles of the South and found a grave when *her* battles were ended.

The Lieutenant challenged the Captain, but the question of its acceptance was decided even before the challenge was received. These were the terms: At daylight the principals were to meet one mile from the camp upon the prairie, armed each with a revolver and saber. They were to be mounted and stationed twenty paces apart, back to back. At the word they were to wheel and fire, advancing if they chose or remaining stationary if they chose. In no event were they to pass beyond a line two hundred yards in the rear of each position. This space was accorded as that in which the combatants might rein up and return again to the attack.

So secret were the preparations, and so sacred the honor of the two men, that, although the difficulty was known to 300 soldiers, not one of them informed Shelby. He would have instantly arrested the principals and forced a compromise, as he had done once before under circumstances as urgent but in no ways similar.

It was a beautiful morning, all balm and bloom and verdure. There was not wind enough to shake the sparkling dew-drops from the grass, not wind enough to lift breast high the heavy odor of the flowers. The face of the sky was placid and benignant. Some red like a blush shone in the east, and some clouds, airy and gossamer, floated away to the west. Some birds sang, too, hushed and far apart. Two and two, and in groups, men stole away from the camp and ranged themselves on either flank. A few rude jokes were heard, but they died out quickly as the combatants rode up to the dead line. Both were calm and cool, and on the Captain's face there was a half smile. Poor fellow, there was already the scars of three honorable wounds upon his body; the fourth would be his death wound.

They were placed, and sat their horses like men who are about to charge. Each head was turned a little to one side, the feet rested lightly in the stirrups, the left hands grasped the reins well gathered up, the right hands held the deadly pistols, loaded fresh an hour before.

"Ready—*wheel!*" The trained steeds turned upon a pivot as one steed. "Fire!"

The Lieutenant never moved from his tracks. The Captain dashed down upon him at a full gallop, firing as he came on. Three chambers were emptied, and three bullets sped away over the prairie, harmless. Before the fourth fire was given the Captain was abreast of the Lieutenant, and aiming at him at deadly range. Too late! The Lieutenant threw out his pistol until the muzzle almost touched the Captain's hair, and fired. The mad horse dashed away riderless, the Captain's lifeblood upon his trappings and his glossy hide. There was a face in the grass, a widowed woman in Missouri, and a soul somewhere in the white hush and waste of eternity. A great dragoon ball had gone directly through his brain, and the Captain was dead before he touched the ground. They buried him before the sun rose, before the dew was dried upon the grass that grew upon his premature and bloody grave. There was no epitaph, yet this might have been lifted there, ere the grim soldiers marched away again to the South:

"Ah, soldier, to your honored rest,
    Your truth and valor bearing;
The bravest are the tenderest,
    The loving are the daring."

CHAPTER III.

At Houston, Texas, there was a vast depot of supplies filled with all kinds of quartermaster and commissary stores. Shelby desired that the women and children of *true* soldiers should have such of these as would be useful and beneficial, and so issued his orders. These were disputed by a thousand or so refugees or renegades whose heads were beginning to be lifted up everywhere as soon as the last mutterings of the war storm were heard in the distance.

He called to him two captains—James Meadow and James Wood—two men known of old as soldiers fit for any strife. The first is a farmer now in Jackson, the last a farmer in Pettis, both young, brave, worthy of all good luck or fortune.

They came speedily; they saluted and waited for orders.

Shelby said:

"Take one hundred men and march quickly to Houston. Gallop oftener than you trot. Proclaim to the Confederate women that on a certain day you will distribute to them whatever of cloth, flour, bacon, medicines, clothing or other supplies they may need or that are in store. Hold the town until that day, and then obey my orders to the letter."

"But if we are attacked?"

"Don't wait for that. Attack first."

"And fire ball cartridges?"

"And fire nothing else. Bullets first, speeches afterward."

They galloped away to Houston. Two thousand greedy and clamorous ruffians were besieging the warehouses. They had not fought for Texas and not one dollar's worth of Texas property should they have. Wood and Meadow drew up in front of them.

"Disperse!" they ordered.

Wild, vicious eyes glared out upon them from the mass, red and swollen by drink. They had rifled an arsenal, too, and all had muskets and cartridges.

"After we have seen what's inside this building, and taken what's best for us to take," the leader answered, "we will disperse. The war's over, young fellows, and the strongest party takes the plunder. Do you understand our logic?"

"Perfectly," replied Wood, as cool as a grenadier, "and it's bad logic if you were a Confederate, good logic if you are a thief. Let *me* talk a little.

We are Missourians, we are leaving Texas, we have no homes, but we have our orders and our honor. Not so much as one percussion cap shall you take from this house until you bring a written order from Jo Shelby, and one of Shelby's men along with you to prove that you did not forge that order. Do you understand *my* logic?"

They understood him well, and they understood better the one hundred stern soldiers, drawn up ten paces to the rear, with eyes to the front and revolvers drawn. Shrill voices from the outside of the crowd urged those nearest to the detachment to fire, but no weapon was presented. Such was the terror of Shelby's name, and such the reputation of his men for prowess, that not a robber stirred. By and by, from the rear, they began to drop away one by one, then in squads of tens and twenties, until before an hour, the streets of Houston were as quiet and as peaceful as the cattle upon the prairies. These two determined young officers obeyed their instruction and rejoined their General.

Similar scenes were enacted at Tyler and Waxahatchie. At the first of these places was an arsenal guarded by Colonel Blackwell, and a small detachment consisting of squads under Captain Ward, Cordell, Rudd, Kirtley and Neale. They were surrounded in the night time by a furious crowd of mountain plunderers and shirking conscripts—men who had dodged both armies or deserted both. They wanted guns to begin the war on their neighbors after the real war was over.

"You can't have any," said Blackwell.

"We will take them."

"Come and do it. These are Shelby's soldiers, and they don't know what being taken means. Pray teach it to us."

This irony was had in the darkness, be it remembered, and in the midst of seven hundred desperate deer-hunters and marauders who had baffled all the efforts of the regular authorities to capture them. Blackwell's detachment numbered thirty eight.[1] And now a deed was done that terrified the boldest in all that band grouped together in the darkness, and waiting to spring upon the little handful of devoted soldiers, true to that country which no longer had either thanks or praise to bestow. James Kirtley, James Rudd, Samuel Downing and Albert Jeffries seized each a keg of powder and advanced in front of the arsenal some fifty paces, leaving behind them from the entrance a dark and ominous train. Where the halt was had a little heap of powder was placed upon the ground, and upon each heap was placed a keg, the hole downward, or connected with the heap upon the ground. The mass of marauders surged back as if the earth had opened at their very feet.

"What do you mean?" they yelled.

"To blow you into hell," was Kirtley's quiet reply, "if you're within range while we are eating our supper. We have ridden thirty miles, we have good consciences, and therefore we are hungry. Good night!" and the reckless soldiers went back singing. One spark would have demolished the town. A great awe fell upon the clamoring hundreds, and they precipitately fled from the deadly spot, not a skulker among them remaining until the daylight.

At Waxahatchie it was worse. Here Maurice Langhorne kept guard. Langhorne was a Methodist turned soldier. He publishes a paper now in Independence, harder work, perhaps, than soldiering. Far be it from the author to say that the young Captain ever fell from grace. His oaths were few and far between, and not the great strapping oaths of the Baptists or the Presbyterians. They adorned themselves with black kids and white neckties, and sometimes they fell upon their knees. Yet Langhorne was always orthodox. His pistol practice was superb. During his whole five years' service he never missed his man.[2]

He held Waxahatchie with such soldiers as John Kritzer, Martin Kritzer, Jim Crow Childs, Bud Pitcher, Cochran and a dozen others. He was surrounded by a furious mob who clamored for admittance into the building where the stores were.

"Go away," said Langhorne, mildly. His voice was soft enough for a preacher's, his looks bad enough for a backslider.

They fired on him a close, hot volley. Wild work followed, for with such men how could it be otherwise? No matter who fell, nor the number of dead and dying, Langhorne held the town that night, the day following and the next night. There was no more mob. A deep peace came to the neighborhood, and as he rode away there were many true, brave Confederates who came to his little band and blessed them for what had been done. In such guise did these last acts of Shelby array themselves. Scorning all who in the name of soldiers plundered the soldiers, he left a record behind him which, even to this day, has men and women rise up and call it noble.

After Houston and Tyler and Waxahatchie came Austin. The march had become an ovation. Citizens thronged the roads, bringing with them refreshments and good cheer. No soldier could pay for anything. Those who had begun by condemning Shelby's stern treatment of the mob, ended by upholding him.

Governor Murrah of Texas still remained at the capital of his State.[3] He had been dying for a year. All those insidious and deceptive approaches of consumption were seen in the hectic cheeks, the large, mournful eyes, the tall, bent frame that quivered as it moved. Murrah was a gifted and brilliant man, but his heart was broken. In his life there was the memory of an unblessed and an unhallowed love, too deep for human sympathy, too sad and passionate for tears. He knew death was near to him, yet he put on his old gray uniform, and mounted his old, tired war horse, and rode away dying to Mexico. Later, in Monterey, the red in his cheeks had burnt itself out. The crimson had turned to ashen gray. He was dead with his uniform around him.

The Confederate government had a sub-treasury in Austin, in the vaults of which were three hundred thousand dollars in gold and silver. Operating about the city was a company of notorious guerrillas, led by Captain Rabb, half *ranchero* and half freebooter. It was a pleasant pasturage over beyond the Colorado river, and thither the Regiment went, for it had marched far, and it was weary. Loitering late for wine and wassail, many soldiers halted in the streets and tarried till the night came—a misty, cloudy, ominous night, full of darkness and dashes of rain.

Suddenly a tremendous battering arose from the iron doors of the vaults in the State House where the money was kept. Silent horsemen galloped to and fro through the gloom; the bells of the churches were rung furiously; a home guard company mustered at their armory to the beat of a long roll, and from beyond the Colorado there arose on the night air the full, resonant blare of Shelby's bugle sounding the well-known rallying call. In some few brief moments more the head of a solid column, four deep, galloped into the Square, reporting for duty to the Mayor of the city—a maimed soldier of Lee's army. Ward led them.

"They are battering down the Treasury doors," said the Mayor.

"I should think so," replied Ward. "Iron and steel must soon give way before such blows. What would you have?"

"The safety of the treasure."

"Forward, men!" and the detachment went off at a trot, and in through the great gate leading to the Capitol. It was surrounded. The blows continued. Lights shone through all the windows; there were men inside gorging themselves with gold. No questions were asked. A sudden, pitiless jet of flame spurted out from two score of Sharp's carbines; there was the sound of falling men on the echoing floor, and then a great darkness. From out of the smoke and gloom and shivered glass and scattered eagles, they dragged the victims forth—dying, bleeding, dead. One among the rest, a great-framed, giant man, had a king's ransom about his person. He had taken off his pantaloons, tied a string around each leg at the bottom and had filled them. An epicure even in death, he had discarded the silver. These white heaps, like a wave, had inundated the room, more precious to fugitive men than food or raiment. Not a dollar was touched, and a stern guard took his post, as immutable as fate, by the silver heaps and the blood puddles. In walking his beat, this blood splashed him to the knees.

Now this money was money of the Confederacy, it belonged to her soldiers, they should have taken it and divided it *per capita*. They did not do this because of this remark. Said Shelby, when they appealed to him to take it as a right:

"I went into the war with clean hands, and by God's blessing, I will go out of the war with clean hands."

After that they would have starved before touching a silver picayune.[4]

Ere marching the next morning, however, Murrah came to Shelby and insisted that as his command was the last organized body of Confederates in Texas, and that as they were on the eve of abandoning the country, he should take this Confederate property just as he had taken the cannon and the muskets. The temptation was strong, and the arguments were strong, but he never wavered. He knew what the world would say, and he dreaded its malice. Not for himself, however, but for the sake of that nation he had loved and fought so hard to establish.

"We are the last of the race," he said, a little regretfully, "but let us be the best as well."

And so he turned his back upon the treasury and its gold, penniless. His soldiers were ragged, without money, exiles, and yet at his bidding they set their faces as iron against the heaps of silver, and the broken doors of the treasury vaults, and rode on into the South.

When the line of demarkation was so clearly drawn between what was supposed, and what was intended—when, indeed, Shelby's line of march was so straight and so steadfast as to no longer leave his destination in doubt, fugitives began to seek shelter under his flag and within the grim ranks of his veterans. Ex-Governor and Ex-Senator Trusten Polk was one of these.[5] He, like the rest, was homeless and penniless, and joined his fortune to the fortunes of those who had just left three hundred thousand dollars in specie in Austin. From all of which Trusten Polk might have argued:

"These fellows will carry me through, but they will find me no gold or silver mines."

Somewhere in the State were other fugitives struggling to reach Shelby—fugitive generals, governors, congressmen, cabinet officers, men who imagined that the whole power of the United States Government was bent upon their capture. Smith was making his way to Mexico, so was Magruder, Reynolds, Parsons, Standish, Conrow, General Lyon of Kentucky; Flournoy,

Terrell, Clark, and Snead, of Texas; General John B. Clark, Sr., General Prevost, of Louisiana; Governor Henry W. Allen, Commodore M. F. Maury, General Bee, General Oscar Watkins, Colonel Wm M. Broadwell, Colonel Peter B. Wilks, and a host of others equally determined on flight and equally out at the elbows.[6] Of money they had scarcely fifty dollars to the man. Magruder brought his superb spirits and his soldierly heart for every fate; Reynolds, his elegant cultivation, and his cool, indomitable courage; Smith, his useless repinings and his rigid West Point courtesy; Allen, his electric enthusiasm and his abounding belief in Providence; Maury, his learning and his foreign decorations; Clark, his inimitable drollery and his broad Southern humor; Prevost, his French gallantry and wit; Broadwell, his generosity and his speculative views of the future; Bee, his theories of isothermal lines and cotton planting; and Parsons and Standish and Conrow the shadow of a great darkness that was soon to envelop them as in a cloud— the darkness of bloody and premature graves.[7]

The command was within three days' march of San Antonio. As it approached Mexico, the grass gave place to *mesquite*[8]—the wide, undulating prairies to matted and impenetrable stretches of *chaparral.*[9] All the rigid requirements of war had been carried out—the picquet guard, the camp guard, the advanced posts, and the outlying scouts, aimless and objectless, apparently, but full of daring, cunning and guile.

Pasturage was scarce on this night, and from water to grass was two good miles. The artillery and commissary teams needed to be fed, and so a strong guard was sent with them to the grazing place. They were magnificent animals, all fat and fine enough to put bad thoughts in the fierce natures of the cow-boys—an indigenous Texas growth—and the unruly borderers.

They had been gone an hour, and the sad roll of the tattoo had floated away on the night air. A scout—Martin Kritzer—rode rapidly up to Shelby and dismounted.

He was dusty and tired, and had ridden far and fast. As a soldier, he was all iron; as a scout, all intelligence; as a sentinel, unacquainted with sleep.

"Well, Martin," his General said.

"They are after the horses," was the sententious reply.

"What horses?"

"Those of the artillery."

"Why do they want them?"

The cavalry soldier looked at his General in surprise. It was the first time in his life he had ever lost confidence in him. Such a question from such a source was more than he could well understand. He repeated slowly, a look of honest credulity on his bronzed face:

"Why do they want them?—well, because they are fine, fat, trained in the harness, scarce to find, and worth half their weight in gold. Are these reasons enough?"

Shelby did not reply. He ordered Langhorne to report to him. He came up as he always came, smiling.

"Take fifty men," were the curt instructions, "and station them a good half mile in front of the pasturing-place. There must be no bullets dropping in among our stock, and they must have plenty of grass room. You were on duty last night, I believe."

"Yes, General."

"And did not sleep?"

"No, General."

"Nor will you sleep to-night. Station the men, I say, and then station yourself at the head of them. You will hear a noise in the night—late in the night—and presently a dark body of horsemen will march up, fair to see between the grass and the sky-line. You need not halt them. When the range gets good, fire and charge. Do you understand?"

"Perfectly."

In an hour Langhorne was at his post, silent as fate and as terrible, crouching there in his lair, with fifty good carbines behind him. About midnight a low note like thunder sprang up from toward San Antonio. The keen air of the practiced soldier took in its meaning, as a sailor might the speech of the sea.

"Get ready—they are coming."

The indolent forms lifted themselves up from the great shadow of the earth. When they were still again they were mounted.

The thunder grew louder. What had before been noise was now shape and substance. Seventy-eight border men were riding down to raid the herders.

"Are you all loaded?" asked Langhorne.

"All. Have been for four years."

From the mass in front plain figures evolved themselves. Under the stars their gun-barrels shone.

"They have guns," sneered Langhorne, "but no scouts in front. What would Old Joe say to that?"

"He would dismount them and send them to the infantry," laughed John Kritzer.

The leading files were within fifty yards, near enough for a volley. They had not heard this grim by-play, rendered under the night and to the ears of an unseen death crouching in the prairie grass.

"Make ready!" Langhorne's voice had a gentleness in it, soft as a caress. The Methodist had turned lover.

Fifty dark muzzles crept out to the front, and waited there gaping.

"Take aim!" The softest things are said in whispers. The Methodist was about to deliver the benediction.

"Fire!"

A red cleft in the heart of the midnight—a murky shroud of dun and dark that smelt of sulphur—a sudden uprearing of staggering steeds and staggering riders—a wild, pitiful panic of spectres who had encountered the unknown—and fifty terrible men dashed down to the charge. Why follow the deadly work under the sky and the stars? It was providence fulfilling a vow—fate restoring the equilibrium of justice—justice vindicating the supremacy of its immortal logic. Those who came to rob had been a scourge more dreaded than the pestilence—more insatiate than a famine. Defying alike civil and martial law, they had preyed alternately upon the people and the soldiers. They were desperadoes and marauders of the worst type, feared and hated or both. Beyond a few scattering shots, fired by the boldest of them in retreat, they made no fight. The dead were not buried. As the regiment moved on toward San Antonio, thirty-nine could have been counted lying out in the grass—booted and spurred, and waiting the Judgment Day.

CHAPTER IV.

San Antonio, in the full drift of the tide which flowed in from Mexico, was first an island and afterward an oasis. To the hungry and war-torn soldiers of Shelby's expedition it was a Paradise. Mingo, the unparalleled host of Mingo's Hotel, was the guardian angel, but there was no terror in his looks, nor any flaming sword in his hand.[1] Here, everything that European markets could afford was found in abundance. Cotton, magnificent even in its overthrow, had chosen this last spot as the city of its refuge and its caresses. Fugitive generals had gathered here, and fugitive senators and fugitive governors and fugitive desperadoes, as well, men sententious of speech and quick of pistol practice. These last had taken immediate possession of the city, and were rioting in the old royal fashion, sitting in the laps of courtesans and drinking wines fresh through the blockade from France. Those passers-by who jeered at them as they went to and fro received a fusillade for their folly. Seven even had been killed—seven good Texan soldiers—and a great tear had fallen upon the place, this antique, half-Mexican city which had seen Fannin's new Thermopylae, and the black Spanish death-flag wind itself up into the Alamo. When the smoke had cleared away and the powder-pall had been lifted, the black had become crimson.[2]

First a speck and then a vulture, until the streets had become dangerous with desperadoes. They had plundered a dozen stores, had sacked and burnt a commissary train, had levied a *prestamo*[3] upon the citizens, and had gone one night to "smoke out Tom Hindman," in their rough border dialect. Less fortunate than Putnam, they found the wolf's den, and the wolf was within, but he showed his teeth and made a fight. They hammered at his door furiously. A soft musical voice called out:

"What do you want?"

Hindman was a small man, having the will and the courage of a Highlander.[4] Eloquent of speech, cool, a colloquial swordman whose steel had poison on it from point to hilt, audacious in plot, imperturbable in *finesse,* gray-eyed, proud at times to isolation, unsuccessful in the field, and incomparable in the cabinet, it was this manner of man who had called out from behind his barricade.

The leader of the attacking party answered him:

"It is said that you have dealt in cotton, that you have gold, that you are leaving the country. We have come for the gold—that is all."

"Indeed!" and the soft voice was strangely harsh and guttural now.

"Then, since you have come for the gold, suppose you take the gold. In the absence of all law, might makes right."

He spoke to them not another word that night, but no man advanced to the attack upon the building, and when the daylight came, Shelby was in possession of the city. A deputation of citizens had traveled nearly twenty miles that day to his camp, and besought him to hasten forward, that their lives and their property might be saved. The camp was in deep sleep, for the soldiers had traveled far, but they mustered to the shrill bugle call, and rode on through the long night afterwards, for honor and for duty.

Discipline is a stern, chaste queen—beautiful at times as Semiramis, ferocious as Medea.[5] Her hands are those of the priest and executioner. They excommunicate, which is a bandage over the eyes and a platoon of musketry; they make the sign of the cross, which is the acquittal of a drum-head court-martial. Most generally the excommunications outnumber the genuflections.

D. A. Williams did provost duty on one side of the river, A. W. Slayback upon the other. What slipped through the hands of the first fell into those of the last. What escaped both fell into the water. Some men are born to be shot, some to be hung, and some to be drowned. Even desperadoes have this fatality in common with the Christians, and thus in the ranks of the plunderers there is predestination. Peace came upon the city as the balm of a southeast trade wind, and after the occupation there was an ovation. Women walked forth as if to a festival. The Plaza transformed itself into a *parterre*.[6] Roses bloomed in the manes of the horses—these were exotic; roses bloomed in the faces of the maidens—these were divine. After Cannae there was Capua.[7] Shelby had read of Hannibal, the Carthagenian, and had seen Hannibal the elephant, and so in his mind there was no more comparison between the battle and the town than there was between the man and the animal. He would rest a little, much, many, glad and sun-shiny days, filled full of dalliance, and dancing, and music.

Mingo's Hotel from a cloister had come to be a cantonment. It was noisy like a hive, vocal like a morning in May. Serenading parties improvised themselves. Jake Connor led them, an artillery officer, who sang like Mario and fought like Victor Emmanuel.[8] In his extremes he was Italian. On the edge of all this languor and love, discipline, like a fringe, arrayed itself. Patrols paraded the streets, sentinels stood at the corners, from post to post martial feet made time, and in the midst of a flood of defeat, disaster, greed, overthrow, and rending asunder, there was one ark which floated hither and thither armed in a fashion unknown to Noah, bearing a strange barred banner at the fore—the Banner of the Bars. When its Ararat was found, there was no longer any more Ark.[9]

On the evening of the second day of occupation, an ambulance drew up in front of the Mingo House. Besides the driver, there alighted an old man, aged, bent, spent with fatigue, and dusty as a foot soldier. Shelby sat in the balcony watching him, a light of recognition in his calm, cold eyes. The old man entered, approached the register, and wrote his name. One having curiosity enough to look over his shoulder might have read:

"WILLIAM THOMPSON."

Fair enough name and honest. The old man went to his room and locked his door. The windows of his room looked out upon the plaza. In a few moments it was noticed that the blinds were drawn, the curtains down. Old men need air and sunlight; they do not commence hibernating in June.

When he had drawn his blinds, Shelby called up Connor. "Get your band together, Lieutenant," was the order.

"For what, General?"

"For a serenade."

"A serenade to whom?"

"No matter, but a serenade just the same. Order, also as you go out by headquarters, that all the men not on duty, get under arms immediately and parade in front of the balcony."

The assembly blew a moment afterwards, and as the sun set a serried mass of soldiers, standing shoulder to shoulder, were in line, waiting. Afterwards, the band marched into the open place reserved for it, Connor leading.

Shelby pointed up to the old man's window, smiling.

"Play 'Hail to the Chief,'" he said.

It was done. No answering signals at the window. The blinds from a look of silence had put on one of selfishness.

Shelby spoke again:

"Try 'Dixie,' boys. If the old man were dead, it would bring him to life again."

The sweet, familiar strains rose up rapid and exultant, filling all the air with life and the pulses with blood. When they had died with the sunset, there was still no answer.

Shelby spoke again:

"That old man up there is Kirby Smith. I would know him among a thousand. Shout for him until you are hoarse."

A great roar burst forth like a tempest, shaking the house, and in the full torrent of the tide, and borne aloft as an awakening cry, could be heard the name of "Smith! Smith!"

The blinds flew open, the curtains were rolled up, and in plain view of the last remnant of his magnificent army of fifty thousand men, General E. Kirby Smith came forth undisguised, a look full of eagerness and wonderment on his weary and saddened face. He did not understand the greeting, the music, the armed men, the eyes that penetrated his disguise, the shouts that had invaded his retreat. Threatened with death by roving and predatory bands from Shreveport to San Antonio, he knew not whether one friend remained to him of all the regiments he had fed, clothed, flattered, and left unfought.

Shelby rose up in his place, a great respect and tenderness at work in his heart for this desolate and abandoned man who had lived the military life that was in him, and who—a stranger in a land full of his soldiers—had not so much as a broken flag staff to lean upon. Given not overmuch to speaking and brief of logic and rhetoric, he won the exile when he said to him:

"General Smith, you are the ranking officer in the Trans-Mississippi Department. These are your soldiers, and we are here to report to you. Command, and we obey; lead us, and we will follow. In this public manner, and before all San Antonio, with music and with banners, we come to proclaim your arrival in the midst of that little band which knows neither dishonor nor surrender. You were seeking concealment, and you have found a noontide of soldierly obedience and devotion. You were seeking the night and the obscurity of self-appointed banishment and exile, and you have found guards to attend you, and the steadfast light of patriotism to make your pathway plain. We bid you good morning instead of good night, and await, as of old, your further orders."

Shouts arose upon shouts, triumphal music filled all the air again; thrice Smith essayed to speak, and thrice his tears mastered him. In an hour he was in the ranks of his happy soldiers as safe and as full of confidence as a king upon his throne.

There came also to San Antonio, before the march was resumed, an Englishman who was a mystery and an enigma. Some said he was crazy, and he might have been, for the line of demarkation is so narrow and so fine between the sound and the unsound mind, that analysis, however acute, fails often to ascertain where the first ends and the last begins. This Englishman, however, was different from most insane people in this—that he was an elegant and accomplished linguist, an extensive traveler, a soldier who had seen service in Algeria with the French, and in the Crimea with the British, and a hunter who had known Jules Girard and Gordon Cummings. His views upon suicide were as novel as they were logically presented. His knowledge of chemistry, and the intricate yet fascinating science of toxicology, surprised all who conversed with him. He was a man of middle age, seemingly rich, refined in all of his habits and tastes, and singularly winning and fascinating in his intercourse with the men. Dudley, that eminent Kentucky physician, known of most men in America, declared, after the observations of a long life, that every man born of a woman was crazy upon some one subject.[10] This Englishman, therefore, if he was crazy at all, was crazy upon the subject of Railroad Accidents. He had a feverish desire to see one, be in one, enjoy one, and run the risk of being killed by one. He had traveled, he said, over two continents, pursuing a phantom which always eluded him. Now before and now behind him, and then again upon the route he had just passed over, he had never so much as seen an engine ditched. As for a real, first-class collision, he had long ago despaired of its enjoyment. His talk never ended of wrecked cars and shattered locomotives. With a sigh he abandoned his hopes of a luxury so peculiar and unnatural, and came as a private to an expedition which was taking him away from the land of railroads. Later, this strange Englishman, this traveler, linguist, soldier, philosopher, chemist—this monomaniac, too, if you will—was foremost in the battle of the Salinas, fighting splendidly, and well to the front. A musket ball killed his horse. He mounted another and continued to press forward. The second bullet shattered his left leg from the knee to the ankle. It was not known that he was struck until a third ball, entering the breast fairly, knocked him clear and clean from the saddle, dying. He lived until the sun went down—an hour and more. Before he died, however, the strangest part of his life was to come—that of his confession. When related, in its proper sequence, it will be found how prone the best of us are to forget that it is the heart which is oftener diseased than the head. He had suffered much in his stormy lifetime, had sinned not a little, and had died as a hunted wolf dies, viciously and at bay.

At San Antonio, also, Governor Reynolds and General Magruder joined the expedition. The first was a man whose character had to be tried in the fiery crucible of military strife and disaster, that it might stand out grand, massive and indomitable. He was a statesman and a soldier. Much residence abroad had made him an accomplished diplomatist. He spoke three foreign languages fluently. To the acute analysis of a cultivated and expanded mind, he had added the exacting logic of the law. Poetry, and all the natural and outward forms of beauty, affected him like other imaginative men, but in his philosophy he discarded the ornate for the strong, the Oriental architecture for the Corinthian. Revolution stood revealed before him, stripped of all its glare and tinsel. As a skillful physician, he laid his hand upon the pulse of war and told the fluctuations of the disease from the symptoms of the patient. He knew the condition of the Confederacy better than its President, and worked like a giant to avert catastrophe.

Shams fled before him as shadows before the sun. He heard no voice but of patriotism, knew no word but devotion, had no ambition but for his country, blessed no generals without victorious battle fields, and exiled himself before he would surrender. His faith was spotless in the sight of that God of battles in whom he put his trust, and his record shone out through all the long, dark days as a light that was set upon a hill.

Magruder was a born soldier, dead now and gone to heaven. He had a figure like a Mars divested of immortality. He would fight all day and dance all night. He wrote love songs and sang them, and won an heiress rich beyond comparison. The wittiest man in the old army, General Scott adored him. His speech had a lisp that was attractive, inasmuch as it lingered over its puns and caressed its rhetoric. Six feet in height, and straight as Tecumseh, Magruder, in full regimentals, was the handsomest soldier in the Confederacy. Not the fair, blonde beauty of the city, odorous of perfume and faultless in tailor-fashion, but a great, bronzed Ajax, mighty thewed, and as strong of hand as strong of digestion. He loved women, too, and was beloved of them. After Galveston, with blood upon his garments, a bullet wound upon his body, and victory upon his standards, he danced until there was daybreak in the sky and sunlight upon the earth. From the fight to the frolic it had been fifty-eight hours since he had slept. A boy at sixty-four, penniless, with a family in Europe, homeless, bereft of an avocation he had grown gray in following, having no country and no calling, he, too, had come to his favorite officer to choose his bivouac and receive his protection.[11] The ranks opened eagerly for this wonderful recruit, who carried in his old-young head so many memories of the land towards which all were journeying.

CHAPTER V.

From San Antonio to Eagle Pass was a long march made dreary by mesquite and chaparral. In the latter, war laggards abounded, sleeping by day and devouring by night. These hung upon the flanks and upon the rear of the column, relying more upon force than stratagem—more upon surprises for capture than saber work or pistol practice. Returning late one night from extra duty, D. A. Williams with ten men met a certain Captain Bradford with thirty-two. Williams had seven mules that Bradford wanted, and to get them it was necessary to take them. This he tried from an ambush, carefully sought and cunningly planned—an ambush all the more deadly because the superb soldier Williams was riding campward under the moon, thinking more of women than of war.

In front, and back from the road upon the right, was a clump of mesquite too thick almost for a centipede to crawl through. When there was water, a stream bounded from one edge of this undergrowth; when there was no water, the bed of this stream was a great ditch. When the ambushment was had, instead of water there was sand. On guard, however, more from the force of habit than from the sense of danger, Williams had sent a young soldier forward to reconnoitre and to stay forward, watching well upon the right hand and upon the left. George R. Cruzen was his name, and a braver and better never awoke to the sound of the *reveille.* Cruzen had passed the mesquite, passed beyond the line of its shadows, passed out into the glare of a full harvest moon, when a stallion neighed fiercely to the right of him. He halted by instinct, and drew himself together, listening. Thanks to the sand, his horse's feet had made no noise; thanks to the stallion, he had stopped before the open jaws of the defile had closed upon their prey. He rode slowly back into the chaparral, dismounted, tied his horse, and advanced on foot to the brink of the ravine just where it skirted the edge of the brush. As he held his breath he counted thirty stalwart men crouching in the moonlight. Two he did not see. These men were on guard where the road crossed the dry bed of the creek. Cruzen's duty was plain before him. Regaining his horse speedily, he galloped back to where Williams had halted for a bit of rest. "Short greeting serves in time of strife," and Cruzen stated the case so plainly that Williams could almost see the men as they waited there for his little band. He bade his soldiers dismount, take a pistol in each hand, and follow him. Before doing this the horses and led mules were securely fastened.

Stealing round the point of the chaparral noiselessly as the flight of birds through the air, he came upon the left flank of the marauders, upon that flank which had been left unprotected and unguarded. He was within five paces of them before he was discovered. They fired a point blank volley full in his face, but his detachment fell forward and escaped untouched. As they arose they charged. The *melee* was close and suffocating. Three of Williams' soldiers died in the ravine, two scrambled out wounded to the death, one carries yet a bullet in his body. But he triumphed. Never was there a fight so small, so rapid and desperate. Cruzen killed three, Cam. Boucher three, Williams four, Ras. Woods five with one pistol, a heavy English dragoon, and other soldiers of the ten two apiece. Out of the thirty-two, twenty-seven lay dead in a space three blankets might have covered. Shelby heard the firing, and sent swift succor back, but the terrible work was done. Williams rarely left a fight half finished. His deeds that night were the talk of the camp for many long marches thereafter.

The next day at noon, while halting for dinner, two scouts from the rear—James Kirtley and James Rudd—galloped in with the news that a federal force, 3,000 strong, with a six gun battery, was marching to overtake the column.

"Who commands?" asked Shelby.

"Colonel Johnson," replied Rudd.

"How far in the rear did you see him?"

"About seventeen miles."

"Mount your horse again, Rudd, you and Kirtley, and await further orders."

Shelby then called one who had been his ordnance master, Maj. Jos. Moreland. Moreland came, polite, versatile, clothed all in red and gold lace. Fit for any errand, keen for any frolic, fond of any adventure, so only there were wine and shooting in it, Moreland reported.

"I believe," said Shelby, "you can turn the prettiest period, make the grandest bow, pay the handsomest compliment, and drink the pleasantest toast of any man in my command. Take these two soldiers with you, ride to the rear seventeen miles, seek an interview with Colonel Johnson and give him this."

It was a note which he handed him—a note which read as follows:

"COLONEL: My scouts inform me that you have about three thousand men, and that you are looking for me. I have only one thousand men, and yet I should like to make your acquaintance. I will probably march from my present camp about ten miles further to-day, halting on the high road between San Antonio and Eagle Pass. Should you desire to pay me a visit, you will find me at home until day after to-morrow."

Moreland took the message and bore it speedily to its destination. Amid many profound bows, and a multitude of graceful and complimentary words, he delivered it. Johnson was a gentleman, and dismissed the embassy with many promises to be present. He did not come. That night he went into camp five miles to the rear, and rested there all the next day. True to his word, Shelby waited for him patiently, and made every preparation for a stubborn fight. Once afterwards Colonel Johnson came near enough to indicate business, but he halted again at the eleventh hour and refused to pick up the gage of battle. Perhaps he was nearer right than his antagonist. The war was over, and the lives of several hundred men were in his keeping. He could afford to be lenient in this, the last act of the drama, and he was. Whatever his motives, the challenge remained unaccepted. As for Shelby, he absolutely prayed for a meeting. The old ardor of battle broke out like a hidden fire, and burnt up every other consideration. He would have staked all and risked all upon the issue of the fight—one man against three.

The march went rapidly on. But one adventure occurred after Williams' brief battle, and that happened in this wise: Some stores belonging to the families of Confederate soldiers had been robbed by renegades and deserters a few hours previous to Shelby's arrival in the neighborhood. A delegation of women came to his camp seeking restitution. He gave them retribution. Eleven miles from the plundered habitations was a rugged range of hills, inaccessible to most soldiers who had ridden and raided about its vicinity. Here, as another Rob Roy,[1] the leader of the robber band had his rendezvous. This band numbered, all told, nearly three hundred, and a motley band it was, composed of Mexicans, deserters from both armies, Indians, men from Arizona and California, and desperate fugitives from justice, whose names were changed, and whose habitations had been forgotten. To these hills the property had been taken, and to these hills went Slayback with two hundred men. He found the goods piled up breast high, and in front of them, to defend them, were about two hundred robbers. They scarcely waited for a fire. Slayback charged them with a great rush, and with the revolver solely. The nature of the ground alone prevented the attack from becoming an extermination. Slayback finished his work, as he always did, thoroughly and well, and returned to the command without the loss of a man.

About this time three men came to Shelby and represented themselves as soldiers of Lee's army who were abandoning the country, and who wished to go with him to Mexico. They were enrolled at once and assigned to a company. In a day or two some suspicions were aroused from the fact of their being well acquainted with the Spanish language, speaking it fluently upon every occasion when an opportunity offered. Now Lee's soldiers had but scant time for the acquirement of such accomplishments, and it became at last a question of some doubt as to the truth of the statements of these three men. To expose them fully it cost one of them his arm, the other two their lives, together with the lives of thirteen Mexicans who, guiltless of intention, yet sinned in the act.

When within three days' journey of the Rio Grande, General Smith expressed a desire to precede the regiment into Mexico, and asked for an escort. This was cheerfully furnished, and Langhorne received his orders to guard the Commander-in-Chief of the Trans-Mississippi Department safely to the river, and as far beyond as the need might be, if it were to the Pacific Ocean. There was not a drop of the miser's blood in Shelby's veins. In everything he was prodigal—of his money, when he had any, of his courage, of his blood, of his men, of his succor, of his influence, of his good deeds to his comrades and superior officers, and of his charities to others not so strong and so dauntless as himself. With Smith there went also Magruder, Prevost, Wilcox, Bee and a score of other officers who had business with certain French and Mexican officers at Piedras Negras, and who were tired of the trained marching and the regular encampments of the disciplined soldiers.

Langhorne did his duty well. Rigid in all etiquette, punctilious in the performance of every obligation, as careful of his charges as he could have been of a post of honor in the front of battle, Smith said to him, when he bade him good-bye:

"With an army of such soldiers as Shelby has, and this last sad act in the drama of exile would have been left unrecorded."

CHAPTER VI.

Eagle Pass is on one side of the Rio Grande River, Piedras Negras upon the other. The names indicate the two countries. Wherever there is an American, there is always an eagle. Two thousand Mexican soldiers held Piedras Negras—followers of Juarez—quaint of costume and piratical of aspect. They saw the head of Shelby's column *debouching*[1] from the *plateau* above the river—they saw the artillery planted and commanding the town—they saw the trained soldiers form up rapidly to the right and left, and they wondered greatly thereat. No boats would come over. Not a skiff ventured beyond the shade of the Mexican shore, and not a sign of life, except the waving of a blanket at intervals, or the glitter of a sombrero through the streets, and the low, squat adobes.

How to get over was the question. The river was high and rapid.

"Who can speak Spanish?" asked Shelby.

Only one man answered—him of the senorita of Senora—a recruit who had joined at Corsicana, and who had neither name nor lineage.

"Can you swim?" asked Shelby.

"Well."

"Suppose you try for a skiff, that we may open negotiations with the town."

"I dare not. I am afraid to go over alone."

Shelby opened his eyes. For the first time in his life such answer had been made by a soldier. He scarcely knew what the man was saying.

"Afraid!" This with a kind of half pity. "Then stand aside." This with cold contempt. Afterwards his voice rang out with its old authority.

"Volunteers for the venture—swimmers to the front." Fifty stalwart men dashed down to the water, dismounted—waiting. He chose but two—Dick Berry and George Winship—two dauntless young hearts fit for any forlorn hope beneath the sun. The stream was wide, but they plunged in. No matter for the drowning. They took their chances as they took the waves. It was only one more hazard of battle. Before starting, Shelby had spoken to Collins:

"Load with canister. If a hair of their heads is hurt, not one stone upon another shall be left in Piedras Negras."

The current was strong and beat the men down, but they mastered it, and laid hands upon a skiff whose owner did not come to claim it. In an hour a flag of truce was carried into the town, borne by Colonel Frank Gordon, having at his back twenty-five men with side arms alone.

Governor Biesca, of the State of Coahuila, half soldier and half civilian, was in command—a most polished and elegant man, who quoted his smiles and italicised his gestures. Surrounded by a glittering staff, he dashed into the Plaza and received Gordon with much pomp and circumstance. Further on in the day, Shelby came over, when a long and confidential interview was held between the American and the Mexican—between the General and the Governor—one blunt, abrupt, a little haughty and suspicious—the other suave, voluble, gracious, in promises, and magnificent in offers and inducements.

Many good days before this interview—before the terrible tragedy at that Washington theatre where a President fell dying in the midst of his army and his capital—Abraham Lincoln had made an important revelation, indirectly, to some certain Confederate chieftains. This came through General Frank P. Blair[2] to Shelby, and was to this effect: The struggle will soon be over. Overwhelmed by the immense resources of the United States, the Southern government is on the eve of utter collapse. There will be a million men disbanded who have been inured to the license and the passions of war, and who may be troublesome if nothing more. An open road will be left through Texas for all who may wish to enter Mexico. The Confederates can take with them a portion or all of the arms and war munitions now held by them, and when the days of their enlistment are over, such Federal soldiers as may desire shall also be permitted to join the Confederates across the Rio Grande, uniting afterwards in an effort to drive out the French and re-establish Juarez and the Republic. Such guarantees had Shelby received, and while on the march from Corsicana to Eagle Pass, a multitude of messages overtook him from Federal regiments and brigades, begging him to await their arrival—a period made dependent upon their disbandment. They wished above all things to take service with him, and to begin a war upon imperialism after the war upon slavery.

Governor Biesca exhibited his authority as Governor of Coahuila, and as Commander-in-Chief of Coahuila, Tamaulipas and New Leon, and offered Shelby the military control of these three States, retaining to himself only the civil. He required of him but one thing, a full, free and energetic support of Benito Juarez. He suggested, also, that Shelby should remain for several months at Piedras Negras, recruiting his regiment up to a division, and that when he felt himself sufficiently strong to advance, he should move against Monterey, held by General Jeanningros, of the Third French Zouaves, and some two thousand soldiers of the Foreign Legion.[3]

The picture, as painted by this fervid Mexican, was a most attractive one, and to a man like Shelby, so ambitious of military fame, and so filled with the romance and the adventure of his situation, it was doubly so. At least he was a devout Liberal. Having but little respect for Mexican promises or Mexican civilization, he yet knew that a corps of twenty thousand Americans could be easily recruited, and that after he once got a foothold in the country, he could preserve it for all time. His ideas were all of conquest. If he dreamed at all, his dreams were of Cortez. He saw the golden gates of Sonora rolled back at his approach, and in his visions, perhaps, there were glimpses of those wonderful mines guarded even now as the Persians guarded the sacred fire of their gods.

The destiny of the expedition was in this interview. Looking back now through the placid vista of the peace years, there are but few of all that rugged band who would speak out to-day as they did about the council board on the morrow after the American and the Mexican had shaken hands and went their separate ways.

The council was long, and earnest, and resolute. Men made brief speeches, but they counted as so much gold in the scales that had the weighing of the future. If Shelby was more elaborate and more eloquent, that was his wont, be sure there were sights his fervid fancy saw that to others were unrevealed, and that evolving itself from the darkness and the doubts of the struggle ahead, was the fair form of a new empire, made precious by knightly deeds, and gracious with romantic perils and achievements.

Shelby spoke thus to his followers, when silence had fallen, and men were face to face with the future:

"If you are all of my mind, boys, and will take your chances along with me, it is Juarez and the Republic from this time on until we die here, one by one, or win a kingdom. We have the nucleus of a fine army—we have cannon, muskets, ammunition, some good prospects for recruits, a way open to Sonora, and according to the faith that is in us will be the measure of our loss or victory. Determine for yourselves. You know Biesca's offer. What he failed to perform we will perform for ourselves, so that when the game is played out there will be scant laughter over any Americans trapped or slain by treachery."

There were other speeches made, briefer than this one by the leader, and some little whispering apart and in eagerness. At last Elliott stood up—the spokesman. He had been a fighting colonel of the Old Brigade, he had been wounded four times, he was very stern and very true, and so the lot fell to him to make answer.

"General, if you order it, we will follow you into the Pacific Ocean; but we are all Imperialists, and would prefer service under Maximilian."

"Is this your answer, men?" Shelby's voice had come back to its old cheery tones.

"It is."

"Final?"

"As the grave."

"Then it is mine, too. Henceforth we will fight under Maximilian. To-morrow, at four o'clock in the afternoon, the march shall commence for Monterey. Let no man repine. You have chosen the Empire, and, perhaps, it is well, but bad or good, your fate shall be my fate, and your fortune my fortune."

The comrade spoke then. The soldier had spoken at Marshall, at Corsicana, at San Antonio, and in the long interview held with Biesca. Time has revealed many things since that meeting in June, 1865—many things that might have been done and well-done, had the frank speech of Elliott remained unspoken—had the keen feeling of sympathy between the French and the Confederates been less romantic. Shelby was wiser then than any man who followed him, and strong enough to have forced them in the pathway that lay before *his* eyes so well revealed, but would not for the richest province in Mexico. And as the conference closed, he said, in passing out:

"Poor, proud fellows—it is principle with them, and they had rather starve under the Empire than feast in a republic. Lucky, indeed, for many of them if to famine there is not added a fusillade."

Governor Biesca's bland face blankly fell when Shelby announced to him the next morning the decision of the conference. He had slept upon the happiness of a *coup d'etat;* when he awoke it was a phantasy. No further arguments availed him, and he made none. When a Mexican runs his race, and comes face to face with the inevitable, he is the most indifferent man in the world. A muttered *bueana,*[4] a folded cigarrito, a bow to the invisible, and he has made his peace with his conscience and his God, and lies or sighs in the days that come after as the humor of the fancy takes him.

Biesca had all of his nation's *nonchalance,* and so, when for his master's service he could not get men, he tried for munitions of war. Negotiations for the purchase of the arms, the artillery and the ammunition were begun at once. A *prestamo* was levied. Familiarity with this custom had made him an adept. Being a part of the national education, it was not expected that one so high in rank as a governor would be ignorant of its rudiments.

Between Piedras Negras and Monterey the country was almost a wilderness. A kind of debatable ground—the robbers had raided it, the Liberals had plundered it, and the French had desolated it. As Shelby was to pass over it, he could not carry with him his teams, his wagons, his artillery, and his supply trains. Besides he had no money to buy food, even if food was to be had, and as it had been decided to abandon Juarez, it was no longer necessary to retain the war material. Hence the *prestamo.* A list of the merchants was made; the amount assessed to each was placed opposite his name; an adjutant with a file of soldiers called upon the interested party; bowed to him; wished him happiness and high fortune; pointed to the ominous figures, and waited. Generally they did not wait long. As between the silver and the guard house the merchant chose the former, paid his toll, cursed the Yankees, made the sign of the cross, and went to sleep.

By dint of much threatening, and much mild persuasiveness—such persuasiveness as bayonets give—sixteen thousand dollars were got together, and for safety were deposited in the custom house. On the morrow they were to be paid out.

The day was almost a tropical one. No air blew about the streets, and a white glare came over the sands and settled as a cloud upon the houses and upon the water. The men scattered in every direction, careless of consequences and indifferent as to results. The cafes were full. Wine and women abounded. Beside the bronzed faces of the soldiers were the tawny faces of the senoritas. In the passage of the drinking-horns the men kissed the women. Great American oaths came out from the *tiendas*,[5] harsh at times, and resonant at times. Even in their wickedness they were national.

A tragedy was making head, however, in spite of the white glare of the sun, and the fervid kisses under the rose. The three men, soldiers of Lee's army ostensibly—men who had been fed and sheltered—were tempting Providence beyond the prudent point. Having the hearts of sheep, they were dealing with lions. To their treachery they were about to add bravado—to the magazine they were about to apply the torch.

There is a universal Mexican law which makes a brand a Bible. From its truth there is no appeal. Every horse in the country is branded, and every brand is entered of record, just as a deed or a legal conveyance. Some of these brands are intricate, some unique, some as fantastic as a jester's cap, some a single letter of the alphabet, but all legal and lawful brands just the same, and good to pass muster anywhere so only there are alcaldes and sandaled soldiers about. Their logic is extremely simple, too. You prove the brand and take the horse, no matter who rides him, nor how great the need for whip and spur.

In Shelby's command there were a dozen magnificent horses, fit for a king's race, who wore a brand of unusual fashion—many-lined and intricate as a column of Arabesque. They had been obtained somewhere above San Antonio, and had been dealt with as only cavalry soldiers know how to deal with horses. These the three men wanted. With their knowledge of Spanish, they had gone among the Mexican soldiers, poisoning their minds with tales of American rapine and slaughter, depicting, with not a little of attractive rhetoric, the long and weary march they had made with these marauders that their beloved steeds might not be taken entirely away from them.

The Mexicans listened, not from generosity, but from greed, and swore a great oath by the Virgin that the *gringos* should deliver up every branded horse across the Rio Grande.

Ike and Dick Berry rode each a branded horse, and so did Armistead, Kirtley, Winship, Henry Chiles, John Rudd, Yowell and two-score more, perhaps, equally fearless, and equally ignorant of any other law besides the law of possession.

The afternoon drill was over. The hot glare was still upon the earth and the sky. If anything, the noise from the cafes came louder and merrier. Where the musical voices were the sweetest, were the places where the women abounded with disheveled hair and eyes of tropical dusk.

Ike Berry had ridden one of these branded horses into the street by regimental headquarters, and sat with one leg crossed upon the saddle, lazily smoking. He was a low, squat Hercules, free of speech and frank of nature. In battle he always laughed; only when eating was he serious. What reverence he had came from the appetite. The crumbs that fell from his long, yellow beard were his benediction.

Other branded horses were hitched about, easy of access and unnoted of owner. The three men came into the street, behind them a young Mexican captain handsome as Adonis. This captain led thirty-five soldiers, with eyes to the front and guns at a trail.

Jim Wood lounged in the door of a *cafe* and remarked them as they filed by. As he returned, he spoke to Martin Kritzer, toying with an Indian girl, beaded and beautiful.

"They are in skirmishing order. Old Jo has delivered the arms; it may be we shall take them back again."

One of the men went straight up to Ike Berry, as he sat cross-legged upon his horse, and laid his hand upon the horse's bridle.

Ike knew him and spoke to him cheerily:

"How now, comrade?"

Short answer, and curt:

"This is my horse; he wears my brand; I have followed him to Mexico. Dismount!"

A long white wreath of smoke curled up from Ike's meerschaum in surprise. Even the pipe entered a protest. The old battle-smile came back to his face, and those who were nearest and knew him best, knew that a dead man would soon lay upon the street. He knocked the ashes from his pipe musingly; he put the disengaged foot back gently in the stirrup; he rose up all of a sudden, the very incarnation of murder; there was a white gleam in the air; a heavy saber that lifted itself up and circled, and when it fell a stalwart arm was shredded away, as a girl might sever a silken chain or the tendrils of a vine. The ghastly stump, not over four inches from the shoulder, spouted blood at every heart throb. The man fell as one paralyzed. A shout arose. The Mexicans spread out like a fan, and when the fan closed it had surrounded Berry and Williams and Kirtley and Collins and Armistead and Langhorne and Henry Childs and Jim Wood and Rudd and Moreland and Boswell and McDougall and the brothers Kritzer. Yowell alone broke through the cordon and rushed to Shelby.

Shelby was sitting in a saloon discussing cognac and catalan with the Englishman. On the face of the last there was a look of sorrow. Could it have been possible that the somber shadows of the Salinas were already beginning to gather about his brow?

A glance convinced Shelby that Yowell was in trouble.

"What is it?" he asked.

"They are after the horses."

"What horses?'

"The branded horses; those obtained from the Rosser ranch."

"Ah! and after we have delivered the arms, too Mexican like—Mexican like."

He arose as he spoke and looked out upon the street. Some revolvers were being fired. These, in the white heat of the afternoon, sounded as the tapping of woodpeckers. Afterward a steady roar of rifles told how the battle went.

"The rally! the rally!—sound the rally!" Shelby cried to his bugler, as he dashed down to where the Mexicans were swarming about Berry and the few men nearest to him. "We have eaten of their salt, and they have betrayed us; we have come to them as friends, and they would strip us like barbarians. It is war again—war to the knife!"

At this moment the wild, piercing notes of an American bugle were heard—clear, penetrating, defiant—notes that told of sore stress among comrades, and pressing need of succor.

The laughter died in the *cafes* as a night wind when the morning comes. The bugle sobered all who were drunk with drink or dalliance. Its voice told of danger near and imminent—of a field needing harvesters who knew how to die.

The men swarmed out of every door-way—poured from under every *portal*—flushed, furious, ravenous for blood. They saw the Mexicans in the square, the peril of Berry and those nearest to him, and they asked no further questions. A sudden crash of revolvers came first, close and deadly; a yell, a shout, and then a fierce, hot charge. Ras. Woods, with a short Enfield rifle in his hand, stood fair in the street looking up at the young Mexican Captain with his cold gray eyes that had in them never a light of pity. As the press gathered about him, the rifle crept straight to the front and rested there a moment, fixed as fate. It looked as if he was aiming at a flower—the dark olive beauty of the Spaniard was so superb.

"Spare him!" shouted a dozen reckless soldiers in a breath, "he is too young and too handsome to die."

In vain! A sharp, sudden ring was the response; the Captain tossed his arms high in the air, leaped up suddenly as if to catch something above his head, and fell forward upon his face, a corpse. A wail of women arose upon the sultry evening—such as may have been heard in David's household when back from the tangled brushwood they brought the beautiful Absalom.

> "The life upon his yellow hair,
> But not within his eyes."

The work that followed was quick enough and deadly enough to appal the stoutest. Seventeen Mexicans were killed, including the Captain, together with the two Americans who had caused the encounter. The third, strange to say, recovered from his ghastly wound, and can tell to this day, if he still lives, of the terrible prowess of that American soldier who shredded his arm away as a scythe blade might a handful of summer wheat.

A dreadful commotion fell upon Piedras Negras after the battle in the street had been finished. The long roll was beaten, and the Mexican garrison rushed to arms. Shelby's men were infuriated beyond all immediate control, and mounted their horses without orders for further battle. One detachment, led by Williams, swept down to where the artillery and ammunition wagons were packed and dispersed the guard after a rattling broadside. Langhorne laid hands upon the Custom-house and huddled its sentinels in a room as so many boys that needed punishment. Separate parties under Fell, Winship, Henry Chiles, Kirtley, Jim Wood and Martin Kritzer seized upon the skiffs and the boats at the wharf. They meant to pillage and sack the town, and burn it afterward. Women went wailing through the streets; the church bells rang furiously; windows were darkened and barricaded; and over all the din and turmoil—the galloping of horses, and the clanking of steel—arose the harsh, gathering cry of the Mexican long roll—sullen, hoarse, discordant. Shelby stormed at his men, and threatened. For the first and the last time of his career, they had passed beyond his keeping. At a critical juncture, Governor Biesca rushed down into the square, pale, his hat off, pleading in impassioned Spanish, apologizing in all the soft vowels known to that soft and sounding language.

Shelby would bow to him in great gravity, understanding not one word, conversing in English when the tide of Spanish had run itself out:

"It's mostly Greek to me, Governor, but the devil is in the boys, for all that."

Discipline triumphed at last, however, and one by one the men came back to their duty and their obedience. They formed a solid, ominous looking column in front of headquarters, dragging with them the cannon that had been sold, and the cannon they had captured from the enemy.

"We want to sleep to-night," they said, in their grim soldier humor, "and for fear of Vesuvius, we have brought the crater with us."

As the night deepened, a sudden calm fell upon the city. Biesca had sent his own troops to barracks, and had sworn by every saint in the calendar that for the hair of every American hurt he would sacrifice a hecatomb of Mexicans. He feared, and not without cause, the now thoroughly aroused and desperate men who were inflamed by drink, and who had good reason for much ill-will and hatred. To Shelby's assurances of safety he offered a multitude of bows, each one more profound and more lowly than the other, until at last, from the game of war, the two chiefs had come to play a game of diplomacy. Biesca wanted his cannon back, and Shelby wanted his money for them. In the end, both were satisfied.

The men had gone to quarters, and supper was being cooked. To the feeling of revenge had been added at last one of forgiveness. Laughter and songs issued again from the wine-shops. At this moment a yell was heard— a yell that was a cross between an Indian war-whoop and a Mexican cattle-call. A crowd of soldiers gathered hastily in the street. Again the yell was repeated, this time nearer, clearer, shriller than before. Much wonderment ensued. The day had been one of surprises. To a fusillade there was to be added a frolic. Up the street leading from the river, two men approached slowly, having a third man between them. When near enough, the two first were recognized as the soldiers, Joseph Moreland and William Fell. The other man, despite the swarthy hue of his countenance, was ghastly pale. He had to be dragged rather than led along. Fell had his saber drawn, Moreland his revolver. The first was fierce enough to perform amputation; the last suave enough to administer chloroform.

When Moreland reached the edge of the crowd he shouted:

"Make way, Missourians, and therefore barbarians, for the only living and animated specimen of the *genus* Polyglott now upon the North American continent. Look at him, you heathens, and uncover yourselves. Draw nigh to him, you savages, and fall upon your knees. Touch him, you blood-drinkers, and make the sign of the cross."

"What did you call him?" asked Armistead.

"A Polyglott, you Fejee Islander; a living dictionary; a human mausoleum with the bones of fifty languages; a *lusus naturae*[6] in a land of garlic, stilettos and straw hats."

The man himself was indeed a curiosity. Born of Creole parents in New Orleans, he had been everywhere and had seen everything. When captured, he was a clerk in the custom house. French, Spanish, English, Italian, German, modern Greek, Gumbo French, Arabic, Indian dialects without number, and two score or so of *patois* rolled off from his tongue in harsh or hurried accents accordingly as the vowels or the consonants were uppermost. He charmed Shelby from the beginning. When he felt that he was free, his blood began to circulate again like quicksilver. Invited to supper, he remained late over his wine, singing songs in all manner of languages, and boasting in all manner of tongues. When he bowed himself out, his voice had in it the benediction that follows prayer.

That night he stole $2,000.

The money for the arms and the ammunition had been stored in the custom house and he had the key. The next morning a sack was missing. Biesca swore, Shelby seemed incredulous, the Polyglott only smiled. Between the oath and the smile there was this difference: the first came from empty pockets, the last from more money than the pockets could hold. Master of many languages, he ended by being master of the situation.

In the full flow of the Polyglott's eloquence, however, Shelby forgot his loss, and yielded himself again to the invincible charms of his conversation. When they parted for the last time, Shelby had actually given him a splendid pistol, ivory-handled and wrought about the barrel with gold and figure work. So much for erudition. Even in the desert there are date and palm trees.

The formal terms of the transfer were concluded at last. Biesca received his arms, paid his money, buried the dead soldiers, and blessed all who came into Piedras Negras and went out from it. His last blessings were his best. They came from his heart and from the happy consciousness that the Americans were about to depart forever from the midst of his post of honor and his possessions.

Marching southward from the town, the column had reached the rising ground that overlooked the bold sweep of the rapid river, the green shores of Texas beyond, the fort on the hill, from which a battered Confederate flag yet hung, and a halt was called.[7] Rear and van the men were silent. All eyes were turned behind them. Some memories of home and kindred may have come then as dreams come in the night; some placid past may have outlined itself as a mirage against the clear sky of the distant north; some voice may have spoken even then to ears that heard and heeded, but the men made no sign. The bronzed faces never softened. As the ranks closed up, waiting, a swift horseman galloped up from the town—a messenger. He sought the leader and found him by instinct.

"Amigo," he said, giving his hand to Shelby.

"Friend, yes. It is a good name. Would you go with us?"

"No."

"What will you have?"

"One last word at parting. Once upon a time in Texas an American was kind to me. Maybe he saved my life. I would believe so, because I want a reason for what is done between us."

"Speak out fairly, man. If you need help, tell me."

"No help, Senor, no money, no horses, no friendship—none of these. Only a few last words."

"What are they?"

"Beware of the Salinas!"

CHAPTER VII.

The Salinas was a river, and why should one be beware of it? Its water was cool, the shade of its trees grateful, its pasturage abundant, and why then should the command not rest some happy days upon its further banks, sleeping and dreaming? Because of the ambush.

Where the stream crossed the high, hard road leading down to Monterey, it presented on either side rough edges of rock, slippery and uncertain. To the left some falls appeared. In the mad vortex of water, ragged pinnacles reared themselves up, hoary with the white spray of the breakers—grim cut-throats in ambush in mid-river.

Below these falls there were yet other crossings, and above them only two. Beyond the fords no living thing could make a passage sure. Quicksands and precipices abounded, and even in its solitude the river had fortified itself. Tower and moat and citadel all were there, and when the flood-time came the Salinas was no longer a river—it was a barrier that was impassable.

All the country round about was desolate. What the French had spared the guerrillas had finished. To be sure that no human habitation was left, a powerful war party of Lipan Indians came after the guerrillas, spearing the cattle and demolishing the farming implements. These Lipans were a cruel and ferocious tribe, dwelling in the mountains of Sonora, and descending to the plains to slaughter and desolate.[1] Fleetly mounted, brave at an advantage, shooting golden bullets oftener than leaden ones, crafty as all Indians are, superior to all Mexicans, served by women whom they had captured and enslaved, they were crouched in ambush upon the further side of the Salinas, four hundred strong.

The weaker robber when in presence of the stronger is always the most blood-thirsty. The lion will strike down, but the jackal devours. The Lipan butchered and scalped, but the Mexicans mutilated the dead and tortured the living.

With the Lipans, therefore, there were three hundred native Mexicans, skilled in all the intricacies of the chaparral—keen upon all the scents that told of human prey or plunder. As ghastly skirmishers upon the outposts of the ambushment, these had come a day's march from the river to where a little village was at peace and undefended. As Shelby marched through, there was such handiwork visible of tiger prowess that he turned to Elliott, that grim Saul who never smiled, and said to him, curtly:

"Should the worst come to the worst, keep one pistol ball for yourself, Colonel. Better suicide than a fate like this."

The spectacle was horrible beyond comparison. Men hung suspended from door-facings literally flayed alive. Huge strips of skin dangled from them as tattered garments might hang. Under some a slow fire had been kindled, until strangulation came as a tardy mercy for relief. There were the bodies of some children among the slain, and one beautiful woman, not yet attacked by the elements, seemed only asleep. The men hushed their rough voices as they rode by her, and more than one face lit up with a strange pity that had in it the light of a terrible vengeance.

The village with its dead was left behind, and a deep silence fell upon the column, rear and van. The mood of the strange Englishman grew sterner and sadder, and when the night and the camp came he looked more keenly at his arms than was his wont, and seemed to take a deeper interest in his horse.

Gen. Magruder rode that day with the men—the third of July. "To-morrow will be the Fourth, boys," he said, when dismounting, "and perhaps we shall have fire works."

Two deserters—two Austrians from the Foreign Legion under Jeanningros at Monterey—straggled into the picket lines before tattoo and were brought directly to Shelby. They believed death to be certain and so they told the truth.[2]

"Where do you go?" asked Shelby.

"To Texas."

"And why to Texas?"

"For a home; for any life other than a dog's life; for freedom, for a country."

"You are soldiers, and yet you desert?"

"We were soldiers, and yet they made robbers of us. We do not hate the Mexicans. They never harmed Austria, our country."

"Where did you cross the Salinas?"

"At the ford upon the main road."

"Who were there and what saw you?"

"No living thing, General. Nothing but trees and rocks and water."

They spoke the simple truth. Safer back from an Indian jungle might these men have come, than from a passage over the Salinas with a Lipan and Mexican ambushment near at hand.

It was early in the afternoon of the Fourth of July, 1865, when the column approached the Salinas river. The march had been long, hot and dusty. The men were in a vicious humor, and in excellent fighting condition. They knew nothing of the ambushment, and had congratulated themselves upon plentiful grass and refreshing water.

Shelby called a halt and ordered forward twenty men under command of Williams to reconnoitre. As they were being told off for the duty, the commander spoke to his subordinate:

"It may be child's play or warrior's work, but whatever it is, let me know quickly."

Williams' blue eyes flashed. He had caught some glimpses of the truth, and he knew there was danger ahead.

"Any further orders, General?" he asked as he galloped away.

"None. Try the ford and penetrate the brush beyond. If you find one rifle barrel among the trees, be sure there are five hundred close at hand. Murderers love to mass themselves."

Williams had ridden forward with his detachment some five minutes space, when the column was again put in motion. From the halt to the river's bank was an hour's ride. Before commencing the ride, however, Shelby had grouped together his officers, and thus addressed them:

"You know as well as I do what is waiting for you at the river, which knowledge is simply nothing at all. This side of Piedras Negras, a friendly Mexican spoke some words at parting, full of warning, and doubtless sincere. He at least believed in danger, and so do I. Williams has gone forward to flush the game, if game there be, and here before separating I wish to make the rest plain to you. Listen, all. Above and below the main road, the road we are now upon, there are fords where men might cross at ease and horses find safe and certain footing. I shall try none of them. When the battle opens, and the bugle call is heard, you will form your men in fours and follow me. The question is to gain the further bank, and after that we shall see."

Here something of the old battle ardor came back to his face, and his eyes caught the eyes of the officers. Like his own they were full of fire and high resolve.

"One thing more," he said, "before we march. Come here, Elliott."

The scarred man came, quiet as the great horse he rode.

"You will lead the forlorn hope. It will take men to form it. That is enough to give up of my precious ones. Call for volunteers—for men to take the water first, and draw the first merciless fire. After that we will all be in at the death."

Ten were called for, two hundred responded. They had but scant knowledge of what was needed, and scantier care. In the ranks of the ten, however, there were those who were fit to fight for a kingdom. They were Maurice Langhorne, James Wood, George Winship, William Fell, Ras.

Woods, James Kirtley, John McDougall, James Rudd, James Chiles and James Cundiff.

Cundiff is staid, and happy, and an editor *sans peur et sans reproche* to-day in St. Joseph. He will remember, amid all the multifarious work of his hands—his locals, his editorials, his type-setting, his ledger, his long nights of toil and worry—and to his last day, that terrible charge across the Salinas, water to the saddle-girths, and seven hundred muskets pouring forth an unseen and infernal fire.

The march went on, and there was no news of Williams. It was three o'clock in the afternoon. The sun's rays seemed to penetrate the very flesh. Great clouds of dust arose, and as there was no wind to carry it away, it settled about the men and horses as a garment that was oppressive.

Elliott kept right onward, peering straight to the front, watching. Between the advance and the column some two hundred paces intervened. When the ambush was struck this distance had decreased to one hundred paces—when the work was over the two bodies had become one. Elliott was wounded and under his dead horse. Cundiff was wounded, Langhorne was wounded, Winship was wounded, and Wood, and McDougall, and Fell. Some of the dead were never seen again. The falls below the ford received them, and the falls buried them. Until the judgment day, perhaps, will they keep their precious sepulchres.

Over beyond the yellow dust, a long green line arose against the horizon. This was the further edge of the Salinas, dense with trees, and cool in the distance. The column had reached its shadow at last. Then a short, sharp volley came from the front, and then a great stillness. One bugle note followed the volley. The column, moved by a viewless and spontaneous impulse, formed into fours and galloped on to the river—Elliott leading, and keeping his distance well.

The volley which came from the front had been poured suddenly into the face of Williams. It halted him. His orders were to uncover the ambush, not to attack it, and the trained soldier knew as well the number waiting beyond the river by the ringing of their muskets as most men would have known after the crouching forms had been seen and counted.

He retreated beyond range and waited. Elliott passed on beyond and formed his little band—the ten dauntless volunteers who were anxious to go first and who were not afraid to die.

Shelby halted the main column still further beyond rifle range and galloped straight up to Williams.

"You found them, it seems."

"Yes, General."

"How many?"

"Eight hundred at the least."

"How armed?"

"With muskets."

"Take your place in the front ranks. I shall lead the column."

Turning to Elliott, he continued:

"Advance instantly, Colonel. The sooner over, the sooner to sleep. Take the water as you find it, and ride straight forward. Williams says there are eight hundred, and Williams is rarely mistaken. Forward!"

Elliott placed himself at the head of his forlorn hope and drew his saber. With those who knew him, this meant grim work somewhere. Cundiff spoke to Langhorne upon his right:

"Have you said your prayers, Captain?"

"Too late now. Those who pray best, pray first."

From a walk the horses moved into a trot. Elliott threw his eyes backward over his men and cried out:

"Keep your pistols dry. It will be hot work on the other side."

As they struck the water some Indian skirmishers in front of the ambush opened fire. The bullets threw white foam up in front of the leading files, but did no damage. By and by the stray shots deepened into a volley.

Elliott spoke again, and no more after until the battle was finished:

"Steady men!"

Vain warning! The rocks were not surer and firmer. In the rear the column, four deep and well in hand, thundered after the advance. Struggling through the deep water, Elliott gained the bank unscathed. Then the fight grew desperate. The skirmishers were driven in pell-mell, the ten men pressing on silently. As yet no American had fired a pistol. A yell rose from the woods, long, wild, piercing—a yell that had exultation and murder in it. Wildly shrill and defiant, Shelby's bugle answered it. Then the woods in a moment started into infernal life. Seven hundred muskets flashed out from the gloom. A powder pall enveloped the advance, and when the smoke lifted Elliott was under his dead horse, badly wounded; Cundiff's left arm was dripping blood; Langhorne and Winship and McDougall were down and bleeding; Fell, shot through the thigh, still kept his seat; and Wood, his left wrist disabled, pressed on with the bridle in his teeth, and his right arm using his unerring revolver. Kirtley and Rudd and Chiles and Ras. Woods alone of the ten were untouched, and they stood over their fallen comrades, fighting desperately.

The terrible volley had reached the column in the river, and a dozen saddles were emptied. The dead the falls received; the wounded were caught up by their comrades and saved from death by drowning. Shelby pressed right onward. At intervals the stern notes of the bugles rang out, and at intervals a great hearty cheer came from the ranks of the Americans. Some horses fell in the stream never to rise again, for the bullets plowed up the column and made stark work on every side. None faltered. Pouring up from the river as a great tide, the men galloped into line on the right and left of the road and waited under fire until the last man had made his landing sure. The Englishman rode by Shelby's side, a battle-light on his fair face— a face that was, alas! too soon to be wan and gray and drawn with agony.

The attack was a hurricane. Thereafter no man knew how the killing went on. The battle was a massacre. The Mexicans first broke, and after them the Indians. No quarter was shown. "Kill! Kill!" resounded from the woods, and the roar of the revolver volleys told how the Americans were at work. The Englishman's horse was killed. He seized another and mounted it. Fighting on the right of the road, he went ahead even of his commander. The mania of battle seemed to have taken possession of his brain. A musket ball shattered his left leg from the ankle to the knee. He turned deadly pale, but he did not halt. Fifty paces further, and another ball, striking him fair in the breast, knocked him clear from the saddle. This time he did not rise. The blood that stained all his garments crimson was his life's blood. He saw death creeping slowly towards him with outstretched skeleton hands, and he faced him with a smile. The rough, bearded men took him up tenderly and bore him back to the river's edge. His wounds were dressed and a soft bed of blankets made for him. In vain. Beyond human care or skill, he lay in the full glory of the summer sunset, waiting for something he had tried long and anxiously to gain.

The sounds of the strife died away. While pursuit was worth victims, the pursuit went on—merciless, vengeful, unrelenting. The dead were neither counted nor buried. Over two hundred fell in the chaparral and died there. The impenetrable nature of the undergrowth alone saved the remainder of the fugitives. Hundreds abandoned their horses and threw away their guns. Not a prisoner remained to tell of the ambush or the number of the foe. The victory was dearly bought, however. Thirty-seven wounded on the part of Shelby needed care; nineteen of his dead were buried before the sun went down; and eight the waters of the river closed over until the judgment day.

An hour before sunset the Englishman was still alive.

"Would you have a priest?" Shelby asked him, as he bent low over the wounded man, great marks of pain on his fair, stern face.

"None. No word nor prayer can avail me now. I shall die as I have lived."

"Is there any message you would leave behind? Any token to those who may watch and wait long for your coming? Any farewell to those beyond the sea, who know you and love you?"

His eyes softened just a little, and the old hunted look died out from his features.

"Who among you speaks French?" he asked.

"Governor Reynolds," was the reply.

"Send him to me, please."

It was done. Governor Reynolds came to the man's bedside, and with him a crowd of soldiers. He motioned them away. His last words on earth were for the ears of one man alone, and this is a confession, a free translation of which was given the author by Governor Reynolds, the original being placed in the hands of the British Minister in Mexico, Sir James Scarlett:

"I was the youngest son of an English Baron, born, perhaps, to bad luck, and certainly to ideas of life that were crude and unsatisfactory. The army was opened to me, and I entered it. A lieutenant at twenty-two in the Fourth Royals, I had but one ambition, that to rise in my profession and take rank among the great soldiers of the nation. I studied hard, and soon mastered the intricacies of the art, but promotion was not easy, and there was no war.

"In barracks the life is an idle one with the officers, and at times they grow impatient and fit for much that is reprehensible and unsoldierly. We were quartered at Tyrone, in Ireland, where a young girl lived who was faultlessly fair and beautiful. She was the toast of the regiment. Other officers older and colder than myself admired her and flattered her; I praised her and worshiped her. Perhaps it was an infatuation; to me at least it was immortality and religion.

"One day, I remember it yet, for men are apt to remember those things which change the whole current of the blood, I sought her out and told her of my love. Whether at my vehemence or my desperation, I know not, but she turned pale and would have left me without an answer. The suspense was unbearable, and I pressed the poor thing harder and harder. At last she turned at bay, wild, tremulous, and declared through her tears that she did not and could not love me. The rest was plain. A young cornet in the same regiment, taller by a head than I, and blonde and boyish, had baffled us all, and had taken from me, what in my bitter selfishness, I could not see that I never had.

"Maybe my brain has not been always clear. Sometimes I have thought that a cloud would come between the past and present, and that I could not see plainly what had taken place in all the desolate days of my valueless life. Sometimes I have prayed, too. I believe even the devils pray no matter how impious or useless such prayer may be.

"I need not detail all the ways a baffled lover has to overthrow the lover who is successful. I pursued the cornet with insults and bitter words, and yet he avoided me. One day I struck him, and such was the indignation exhibited by his comrades, that he no longer considered. A challenge followed the blow, and then a meeting. Good people say that the devil helps his own. Caring very little for God or devil, I fought him at daylight and killed him. Since then I have been an outcast and a wanderer. Tried by a military commission and disgraced from all rank. I went first to India and sought desperate service wherever it was to be found. Wounded often and scorched by fever, I could not die. In the Crimea the old, hard fortune followed me, and it was the same struggle with bullets that always gave pain without pain's antidote. No rest anywhere. Perhaps I lived the life that was in me. Who knows? Let him who is guiltless cast the first stone. There is much blood upon my hands, and here and there a good deed that will atone a little, it may be, in the end. Of my life in America it is needless to talk. Aimless, objectless, miserable, I am here dying to-day as a man dies who has neither fear nor hope. I thank you very much for your patience, and for all these good men would have done for me, but the hour has come. Good-bye."

He lifted himself up and turned his face fair to the west. Some beams of the setting sun, like a benediction, rested upon the long blonde hair, and upon the white set lips, drawn now and gray with agony. No man spoke in all the rugged band, flushed with victory, and weary with killing. In the trees a little breeze lingered, and some birds flitted and sang, though far apart.

For a few moments the Englishman lay as one asleep. Suddenly he roused himself and spoke:

"It is so dreary to die in the night. One likes to have the sunlight for this."

Governor Reynolds stooped low as if to listen, drew back and whispered a prayer. The man was dead!

CHAPTER VIII.

Evil tidings have wings and fly as a bird. Through some process, no matter what, and over some roads, no matter where, the news was carried to General Jeanningros, holding outermost watch at Monterey, that Shelby had sold all his cannon and muskets, all his ammunition and war supplies, to Governor Biesca, a loyal follower of Benito Juarez. Straightway the Frenchman flew into a passion and made some vows that were illy kept.

"Let me but get my hands upon these Americans," he said, "these *canaille*,[1] and after that we can see."

He did get his hands upon them, but in lieu of the sword they bore the olive branch.

The march into the interior from the Salinas river was slow and toilsome. Very weak and sore, the wounded had to be waited for and tenderly carried along. To leave them would have been to murder them, for all the country was up in arms, seeking for some advantage which never came to gain the mastery over the Americans. At night and from afar, the outlying guerrillas would make great show of attack, discharging platoons of musketry at intervals, and charging upon the picquets at intervals, but never coming seriously to blows. This kind of warfare, however, while it was not dangerous, was annoying. It interfered with the sleep of the soldiers and kept them constantly on the alert. They grew sullen in some instances and threatened reprisals. Shelby's unceasing vigilance detected the plot before it had culminated, and one morning before reaching Lampasas, he ordered the column under arms that he might talk to the men.

"There are some signs among you of bad discipline," he said, "and I have called you out that you may be told of it. What have you to complain about? Those who follow on your track to kill you? Very well, complain of them if you choose, and fight them to your heart's content, but lift not a single hand against the Mexicans who are at home and the non-combatants. We are invaders, it is true, but we are not murderers. Those who follow me are incapable of this; those who are not shall not follow me. From this moment forward I regard you all as soldiers, and if I am mistaken in my estimate, and if amid the ranks of those who have obeyed me for four years some marauders have crept in, I order now that upon these a soldier's work be done. Watch them well. He who robs, he who insults women, he who oppresses the unarmed and the aged, is an outcast to all the good fellowship of this command and shall be driven forth as an enemy to us all. Hereafter be as you have ever been, brave, true and honorable."

There was no longer any more mutiny. The less disciplined felt the moral pressure of their comrades and behaved themselves. The more unscrupulous set the Mexicans on one side and the Americans on the other, and elected to remain peaceably in the ranks which alone could shelter and protect them. The marches became shorter and the bivouacs less pleasant and agreeable. Although it was not time yet for the rainy season, some rain fell in the more elevated mountain ranges, and some chilling nights made comfort impossible. Now and then some days of camping, too, were requisite—days in which arms were cleaned and ammunition inspected jealously. The American horses were undergoing acclimatization, and in the inevitable fever which develops itself, the affectionate cavalryman sits by his horse night and day until the crisis is passed. Well nursed, this fever is not dangerous. At the crisis, however, woe to the steed who loses his blanket, and woe to the rider who sleeps while the cold night air is driving in death through every pore. Accordingly as the perspiration is checked or encouraged is the balance for or against the life of the horse. There horses were gold, and hence the almost paternal solicitude.

Dr. John S. Tisdale, the lord of many patients and pill-boxes to-day in Platte, was veterinary surgeon, and from the healer of men he had become the healer of horses. Shaggy-headed and wide of forehead in the regions of ideality, he had a new name for every disease, and a new remedy for every symptom. An excellent appetite had given him a hearty laugh. During all the long night watches, he moved about as a Samaritan, his kindly face set in its frame-work of gray—his fifty years resting as lightly upon him as the night air upon the mountains of San Juan de Aguilar. He prayeth well who smoketh well, and the good Doctor's supplications went up all true and rugged many a time from his ancient pipe when the hoar frosts fell and deep sleep came down upon the camp as a silent angel to scatter sweet dreams of home and native land.

Good nursing triumphed. The crisis of the climate passed away, and from the last tedious camp the column moved rapidly on toward Lampasas. Dangers thickened. Content to keep the guerrillas at bay, Shelby had permitted no scouting parties and forbidden all pursuit.

"Let them alone," he would say to those eager for adventure, "and husband your strength. In a land of probable giants we have no need to hunt possible chimeras."

These guerrillas, however, became emboldened. On the trail of a timid or wounded thing they are veritable wolves. Their long gallop can never tire. In the night they are superb. Upon the flanks, in the front or rear, it is one eternal ambush—one incessant rattle of musketry which harms nothing, but which yet annoys like the singing of mosquitoes. At last they brought about a swift reckoning—one of those sudden things which leave little behind save a trail of blood and a moment of savage killing.

The column had reached to within two days' journey of Lampasas. Some spurs of the mountain ran down to the road, and some clusters of palm trees grouped themselves at intervals by the wayside. The palm is a pensive tree, having a voice in the wind that is sadder than the pine—a sober, solemn voice, a voice like the sound of ruffled cerements when the corpse is given to the coffin. Even in the sunlight they are dark; even in the tropics no vine clings to them, no blossom is born to them, no bird is housed by them, and no flutter of wings makes music for them. Strange and shapely, and coldly chaste, they seem like human and desolate things, standing all alone in the midst of luxurious nature, unblessed of the soil, and unloved of the dew and the sunshine.

In a grove of these the column halted for the night. Beyond them was a pass guarded by crosses. In that treacherous land these are a growth indigenous to the soil. They flourish nowhere else in such abundance. Wherever a deed of violence is done, a cross is planted; wherever a traveler is left upon his face in a pool of blood, a cross is reared; wherever a grave is made wherein lies the murdered one, there is seen a cross. No matter who does the deed—whether Indians, or don, or commandante, a cross must mark the spot, and as the pious wayfarer journeys by he lays all reverently a stone at the feet of the sacred symbol, breathing a pious prayer and telling a bead or two for the soul's salvation.

On the left a wooded bluff ran down abruptly to a stream. Beyond the stream and near the palms, a grassy bottom spread itself out, soft and grateful. Here the blankets were spread, and here the horses grazed their fill. A young moon, clear and white, hung low in the west, not sullen or red, but a tender moon full of the beams that lovers seek, and full of the voiceless imagery which gives passion to the songs of the night, and pathos to deserted and dejected swains.

As the moon set, the horses were gathered together and tethered in amid the palms. Then a deep silence fell upon the camp, for the sentinels were beyond its confines, and all withinside slept the sleep of the tired and healthy.

It may have been midnight; it certainly was cold and dark. The fires had gone out, and there was a white mist like a shroud creeping up the stream and settling upon the faces of the sleepers. On the far right a single pistol shot arose, clear and resonant. Shelby, who slumbered like a night bird, lifted himself up from his blankets and spoke in an undertone to Thrailkill:

"Who has the post at the mouth of the pass?"

"Jo. Macey."

"Then something is stirring. Macey never fired at a shadow in his life."

The two men listened. One a grim guerrilla himself, with the physique of a Cossack and the hearing of a Comanche. The other having in his hands the lives of all the silent and inert sleepers lying still and grotesque under the white shroud of the mountain mist.

Nothing was heard for an hour. The two men went to sleep again, but not to dream. Of a sudden and unseen, the mist was lifted, and in its place a sheet of flame so near to the faces of the men that it might have scorched them. Two hundred Mexicans had crept down the mountain, and to the edge of the stream, and had fired point blank into the camp. It seemed a miracle, but not a man was touched. Lying flat upon the ground and wrapped up in their blankets, the whole volley, meant to be murderous, had swept over them.

Shelby was the first upon his feet. His voice rang out clear and faultless, and without a tremor:

"Give them the revolver. Charge!"

Men awakened from sleep grapple with spectres slowly. These Mexicans were spectres. Beyond the stream and in amid the somber shadows of the palms, they were invisible. Only the powder-pall was on the water where the mist had been.

Unclad, barefooted, heavy with sleep, the men went straight for the mountain, a revolver in each hand, Shelby leading. From spectres the Mexicans had become bandits. No quarter was given or asked. The rush lasted until the game was flushed, the pursuit until the top of the mountain was gained. Over ragged rock and cactus and dagger-trees, the hurricane poured. The roar of the revolvers was deafening. Men died and made no moan, and the wounded were recognized only by their voices. When it was over, the Americans had lost in killed eleven and in wounded seventeen, most of the latter slightly, thanks to the darkness and the impetuosity of the attack.[2] In crawling upon the camp, the Mexicans had tethered their horses upon the further side of the mountain. The most of these fell into Shelby's hands, together with the bodies of the two leaders, Juan Anselmo, a renegade priest, and Antonio Flores, a young Cuban who had sold his sister to a wealthy *haciendaro*[3] and turned robber, and sixty-nine of their followers.

It was noon the next day before the march was resumed—noon with the sun shining upon the fresh graves of eleven dauntless Americans sleeping their last sleep, amid the palms and the crosses, until the resurrection day.

There was a grand *fandango*[4] at Lampasas when the column reached the city. The bronzed, foreign faces of the strangers attracted much of curiosity and more of comment; but no notes in the music jarred, no halt in the flying feet of the dancers could be discovered. Shelby camped just beyond the suburbs, unwilling to trust his men to the blandishments of so much beauty, and to the perils of so much nakedness.

Stern camp guards soon sentinelled the soldiers, but as the night deepened their devices increased, until a good company had escaped all vigilance and made a refuge sure with the sweet and swarthy *senoritas* singing:

> "O ven! ama!
> Eres alma,
> Soy corazon."[5]

There were three men who stole out together in mere wantonness and exuberance of life—obedient, soldierly men—who were to bring back with them a tragedy without a counterpart in all their history. None saw Boswell, Walker and Crockett depart—the whole command saw them return again, Boswell slashed from chin to waist, Walker almost dumb from a bullet through the cheeks and tongue, and Crockett, sober and unhurt, yet having over him the somber light of as wild a deed as any that stands out from all the lawless past of that lawless land.

These men, when reaching Lampasas, floated into the flood tide of the *fandango,* and danced until the red lights shone with an unnatural brilliancy—until the fiery *catalan*[6] consumed what little of discretion the dancing had left. They sallied out late at night, flushed with drink, and having over them the glamour of enchanting women. They walked on apace in the direction of the camp, singing snatches of Bacchanal songs, and laughing boisterously under the moonlight which flooded all the streets with gold. In the doorway of a house a young Mexican girl stood, her dark face looking out coquettishly from her fringe of dark hair. The men spoke to her, and she, in her simple, girlish fashion, spoke to the men. In Mexico this meant nothing. They halted, however, and Crockett advanced from the rest and laid his hand upon the girl's shoulder. Around her head and shoulders she wore a *rebosa.*[7] This garment answers at the same time for a bonnet and a bodice. When removed, the head is uncovered and the bosom is exposed. Crockett meant no real harm, although he asked for a kiss. Before she had replied to him, he attempted to take it.

The hot Southern blood flared up all of a sudden at this, and her dark eyes grew furious in a moment. As she drew back from him in proud scorn, the *rebosa* came off, leaving all her bosom bare, the long, luxuriant hair falling down upon and over it as a cloud that would hide its purity and innocence. Then she uttered a low, feminine cry as a signal, followed instantly by a rush of men who drew knives and pistols as they came on. The Americans had no weapons. Not dreaming of danger, and being within sight almost of camp, they had left their revolvers behind. Boswell was stabbed three times, though not seriously, for he was a powerful man, and he fought his assailants off. Walker was shot through his tongue and both cheeks, and Crockett, the cause of the whole *melee*, escaped unhurt. No pursuit was attempted after the first swift work was over. Wary of reprisals, the Mexicans hid themselves as suddenly as they had sallied out. There was a young man, however, who walked close to Crockett—a young Mexican who spoke no word, and who yet kept pace with the American step by step. At first he was not noticed. Before the camp guards were reached, Crockett, now completely sobered, turned upon him and asked:

"Why do you follow me?"

"That you may lead me to your General."

"What do you wish with my General?"

"Satisfaction."

At the firing in the city a patrol guard had been thrown out who arrested the whole party and carried it straight to Shelby. He was encamped upon a wide margin of bottom land, having a river upon one side and some low mountain ridges on the other. The ground where the blankets were spread was velvety with grass. There was a bright moon; the air blowing from the grape gardens and the apricot orchards of Lampasas was fragrant and delicious, and the soldiers were not sleeping.

Under the solace of such surroundings, Shelby had relaxed a little of that grim severity he always manifested toward those guilty of unsoldierly conduct, and spoke not harshly to the three men. When made acquainted with their hurts, he dismissed them instantly to the care of Dr. Tisdale.

Crockett and the Mexican still lingered, and a crowd of some fifty or sixty had gathered around. The first told his story of the *melee*, and told it truthfully. The man was too brave to lie. As an Indian listening to the approaching footsteps of one whom he intends to scalp, the young Mexican listened as a granite pillar vitalized to the whole recital. When it was finished he went up close to Shelby and said to him, pointing his finger at Crockett:

"That man has outraged my sister. I could have killed him, but I did not. You Americans are brave, I know; will you be generous as well, and give me satisfaction?"

Shelby looked at Crockett, whose bronzed face, made sterner in the moonlight, had upon it a look of curiosity. He at least did not understand what was coming.

"Does the Mexican speak the truth, Crockett?" was the question asked by the commander of his soldier.

"Partly; but I meant no harm to the woman. I am incapable of that. Drunk I know I was, and reckless, but not willfully guilty, General."

Shelby regarded him coldly. His voice was so stern when he spoke that the brave soldier hung his head:

"What business had you to lay your hands upon her at all? How often must I repeat to you that the man who does these things is no follower of mine? Will you give her brother satisfaction?"

He drew his revolver almost joyfully and stood proudly up, facing his accuser.

"No! no! not the pistol!" cried the Mexican; "I do not understand the pistol. The knife, Senor General; is the American afraid of the knife?"

He displayed, as he spoke, a keen, glittering knife and held it up in the moonlight. It was white, and lithe, and shone in contrast with the dusky hand that grasped it.

Not a muscle of Crockett's face moved. He spoke almost gently as he turned to his General:

"The knife, ah! well, so be it. Will some of you give me a knife?"

A knife was handed him and a ring was made. About four hundred soldiers formed the outside circle of this ring. These, bearing torches in their hands, cast a red glare of light upon the arena. The ground under foot was as velvet. The moon, not yet full, and the sky without a cloud, rose over all, calm and peaceful in the summer night. A hush, as of expectancy, fell upon the camp. Those who were asleep, slept on; those who were awake seemed as under the influence of an intangible dream.

Shelby did not forbid the fight. He knew it was a duel to the death, and some of the desperate spirit of the combatants passed into his own. He merely spoke to an aide:

"Go for Tisdale. When the steel has finished, the surgeon may begin."

Both men stepped fearlessly into the arena. A third form was there, unseen, invisible, and even in *his* presence the traits of the two nations were uppermost. The Mexican made the sign of the cross, the American tightened his saber belt. Both may have prayed, neither, however, audibly.

They had no seconds; perhaps none were needed. The Mexican took his stand about midway the arena and waited. Crockett grasped his knife firmly and advanced upon him. Of the two, he was the taller by a head and physically the strongest. Constant familiarity with danger for four years had given him a confidence the Mexican may not have felt. He had been wounded three times, one of which wounds had scarcely healed. This took none of his manhood from him, however.

Neither spoke. The torches flared a little in the night wind, now beginning to rise, and the long grass rustled curtly under foot. Afterward its green had become crimson.

Between them some twelve inches of space now intervened. The men had fallen back upon the right and the left for their commander to see, and he stood looking fixedly at the two as he would upon a line of battle. Never before had he gazed upon so strange a sight. That great circle of bronzed faces, eager and fierce in the flare of torches, had something monstrous yet grotesque about it. The civilization of the century had been rolled back, and they were in a Roman circus, looking down upon the arena, crowded with gladiators and jubilant with that strangest of war cries: *Morituri te salutant!*[8]

The attack was the lightning's flash. The Mexican lowered his head, set his teeth hard, and struck fairly at Crockett's breast. The American made a half face to the right, threw his left arm forward as a shield, gathered the deadly steel in his shoulder to the hilt and struck home. How pitiful!

A great stream of blood spurted in his face. The tense form of the Mexican bent as a willow wand in the wind, swayed helplessly, and fell backward lifeless, the knife rising up as a terrible protest above the corpse. The man's heart was found.

Cover him up from sight. No need of Dr. Tisdale here. There was a wail of women on the still night air, a shudder of regret among the soldiers, a dead man on the grass, a sister broken-hearted and alone for evermore, and a freed spirit somewhere out in eternity with the unknown and the infinite.

CHAPTER IX.

General Jeanningros held Monterey with a garrison of five thousand French and Mexican soldiers. Among them was the Foreign Legion—composed of Americans, English, Irish, Arabs, Turks, Germans and Negroes—and the Third French Zouaves, a regiment unsurpassed for courage and discipline in any army in any nation on earth. This regiment afterward literally passed away from service at Gravelotte.[1] Like the Old Guard at Waterloo, it was destroyed.[2]

Jeanningros was a soldier who spoke English, who had gray hair, who drank absinthe, who had been in the army thirty years, who had been wounded thirteen times, and who was only a general of brigade. His discipline was all iron. Those who transgressed, those who were found guilty at night, were shot in the morning. He never spared what the court martial had condemned. There was a ghastly dead wall in Monterey, isolated, lonesome, forbidding, terrible, which had seen many a stalwart form shudder and fall, many a young, fresh, dauntless face go down stricken in the hush of the morning. The face of this wall, covered all over with warts, with excrescences, with scars, had about it a horrible small-pox. Where the bullets had plowed it up were the traces of the pustules. The splashes of blood left by the slaughter dried there. In the sunlight these shone as sinister blushes upon the countenance of that stony and inanimate thing, peering out from an inexorable ambush—waiting.

Speaking no word for the American, and setting down naught to the credit side of his necessities or his surroundings, those who had brought news to Jeanningros of Shelby's operations at Piedras Negras had told him as well of the cannon sold as of the arms and ammunition. Jeanningros had waited patiently and had replied to them:

"Wait awhile. We must catch them before we hang them."

While he was waiting to lay hands upon them, Shelby had marched to within a mile of the French outposts at Monterey. He came as a soldier, and he meant to do a soldier's work. Pickets were thrown forward, the horses were fed, and Governor Reynolds put in most excellent French this manner of a note:

> GENERAL JEANNINGROS, Commander at Monterey.—General: I have the honor to report that I am within one mile of your fortifications with my command. Preferring exile to surrender, I have left my own coun-

try to seek service in that held by His Imperial Majesty, the Emperor Maximilian. Shall it be peace or war between us? If the former, with your permission, I shall enter your lines at once, claiming at your hands that courtesy due from one soldier to another. If the latter, I propose to attack you immediately. Very respectfully yours,

    Jo. O. Shelby

Improvising a flag of truce, two fearless soldiers, John Thrailkill and Rainy McKinney, bore it boldly into the public square at Monterey. This flag was an apparition. The long roll was beaten, the garrison stood to their arms, mounted orderlies galloped hither and thither, and Jeanningros himself, used all his life to surprises, was attracted by the soldierly daring of the deed. He received the message and answered it favorably, remarking to Thrailkill, as he handed him the reply:

"Tell your general to march in immediately. He is the only soldier that has yet come out of Yankeedom."

Jeanningros' reception was as frank and open as his speech. That night, after assigning quarters to the men, he gave a banquet to the officers. Among those present were General Magruder, Ex-Senator Trusten Polk, Ex-Governor Thomas C. Reynolds, General T. C. Hindman, General E. Kirby Smith, General John B. Clark, General Shelby, and many others fond of talk, wine and adventure. Jeanningros was a superb host. His conversation never tired of the Crimea, of Napoleon III's *coup d'etat,* of the Italian campaign, of the march to Pekin, of Algeria, of all the great soldiers he had known, of all the great campaigns he had participated in. The civil war in America was discussed in all of its vivid and somber lights, and no little discussion carried on as to the probable effect peace would have upon Maximilian's occupation of Mexico. Jeanningros was emphatic in all of his declarations. In reply to a question asked by Shelby concerning the statesmanship of the Mexican emperor, the French General replied:

"Ah! the Austrian; you should see him to understand him. More of a scholar than a king, good at botany, a poet on occasions, a traveler who gathers curiosities and writes books, a saint over his wine and a sinner among his cigars, in love with his wife, believing more in manifest destiny than drilled battalions, good Spaniard in all but deceit and treachery, honest, earnest, tender-hearted and sincere, his faith is too strong in the liars who surround him, and his soul is too pure for the deeds that must be done. He can not kill as we Frenchmen do. He knows nothing of diplomacy. In a nation of thieves and cut-throats, he goes devoutly to mass, endows hospitals, laughs a good man's laugh at the praises of the blanketed rabble, says his prayers and sleeps the sleep of the gentleman and the prince. Bah! his days are numbered; nor can all the power of France keep his crown upon his head, if, indeed, it can keep that head upon his shoulders."

The blunt soldier checked himself suddenly. The man had spoken over his wine; the courtier never speaks.

"Has he the confidence of Bazaine?" asked General Clark.

Jeanningros gave one of those untranslatable shrugs which are a volume, and drained his goblet before replying.

"The Marshal, you mean. Oh! the Marshal keeps his own secrets. Besides, I have not seen the Marshal since coming northward. Do you go further, General Clark?"

The diplomatist had met the diplomatist. Both smiled; neither referred to the subject again.

Daylight shone through the closed shutters before the party separated— the Americans to sleep, the Frenchman to sign a death warrant.

A young lieutenant of the Foreign Legion, crazed by that most damnable of drinks, absinthe, had deserted from outpost duty in a moment of temporary insanity. For three days he wandered about, taking no note of men or things, helpless and imbecile. On the morning of the fourth day, his reason was given back to him. None knew better than himself the nature of the precipice upon which he stood. Before him lay the Rio Grande, the succor beyond an asylum, safety; behind him, the court martial, the sentence, the horrible wall, splashed breast high with blood, the platoon, the leveled muskets—death. He never faltered. Returning to the outpost at which he had been stationed, he saluted its officer and said:

"Here I am."

"Indeed. And who are you?"

"A deserter."

"Ah! but Jeanningros shoots deserter. Why did you not keep on, since you had started?"

"No matter. I am a Frenchman and I know how to die."

They brought him in while Jeanningros was drinking his generous wine, and holding high revelry with his guests. When the morning came, he was tried. No matter for anything the poor young soldier could say, and he said but little. At sunrise upon the next morning he was to die.

When Jeanningros awoke late in the afternoon there was a note for him. Its contents, in substance, was as follows:

"I do not ask for my life—only for the means of disposing of it. I have an old mother in France who gave me to the country, and who blessed me as she said good-bye. Under the law, General, if I am shot, my property goes to the State; if I shoot myself, my mother gets it. It is a little thing a soldier asks of his General, who has medals, and honors, and maybe a mother, too—but for the sake of the uniform I wore at Solferino, is it asking more than you can grant when I ask for a revolver and a bottle of brandy?"

Through his sleepy, half-shut eyes Jeanningros read the message to the end. When he had finished he called an aide.

"Take to the commandant of the prison this order."

The order was for the pistol and the brandy.

That afternoon and night the young Lieutenant wrote, and drank, and made his peace with the world. What laid beyond he knew not, nor any man born of woman. There was a little light in the east, and a little brandy in the bottle. But the letters had all been written, and the poor woman in France would get her just due after all.

Turn out the guard!

For what end? No need of soldiers there—rather the coffin, the prayer of the priest, the grave that God blessed, though by man decreed unhallowed. French to the last, the Lieutenant had waited for the daylight, had finished his bottle, and had scattered his brains over the cold walls of his desolate prison. Jeanningros heard the particulars duly related, and had dismissed the Adjutant with an epigram:

"Clever fellow. He was entitled to two bottles, instead of one."

Such is French discipline. All crimes but one may be condoned—desertion never.

Preceding Shelby's arrival in Monterey, there had come also Col. Francois Achille Dupin, a Frenchman who was known as "The Tiger of the Tropics."[3] What he did would fill a volume. Recorded here, no reader would believe it—no Christian would imagine such warfare possible. He was past sixty, tall as Tecumseh, straight as a rapier, with a seat in the saddle like an English guardsman, and a waist like a woman. For deeds of desperate daring, he had received more decorations than could be displayed upon the right breast of his uniform. His hair and beard, snowy white, contrasted strangely with a stern, set face that had been bronzed by the sun and the wind of fifty campaigns.

In the Chinese expedition this man had led the assault upon the Emperor's palace, wherein no defender escaped the bayonet and no woman the grasp of the brutal soldiery. Sack and pillage and murder and crimes without a name all were there, and when the fierce carnage was done, Dupin, staggering under the weight of the rubies and pearls and diamonds, was a disgraced man. The inexorable jaws of a French court martial closed down upon him, and he was dismissed from service. It was on the trial that he parodied the speech of Warren Hastings and declared:

"When I saw mountains of gold and precious stones piled up around me, and when I think of the paltry handfuls taken away, by G—d, Mr. President, I am astonished at my own moderation."[4]

As they stripped his decorations and ribbons from his breast, he drew himself up with a touching and graceful air, and said to the officer, saluting:

"They have left me nothing but my scars."

Such a man, however, tiger and butcher as he was, had need of the army and the army had need of him. The Emperor gave him back his rank, his orders, his decorations, and gave him as well his exile into Mexico.

Maximilian refused him; Bazaine found work for his sword. Even then that fatal quarrel was in its beginning which, later, was to leave a kingdom defenseless, and an Emperor without an arsenal or a siege-gun. Dupin was ordered to recruit a regiment of Contre Guerrillas, that is to say a regiment of Free Companions who were to be superbly armed and mounted, and who were to follow the Mexican guerrillas through copse and chaparral, through lowland and lagoon, sparing no man upon whom hands were laid, fighting all men who had arms in their hands, and who could be found or brought to bay.

Murder with Dupin was a fine art. Mistress or maid he had none. That cold, brown face, classic a little in its outlines, and retaining yet a little of its fierce southern beauty, never grew soft save when the battle was wild and the wreck of the carnage ghastly and thick. On the eve of conflict he had been known to smile. When he laughed or sang his men made the sign of the cross. They knew death was ready at arm's length, and that in an hour he would put his sickle in amid the rows and reap savagely a fresh harvest of simple, yet offending Mexicans. Of all things left to him from the sack of the Pekin palace, one thing alone remained, typical of the tiger thirst of that old age, nor disgrace, nor wounds, nor rough foreign service, nor anything human, had power potent enough to quench or assuage. Victor Hugo, in his "Toilers of the Sea," has woven it into the story after this fashion, looking straight, perhaps, into the eyes of the cruel soldier who, in all his life, has never listened to prayer or priest:

"A piece of silk stolen during the last war from the palace of the Emperor of China represented a shark eating a crocodile, who is eating a serpent, who is devouring an eagle, who is preying on a swallow, who is in his turn eating a caterpillar. All nature which is under our observation is thus alternately devouring and devoured. They prey, prey on each other."[5]

Dupin preyed upon his species. He rarely killed outright. He had a theory, often put into practice, which was diabolical.

"When you kill a Mexican," he would say, "that is the end of him. When you cut off an arm or a leg, that throws him upon the charity of his friends, and then two or three must support him. Those who make corn can not make soldiers. It is economy to amputate."

Hundreds thus passed under the hands of his surgeons. His maimed and mutilated were in every town from Mier to Monterey. On occasions when the march had been pleasant and the wine generous, he would permit chloroform for the operation. Otherwise not. It distressed him for a victim to die beneath the knife.

"You bunglers endanger my theory," he would cry out to his surgeons. "Why can't you cut without killing?"

The "Tiger of the Tropics" also had his playful moods. He would stretch himself in the sun, overpower one with gentleness and attention, say soft things in whispers, quote poetry upon occasions, make of himself an elegant host, serve the wine, laugh low and lightsomely, wake up all of a sudden a demon, and—*kill*.

One instance of this is yet a terrible memory in Monterey.

An extremely wealthy and influential Mexican, Don Vincente Ibarra, was at home upon his *hacienda* one day about noon as Dupin marched by. Perhaps this man was a Liberal; certainly he sympathized with Juarez and had done much for the cause in the shape of recruiting and resistance to the predatory bands of Imperialists. As yet, however, he had taken up no arms, and had paid his proportion of the taxes levied upon him by Jeanningros.

Dupin was at dinner when his scouts brought Ibarra into camp. In front of the tent was a large tree in full leaf, whose spreading branches made an extensive and most agreeable shade. Under this the Frenchman had a camp-stool placed for the comfort of the Mexican.

"Be seated," he said to him in a voice no harsher than the wind among the leaves overhead. "And, waiter, lay another plate for my friend."

The meal was a delightful one. Dupin talked as a subject who had a prince for his guest, and as a lover who had a woman for his listener. In the intervals of the conversation he served the wine. Ibarra was delighted. His suspicious Spanish heart relaxed the tension of its grim defense, and he even stroked the tiger's velvet skin, who closed his sleepy eyes and purred under the caress.

When the wine was at its full, cigars were handed. Behind the white cloud of the smoke, Dupin's face darkened. Suddenly he spoke to Ibarra, pointing up to the tree:

"What a fine shade it makes, Senor? Do such trees ever bear fruit?"

"Never, Colonel. What a question."

"Never? All things are possible with God, why not with a Frenchman?"

"Because a Frenchman believes so little in God, perhaps."

The face grew darker and darker.

"Are your affairs prosperous, Senor?"

"As much so as these times will permit."

"Very good. You have just five minutes in which to make them better. At the end of that time I will hang you on that tree so sure as you are a Mexican. What ho! Captain Jacan, turn out the guard!"

Ibarra's deep olive face grew ghastly white, and he fell upon his knees. No prayers, no agonizing entreaty, no despairing supplication wrung from a strong man in his agony availed him aught. At the appointed time his rigid frame swung between heaven and earth, another victim to the mood of one who never knew an hour of penitence or mercy. The tree had borne fruit.

And so this manner of man—this white-haired Dupin—decorated, known to two continents as the "Tiger of the Tropics," who kept four picked Chasseurs to stand guard about and over him night and day, this old-young soldier, with a voice like a school-girl and a heart like a glacier, came to Monterey and recruited a regiment of Contre Guerrillas, a regiment that feared neither God, man, the Mexicans nor the devil.

Under him as a captain was Charles Ney, the grandson of that other Ney who cried out to D'Erlon at Waterloo, "Come and see how a marshal of France dies on the field of battle."[6]

In Captain Ney's company there were two squadrons—a French squadron and an American squadron, the last having for its commander Capt. Frank Moore, of Alabama. Under Moore were one hundred splendid Confederate soldiers who, refusing to surrender, had sought exile, and had stranded upon that inevitable lee shore called necessity. Between the Scylla of short rations and the Charybdis of empty pockets, the only channel possible was the open sea. So into it sailed John C. Moore, Armistead, Williams and the rest of the American squadron which was to become famous from Matamoras to Matehuala.

This much by way of preface has been deemed necessary in order that an accurate narrative may be made of the murder of Gen. M. M. Parsons, of Jefferson City, his brother-in-law, Colonel Standish, of the same place, the Hon. A. H. Conrow, of Caldwell county, and three gallant young Irishmen, James Mooney, Patrick Langdon, and Michael Monarthy. Ruthlessly butchered in a foreign country, they yet had avengers. When the tale was told to Colonel Dupin, by John Moore, he listened as an Indian in ambush might to the heavy tread of some unwary and approaching trapper. After the story had been finished he asked, abruptly:

"What would you Americans have?"

"Permission," said Moore, "to gather up what is left of our comrades and bury what is left."

"And strike a good, fair blow in return?"

"Maybe so, Colonel."

"Then march at daylight with your squadron. Let me hear when you return that not one stone upon another of the robber's rendezvous has been left."

Gen. M. M. Parsons had commanded a division of Missouri infantry with great credit to himself, and with great honor to the State.[7] He was a soldier of remarkable personal beauty, of great dash in battle, of unsurpassed horsemanship, and of that graceful and natural suavity of manner which endeared him alike to his brother officers and to the men over whom he was placed in command. His brother-in-law, Colonel Standish, was his chief of staff, and a frank, fearless young officer, whom the Missourians knew and admired. Capt. Aaron H. Conrow had, before the war, represented Caldwell county in the Legislature, and had, during the war, been elected to the Confederate Congress.[8] With these three men were three brave and faithful young Irish soldiers—Mooney, Langdon, and Monarthy—six in all, who, for the crime of being Americans, had to die.

Following in the rear of Shelby's expedition in the vain hope of overtaking it, they reached the neighborhood of Piedras Negras too late to cross the Rio Grande there. A strong body of guerrillas had moved up into town and occupied it immediately after Shelby's withdrawal. Crossing the river, however, lower down, they had entered Mexico in safety, and had won their perilous way to Monterey without serious loss or molestation. Not content to go further at that time, and wishing to return to Camargo for purposes of communication with Texas, they availed themselves of the protection of a train of supply wagons sent by Jeanningros, heavily guarded by Imperial Mexican soldiers, to Matamoras. Jeanningros gave them safe conduct as far as possible, and some good advice as well, which advice simply warned them against trusting anything whatever to Mexican courage or Mexican faith.

The wagon train and its escort advanced well on their way to Matamoras—well enough at least to be beyond the range of French succor should the worst come to worst. But on the evening of the fourth day, in a narrow defile at the crossing of an exceedingly rapid and dangerous stream, the escort was furiously assailed by a large body of Juaristas, checked at once, and finally driven back. General Parsons and his party retreated with the rest until the night's camp was reached, when a little council of war was called by the Americans. Conrow and Standish were in favor of abandoning the trip for the present, especially as the whole country was aroused and in waiting for the train, and more especially as the guerrillas, attracted by the scent of plunder, were swarming upon the roads and in ambush by every pass and beside the fords of every stream. General Parsons overruled them, and determined to make the venture as soon as the moon arose, in the direction of Camargo.

None took issue with him further. Accustomed to exact obedience, much of the old soldierly spirit was still in existence, and so they followed him blindly and with alacrity. At daylight the next morning the entire party was captured. Believing, however, that the Americans were but the advance of a larger and more formidable party, the Mexicans neither dismounted nor disarmed them. While at breakfast, and at the word of command from General Parsons, the whole six galloped off under a fierce fire of musketry, unhurt, baffling all pursuit, and gaining some good hours' advantage over their captors. It availed them nothing, however. About noon of the second day they were again captured, this time falling into the hands of Figueroa, a robber chief as notorious among the Mexicans as Dupin was among the French.

Short shrift came afterward. Colonel Standish was shot first. When told of the fate intended for him, he bade good-bye to his comrades, knelt a few moments in silent prayer, and then stood up firmly, facing his murderers. At the discharge of the musketry platoon, he was dead before he touched the ground. Two bullets pierced his generous and dauntless heart.

Capt. Aaron H. Conrow died next. He expected no mercy, and he made no plea for his life. A request to be permitted to write a few lines to his wife was denied him, Figueroa savagely ordering the execution to proceed. The firing party shortened the distance between it and their victim, placing him but three feet away from the muzzles of their muskets. Like Standish, he refused to have his eyes bandaged. Knowing but few words of Spanish, he called out in his brave, quick fashion, and in his own language, "Fire!" and the death he got was certain and instantaneous. He fell within a few paces of his comrade, dead like him before he touched the ground.

The last moments of the three young Irish soldiers had now come. They had seen the stern killing of Standish and Conrow, and they neither trembled nor turned pale. It can do no good to ask what thoughts were theirs, or if from over the waves of the wide Atlantic some visions came that were strangely and sadly out of place in front of the chaparral and the sandaled Mexicans. Monarthy asked for a priest, and received one. He was a kind-hearted, ignorant Indian, who would have saved them if he could, but safe from the bloody hands of Figueroa no foreigner had ever yet come. The three men confessed and received such consolation as the living could give to men as good as dead. Then they joined hands and spoke some earnest words together for the brief space permitted them. Langdon, the youngest, was only twenty-two. A resident of Mobile when the war commenced, he had volunteered in a battery, had been captured at Vicksburg, and had later joined Pindall's battalion of sharpshooters in Parsons' Division. He had a face like a young girl's, it was so fair and fresh. All who knew him loved him. In all the Confederate army there was neither braver nor better soldier. Mooney was a man of fifty-five, with an iron frame and with a gaunt, scarred, rugged face that was yet kindly and attractive. He took Langdon in his arms and kissed him twice, once on each cheek, shook hands with Monarthy, and opened his breast. The close, deadly fire was received standing and with eyes wide open. Langdon died without a struggle, Mooney groaned twice and tried to speak. Death finished the sentence ere it was commenced. Monarthy required the *coup de grace*. A soldier went close to him, rested the muzzle of his musket against his head and fired. He was very quiet then; the murder was done; five horrible corpses lay in a pool of blood; the shadows deepened; and the cruel eyes of Figueroa roamed, as the eyes of a tiger, from the ghastly faces of the dead to the stern, set face of the living. General Parsons felt that for him, too, the supreme moment had come at last.

Left in that terrible period alone, none this side of eternity will ever know what he suffered and endured. Waiting patiently for his sentence, a respite was granted. Some visions of ransom must have crossed Figueroa's mind. Clad in the showy and attractive uniform of a Confederate major-general, having the golden stars of his rank upon his collar, magnificently mounted, and being withal a remarkably handsome and commanding-looking soldier himself, it was for a time at least thought best to hold him a prisoner. His horse even was given back to him, and for some miles further toward Matamoras he was permitted to ride with those who had captured him. The Captain of the guard immediately in charge of his person had also a very fine horse, whose speed he was continually boasting of. Fortunately this officer spoke English, thus permitting General Parsons to converse with him. Much bantering was had concerning the speed of the two horses. A race was at length proposed. The two men started off at a furious gallop, the American steadily gaining upon the Mexican. Finding himself in danger of being distanced, the Captain drew up and ordered his competitor in the race to halt. Unheeding the command, General Parsons dashed on with utmost speed, escaping the shots from the revolver of the Mexican, and eluding entirely Figueroa and his command. Although in a country filled with treacherous and blood-thirsty savages, and ignorant of the roads and the language, General Parsons might have reduced the chances against him in the proportion of ten to one, had he concealed himself in some neighboring chaparral and waited until the night fell. He did not do this, but continued his flight rapidly down the broad highway which ran directly from Monterey to Matamoras. There could be but one result. A large scouting party of Figueroa's forces returning to the headquarters of their chief met him before he had ridden ten miles, again took him prisoner, and again delivered him into the hands of the ferocious bandit.

Death followed almost instantly. None who witnessed the deed have ever told how he died, but three days afterward his body was found stripped by the wayside, literally shot to pieces. Some Mexicans then buried it, marking the unhallowed spot with a cross. Afterward Figueroa, dressed in the full uniform of General Parsons, was in occupation of Camargo, while the same Colonel Johnson, who had followed Shelby southwardly from San Antonio, held the opposite shore of the Rio Grande on the American side. Figueroa, gloating over the savageness of the deed, and imagining, in his stolid Indian cunning, that the Federal officers would pay handsomely for the spoils of the murdered Confederate, proffered to deliver to him General Parsons' coat, pistols and private papers for a certain specified sum, detailing, at the same time, with revolting accuracy, the merciless particulars of the butchery. Horrified at the cool rapacity of the robber, and thinking only of General Parsons as an American and a brother, Colonel Johnson tried for weeks to entice Figueroa across the river, intending to do a righteous vengeance upon him. Too wily and too cowardly to be caught, he moved back suddenly into the interior, sending a message afterward to Colonel Johnson full of taunting and defiance.

Whoso sheddeth man's blood, by man shall his own blood be shed. Dupin's avengers were on the track, imbued with Dupin's spirit, and having over them the stern memory of Dupin's laconic orders. Leave not one stone upon another. And why should there be habitations when the inhabitants were scattered or killed.

Las Flores was a flower town, beautiful in name, and beautiful in the blue of the skies which bent over it: in the blue of the mountains which caught the morning and wove for it a gossamer robe of amethyst and pearl; in the song and flow of running water, where women sat and sang, and combed their dusky hair; and in the olden, immemorial groves, filled with birds that had gold for plumage, and sweet seed and sunshine for mating and wooing songs.

Hither would come Figueroa in the lull of the long marches, and in the relaxation of the nights of ambush, and the days of watching and starving. Booty and beauty, and singing maidens all were there. There, red gold would buy right royal kisses, and there feasting and minstrelsy told of the pillage done, and the rapine and slaughter beyond the sweep of the mountains that had cut the sky line.

God help all of them who tarried till the American squadron charged into town, one hundred rank and file, Frank Moore leading—all who had beard upon their faces or guns within their hands. A trusty guide had made the morning a surprise. It was not yet daylight. Some white mist, like a corpse abandoning a bier, was creeping up from the lowlands. The music and the lights had died out in the streets. The east, not yet awakened, had on its face the placid pallor of sleep. What birds flew were weary of wing and voiceless in the sober hush of dreamless nature.

Leave not one stone upon another. And the faces of the Americans were set as flint and the massacre began. Never were six men so terribly avenged. It need not be told what flames were there, what harsh and guttural oaths, what tawny faces blanched and grew white, what cries and volleys and shrieks, and deaths that made no moan arose on the morning, and scared the mist from the water, the paradise birds from their bowers amid the limes and the orange trees. It was over at last. Call the roll and gather up the corpses. Fifteen Americans dead, eleven wounded, and so many Mexicans that you could not count them. Las Flores, the City of the Flowers, had become Las Cruces, the City of the Crosses.

When the tale was told to Dupin, he rubbed his brown bare hands and lent his arm on his subaltern's shoulder.

"Tell me about it again," he ordered.

The tale was told.

"Oh! brave Americans!" he shouted. "Americans after my own heart. You shall be saluted with sloping standards and uncovered heads.

The bugles ran out "to horse," the regiment got under arms, the American squadron passed in review along the ranks, the flags were lowered and inclined, officers and men uncovered as the files marched down the lines; there were greetings and rejoicings, and from the already lengthened life of the white-haired commander five good years of toil and exposure had been taken. For a week thereafter he was seen to smile and be glad. After that, the old wild work commenced again.

CHAPTER X.

In Monterey, at the time of Shelby's arrival, there was one man who had figured somewhat extensively in a *role* new to most Americans. This man was the Hon. William M. Gwin, ex-United States Senator and ex-Governor of California.[1] He had just been to France and just returned. Accomplished in all of the social graces; an aristocrat born and a bit of an Imperialist as well; full of wise words and sage reflections; graceful in his conversation and charming over his wine; having the political history of his country at heart as a young Catholic does his catechism; fond of the pomp and the paraphernalia of royalty; nothing of a soldier, but much of a diplomatist; a stranger to reverence and a cosmopolitan in religion, he was a right proper man to hold court in Sonora, the Mexican province whose affairs he was to administer upon as a Duke. Napoleon III had granted him letters patent for this, and for this he had ennobled him. It is nowhere recorded that he took possession of his province. Granted an audience by Maximilian, he laid his plans before him and asked for a prompt installment into the administration of the dukedom. It was refused peremptorily. At the mercy of Bazaine, and having no soldiers worthy of the name other than French soldiers, the Mexican Emperor had weighty reasons besides private ones for such refusal. It was not time for the coquetries of empire before that empire had an army, a bank account, and a clean bill of health. Gwin became indignant, Bazaine became amused, and Maximilian became disgusted. In the end the Duke left the country and the guerrillas seized upon the dukedom. When Shelby reached Monterey, ex-Governor Gwin was outward bound for Matamoras, reaching the United States later only to be imprisoned in Fort Jackson, below New Orleans, for several long and weary months. The royal sufferer had most excellent company—although Democratic, and therefore unsympathetic. General John B. Clark, returning about the same time, was pounced upon and duly incarcerated.[2] Gwin attempted to convert him to imperialism, but it ended by Clark bringing Gwin back to Democracy. And a noble Missourian was "Old" General Clark, as the soldiers loved to call him. Lame from a wound received while leading his brigade gallantly into action at Wilson's Creek, penniless in a land for whose sake he had given up gladly a magnificent fortune, proscribed of the Government, a prisoner without a country, an exile who was not permitted to return in peace, dogmatic and defiant to the last, he went into Fort Jackson a rebel, remained a rebel there, came away a rebel, and a rebel he will continue to be as long as life permits him to use the rough Anglo Saxon oaths which go to make up his rebel vocabulary. On the march into Mexico, he had renewed his youth. In the night watches he told tales of his boyhood, and by the camp fires he replenished anew the fires of his memory. Hence all the anecdotes that amused—all the reminiscences which delighted. At the crossing of the Salinas river, he fell in beside General Shelby, a musket in his hand, and the old ardor of battle upon his stern and weather-beaten face.

"Where would you go?" asked Shelby.

"As far as you go, my young man."

"Not this day, my old friend, if I can help it. There are younger and less valuable men who shall take this risk alone. Get out of the ranks, General. The column can not advance unless you do."

Forced against his will to retire, he was mad for a week, and only recovered his amiability after being permitted to engage in the night encounter at the Pass of the Palms.

Before marching northward from Monterey, Shelby sought one last interview with General Jeanningros. It was courteously accorded. General Preston, who had gone forward from Texas to open negotiations with Maximilian, and who had reached Mexico City in safety, had not yet reported the condition of his surroundings. It was Shelby's desire to take military service in the Empire since his men had refused to become the followers of Juarez at Piedras Negras. Knowing that a corps of fifty thousand Americans could be recruited in a few months after a base of operations had once been established, he sought the advice of General Jeanningros to this end, meaning to deal frankly with him, and to discuss fully his plans and purposes.

Jeanningros had grown gray in the service. He acknowledged but one standard of perfection—success. Never mind the means, so only the end was glory and France. The camps had made him cruel; the barracks had given to this cruelty a kind of fascinating rhetoric. Sometimes he dealt in parables. One of these told more of the paymaster than the zouave, more of the Minister Rouher than Marshal McMahon.[3] He would say:

"Napoleon and Maximilian have formed a partnership. To get it well agoing, much money has been spent. Some bargains have been bad, and some vessels have been lost. There is a crisis at hand. More capital is needed to save what has already been invested, and for one, rather than lose the millions swallowed up yesterday, I would put in as many more millions to-day. It is economy to hold on."

Shelby went straight at his work:

"I do not know what you think of things here, General, nor of the outcome the future has in store for the Empire, but one thing is certain, I shall tell you the plain truth. The Federal Government has no love for your French occupation of Mexico. If diplomacy can't get you out, infantry divisions will. I left a large army concentrating upon the banks of the Rio Grande, and all the faces of all the men were looking straight forward into Mexico. Will France fight? For one, I hope so; but it seems to me that if your Emperor had meant to be serious in this thing, his plan should have been to have formed an alliance long ago, offensive and defensive, with Jefferson Davis. This, in the event of success, would have guaranteed you the whole country, and obliged you as well to have opened the ports of Charleston, Savannah, and New Orleans. Better battles could have been fought on the Potomac than on the Rio Grande; surer results would have followed from a French landing at Mobile than at Tampico or Vera Cruz. You have waited too long. Flushed with a triumphant termination of the war, American diplomacy now means the Monroe doctrine, pure and simple, with a little of Yankee brutality and braggadocio thrown in. Give me a port as a basis of operations, and I can organize an American force capable of keeping Maximilian upon his throne. If left discretionary with me, that port shall be either Guaymas or Mazatlan. The Californians love adventure, and many leaders among them have already sent messengers to me with overtures. My agent at the capital has not yet reported, and, consequently, I am uninformed as to the wishes of the Emperor; but one thing is certain, the French can not remain, and he can not rule over Mexicans with Mexicans. Without foreign aid he is lost. You know Bazaine better than I do, and so what would Bazaine say to all this?"

Jeanningros heard him patiently to the end, answering Shelby as frankly as he had been addressed:

"There will be no war between France and the United States, and of this you may rest assured. I can not answer for Marshal Bazaine, nor for his wishes and intentions. There is scant love, however, between his excellency and Maximilian, because one is a scholar and the other is a soldier; but I do not think the Marshal would be averse to the employment of American soldiers in the service of the Empire. You have my full permission to march to the Pacific, and to take such other steps as will seem best to you in the matter of which you have just spoken. The day is not far distant when every French soldier in Mexico will be withdrawn, although this would not necessarily destroy the Empire. Who will take their places? Mexicans. Bah! beggars ruling over beggars, cut-throats lying in wait for cut-throats, traitors on the inside making signs for traitors on the outside to come in. Not thus are governments upheld and administered. Healthy blood must be poured through every effete and corrupted vein of this effete and corrupted nation ere the Austrian can sleep a good man's sleep in his palace of Chapultepec."[4]

The interview ended, and Shelby marched northward to Saltillo. The first camp beyond was upon the battle field of Buena Vista. It was sunset when the column reached the memorable and historic field.[5] A gentle rain in the morning had washed the grass until it shone, had washed the trees until the leaves glistened and smelt of perfume. After the bivouac was made, silence and twilight, as twin ghosts, crept up the glade together. Nest spoke unto nest in the gloaming, and bade good-night as the moon arose. It was an harvest moon, white and splendid and large as a tent-leafed palm. Away over to the left a mountain arose, where the mist gathered and hung dependent as the locks of a giant. The left of the American army had rested there. In its shadows had McKee fallen, and there had Hardin died, and there had the lance's point found Yell's dauntless heart, and there had the young Clay yielded up his precious life in its stainless and spotless prime. The great ravine still cut the level plain asunder. Rank mesquite grew all along the crest of the deadly hill where the Mississippians formed, and where, black-lipped and waiting, Bragg's battery crouched in ambush at its feet. Shining as a satin band, the broad highway lay white under the moonlight toward Saltillo—the highway to gain where Santa Anna dashed his desperate army in vain—the highway which held the rear and the life and the fame of the Northern handful.

General Hindman, a soldier in the regiment of Col. Jefferson Davis, explored the field under the moon and the stars, having at his back a regiment of younger Americans who, although the actors in a direr and more dreadful war, yet clung to their earliest superstitions and their spring-time faith in the glory and the carnage of Buena Vista. He made the camp a long to be remembered one. Here a squadron charged; there a Lancer regiment, gaily caparisoned in scarlet and gold, crept onward and onward until the battery's dun smoke broke as a wave over pennant and plume; here the grim Northern lines reeled and rallied; there the sandaled Mexicans, rent into fragments, swarmed into the jaws of the ravine, crouching low as the hot tempest of grape and canister rushed over and beyond them; yonder, where the rank grass is greenest and freshest, the uncoffined dead were buried; and everywhere upon the right and the left, the little mounds arose, guarding for evermore the sacred dust of the stranger slain.

The midnight came, and the harvest moon, as a spectral boat, was floating away to the west in a tide of silver and gold. The battle-field lay under the great, calm face of the sky—a sepulchre. Looking out from his bivouac, who knows what visions came to the musing soldier, as grave after grave gave up its dead, and as spirit after spirit put on its uniform and its martial array. Pale squadrons galloped again through the gloom of the powder-pall; again the deep roar of the artillery lent its mighty voice to swell the thunder of the gathering battle; again the rival flags rose and fell in the "hot, lit foreground of the fight"; again the Lancers charged, piercing and sweet and wildly shrill, the bugles again called out for victory; and again from out the jaws of the cavernous ravine a tawny tide emerged, clutching fiercely at the priceless road, and falling there in giant windrows as the summer hay when the scythe of the reapers takes the grass that is rankest.

The moon went down. The mirage disappeared, and only the silent and deserted battle-field lay out under the stars, its low trees waving in the night wind, and its droning katydids sighing in the grasses above the graves.

CHAPTER XI.

From Parras there was a broad, national highway running directly to Sonora, and so Shelby marched from Saltillo to Parras, intending to rest there a few days and then continue on to the Pacific, keeping steadily in view the advice and information given him by General Jeanningros.

His entrance into the city was stormy, and his reception there had neither sunlight nor temperate air about it. Indeed, none of the Parras winds blew him good. When, within two days' march of Parras, a sudden rain storm came out of the sky, literally inundating the ground of the bivouac. The watch fires were all put out. Sleep was banished, and in the noisy jubilation of the wind a guerrilla band stole down upon the camp. Dick Collins, James Kirtley, George Winship and James Meadow were on picquet duty at the mouth of the canyon on the north. They were peerless soldiers, and they knew how to keep their powder dry. The unseen moon had gone down, and the rain and the wind warred with each other. Some black objects rose up between the eyes of Winship on the outermost post and the murky clouds, yet a little light, above the darker jaws of the canyon. Weather proof, Winship spoke to Collins:

"There is game afoot. No peaceful thing travels on such a devil's night as this."

The four men gathered closer together, watching. Of a sudden a tawny and straggling kind of flame leaped out from the canyon and showed the faces of the Americans, one to another. They were all resolute and determined. They told how the dauntless four meant to stand there and fight there and die there, if needs be, until the sleeping camp could get well upon its feet. Sheltered a little by the darkness, and more by the rocks before and around them, they held desperately on, four men fighting two hundred. The strange combat waxed hotter and closer. Under the murky night the guerrillas crawled ever nearer and nearer. Standing closely together, the Americans fired at the flashes of the Mexican muskets. As yet they had not resorted to their revolvers. Trained to perfection in the use of Sharp's carbines, their guns seemed always loaded. Collins spoke first in his quaint, characteristic way:

"Boys, it's hot despite the rain."

"It will be hotter," answered Winship.

Then the wild work commenced again. This time they could not load their carbines. The revolvers had taken part in the *melee*. Kirtley was hit badly in the left arm, Collins was bleeding from an ugly wound in the right shoulder, Meadow and Winship each were struck slightly, and the guerrillas were ready for the death grapple. Neither thought of giving one inch of ground. The wind blew furiously and the rain poured down. At the moment when the final rush had come, the piercing notes of Shelby's bugle were heard, and clearer and nearer and deadlier the great shout of an oncoming host, leaping swiftly forward to the rescue. Past the four men on guard, Shelby leading, the tide poured into the pass. What happened there the daylight revealed. It was sure enough and ghastly enough to satisfy all, and better for some if the sunlight had never uncovered to kindred eyes the rigid corpses lying stark and stiff where they had fallen.

All at once a furious fire of musketry was heard in the rear and in amid the tethered horses. Again the bugle's notes were heard, and again Shelby's rallying voice rang out:

"Countermarch for your lives! Make haste!—make haste!—the very clouds are raining Mexicans to-night."

It was a quarter of a mile to the camp. The swiftest men got there first. Sure enough the attack had been a most formidable one. Slayback and Cundiff held the post in the rear and were fighting desperately. On foot, in the darkness, and attacked by four hundred guerrillas well acquainted with the whole country, they had yet neither been surprised or driven back. Woe unto the horses if they had, and horses were as precious as gold. Attracted only by the firing, and waiting for no orders, there had rushed to the rearward post McDougall, Fell, Dorsey, Macey, Ras. Wood, Charley Jones, Vines, Armistead and Elliott. Some aroused from their blankets were hatless and bootless. Inglehardt snatched a lighted torch from a sheltered fire and attempted to light the way. The rain put it out. Henry Chiles, having his family to protect, knew, however, by instinct, that the rear was in danger, and pressed forward with Jim Wood and the Berry brothers. Langhorne, from the left, bore down with John and Martin Kritzer, where he had been all night with the herd, keeping vigilant watch. In the impenetrable darkness, the men mistook each other. Moreland fired upon George Hall and shot away the collar of his overcoat. Hall recognized his voice and made himself known to him. Jake Connor, with the full swell and compass of his magnificent voice, struck up, "Tramp, tramp, the boys are marching," until, guided by the music of the song, the detached parties came together in the gloom and pressed on rapidly to the rear.

It was time. Slayback and Cundiff, having only a detachment of twelve men, nine of whom were killed or wounded, were half surrounded. They, too, had refused to fall back. In the rain, in the darkness, having no authorized commander, fired on from three sides, ignorant of the number and the positions of their assailants, they yet charged furiously in a body and drove everything before them. When Shelby arrived with reinforcements the combat was over. It had been the most persistent and bloody of the expedition. Calculating their chances well, the guerrillas had attacked simultaneously from front and rear, and fought with a tenacity unknown before in their history. The horses were the prize, and right furiously did they struggle for them. Close, reckless fighting alone saved the camp and scattered the desperate robbers in every direction among the mountains.

Colonel Depreuil, with the Fifty-second of the French line, held Parras, an extreme outpost on the north—the key, in fact, of the position toward Chihuahua and Sonora. Unlike Jeanningros in many things, he was yet a fine soldier, a most overbearing and tyrannical man. Gathered together at Parras also, and waiting permission to march to Sonora, was Colonel Terry,[1] one of the famous principals in the Broderick duel, and a detachment of Texans numbering, probably, twenty-five. Terry's own account of this memorable duel was all the more interesting because given by one who, of all others, knew best the causes and the surroundings which rendered it necessary. In substance the following contains the main points of the narrative:

"The political contest preceding the duel was exceptionally and bitterly personal. Broderick recognized the code fully, and had once before fought and wounded his man. He was cool, brave, dangerous and very determined. His influence over his own immediate followers and friends was more marked and emphatic than that exercised by any other man that I have ever known. He excelled in organization and attack, and possessed many of the most exalted qualities of a successful commander. As an orator he was rugged, yet inspired, reminding me somewhat of my own picturings of Mirabeau, without the gigantic persistence and intellect of Mirabeau.[2] I do not desire to enter into even the details which led to the unfortunate meeting, for these have been given again and again in as many false and unnatural ways as possible. After the terms had all been fully discussed and agreed upon, and the time and the place of combat settled, I said confidently to a friend of mine that I did not intend to kill Broderick. This friend seemed greatly surprised, and asked me after a few moments' reflection, what I *really* intended to do in the matter. My answer was that I simply desired to save my own life, and that I should only disable him. 'It is a dangerous game you are playing,' he replied, 'and one likely to bring you trouble. Broderick is no trifling antagonist. He shoots to kill every time.' When I arrived on the field I had not changed my mind, but when I looked into his eyes, I saw murder there as plainly as murder was ever depicted, and then I *knew* that one of us had to die. I put my life fairly against his own. His bearing was magnificent, and his nerve superbly cool. It has been asserted that I remarked to my second, while he was measuring the ground, that he must take short steps. This is untrue, for the ground was measured twice, once by my own second, and once by the second of Broderick. They both agreed perfectly. The distance was ten paces, and in size neither had the advantage. I felt confident of killing him, however, but if required to give a reason for this belief I could not give either a sensible or an intelligent reason. You know the result. He fell at the first fire, shot through the neck and mortally wounded. I did not approach him afterward, nor were any attempts made at reconciliation. At the hands of his friends I received about as large a share of personal abuse as usually falls to the lot of a man; at the hands of my friends I had no reason to complain of their generous support and confidence. When the war commenced I left California as a volunteer in the Confederate army, and am here to-day, like the rest of you, a penniless and an adventurous man. What a strange thing is destiny! I sometimes think we can neither mar nor make our fortunes, but have to live the life that is ordained for us. The future nobody knows. Perhaps it is best to take it as we find it, and bow gracefully when we come face to face with the inevitable."

Colonel Terry had felt his own sorrows, too, in the desperate struggle. One brother had been shot down by his side in Kentucky; a dearly loved child had just been buried in a foreign land; penniless and an exile himself, he had neither home, property, a country, nor a cause. All that was left to him were his honor and his scars.

Before Shelby arrived in Parras, Colonel Depreuil had received an order from Marshal Bazaine intended entirely for the Americans. It was very concise and very much to the point. It commenced by declaring that Shelby's advance was but the commencement of an irruption of Americans— Yankees, Bazaine called them—who intended to overrun Mexico, and to make war alike upon the French and upon Maximilian. Their march to Sonora, therefore, was to be arrested, and if they refused to return to their own country, they were to be ordered to report to him in the City of Mexico. No exceptions were to be permitted, and in any event, Sonora was to be held as forbidden territory.

Used to so many disappointments, and so constantly misunderstood and misinterpreted, Shelby felt the last blow less, perhaps, than some heavier ones among the first of a long series. He called upon Colonel Depreuil, however, for an official confirmation.

This interview, like the night attack, was a stormy one. The Frenchman was drinking and abusive. Uninvited to a seat, Shelby took the nearest one at hand. Upon his entrance into the officer's reception room, he had removed his hat. This was an act of politeness as natural as it was mechanical. Afterward it came near unto bloodshed.

"I have called, Colonel," Shelby began, "for permission to continue my march to Sonora."

"Such permission is impossible. You will turn aside to Mexico City."

"May I ask the reason for this sudden resolution? General Jeanningros had no information to this effect when I left him the other day in Monterey."

At the mention of Jeanningros' name, Depreuil became furious in a moment. It may have been that the subordinate was wanting in respect for his superior, or it may have been that he imagined, in his drunken way, that Shelby sought to threaten him with higher authority. At any rate he roared out:

"What do I care for your information? Let the devil fly away with you and your information. It is the same old game you Americans are forever trying to play—robbing to-day and killing to-morrow—and plundering, plundering, plundering all the time. You shall not go to Sonora, and you shall not stay here; but whatever you do you shall obey."

Shelby's face darkened. He arose as he spoke, put his hat on, and walked some paces toward the speaker. His voice was so cold and harsh when he answered him that it sounded strange and unnatural:

"I am mistaken, it seems. I imagined that when an American soldier called upon a French soldier, he was at least visiting a gentleman. One can not always keep his hands clean, and I wash mine of you because you are a slanderer and a coward."

Depreuil laid his hand upon his sword; Shelby unbuttoned the flap of his revolver scabbard. A rencontre was imminent. Those of Shelby's men who were with him massed themselves in one corner, silent and threatening. A guard of soldiers in an adjoining room fell into line. The hush of expectancy that came over all was ominous. A spark would have exploded a magazine.

Nothing could have surpassed the scornful, insulting gesture of Depreuil as, pointing to Shelby's hat, he ordered fiercely:

"Remove that."

"Only to beauty and to God," was the stern, calm reply; "to a coward, never."

It seemed for a moment afterward that Depreuil would strike him. He looked first at his own guard, then grasped the hilt of his sword, and finally with a fierce oath, he broke out:

"Retire—retire instantly—lest I outrage all hospitality and dishonor you in my own house. You shall pay for this—you shall apologize for this."

Depreuil was no coward. Perhaps there was no braver and more impulsive man in the whole French army. The sequel proved this.

Shelby went calmly from his presence. He talked about various things, but never about the difficulty until he found Governor Reynolds.

"Come apart with me a few moments, Governor," he said.

Reynolds was alone with him for an hour. When he came out he went straight to the quarters of Col. Depreuil. It did not take long thereafter to arrange the terms of a meeting. Governor Reynolds was both a diplomat and a soldier, and so at daylight the next morning they were to fight with pistols at ten paces. In this the Frenchman was chivalrous, notwithstanding his overbearing and insulting conduct at the interview. Shelby's right hand and arm had been disabled by an earlier wound, and this Depreuil had noticed. Indeed, while he was an expert with the sword, Shelby's wrist was so stiff that to handle a sword at all would have been impossible. Depreuil, therefore, chose the pistol, agreed to the distance, talked some brief moments pleasantly with Governor Reynolds, and went to bed. Shelby, on his part, had even fewer preparations to make than Depreuil. Face to face with death for four long years, he had seen him in so many shapes and in so many places that this last aspect was one of his least uncertain and terrifying.

The duel, however, never occurred. That night, about ten o'clock, a tremendous clattering of sabers and galloping of horses were heard, and some who went out to ascertain the cause returned with the information that General Jeanningros, on an inspecting tour of the entire northern line of outposts, had arrived in Parras with four squadrons of the Chasseurs d'Afrique.[3] It was not long before all the details of the interview between Depreuil and Shelby were related to him. His quick French instinct divined in a moment that other alternative waiting for the daylight, and in an instant Depreuil was under arrest, the violation of which would have cost him his life. Nor did it end with arrest simply. After fully investigating the circumstances connected with the whole affair, Jeanningros required Depreuil to make a free and frank apology, which he did most cordially and sincerely, regretting as much as a sober man could the disagreeable and overbearing things he did when he was drunk.

How strange a thing is destiny. About one year after this Parras difficulty, Depreuil was keeping isolated guard above Queretero, threatened by heavy bodies of advancing Juaristas, and in imminent peril of destruction. Shelby, no longer a soldier now but a trader, knew his peril and knew the value of a friendly warning given while it was yet time. Taking all risks, and putting to the hazard not only his own life, but the lives of forty others, Shelby rode one hundred and sixty-two miles in twenty-six hours, saved Depreuil, rescued his detachment, and received in a general order from Bazaine the thanks of the French army.

CHAPTER XII.

Both by education and temperament there were but few men better fitted to accept the inevitable more gracefully than General Shelby. It needed not Depreuil's testimony, nor the immediate confirmation thereof by Jeanningros, to convince him that Bazaine's order was imperative. True enough, he might have marched forth from Parras free to choose whatsoever route he pleased, but to become *en rapport* with the Government it was necessary to obey Bazaine. So when the good-byes were said, and the column well into motion, it was not toward the Pacific that the foremost horsemen rode along.

As the expedition won well its way into Mexico, many places old in local song and story arose, as it were, from the past and stood out, clear-cut and crimson, against the background of a history filled to the brim with rapine, lust, and slaughter. No other land under the sun had an awakening so storm begirt, a christening so bloody and remorseless. First the Spaniards under Cortez—swart, fierce, long of broad-sword and limb; and next the revolution, wherein no man died peacefully or under the shade of a roof. There was Hidalgo, the ferocious priest—shot. Morelos, with these words in his mouth—shot: "Lord, if I have done well, Thou knowest it; if ill, to Thy infinite mercy I commend my soul." Leonardo Bravo, scorning to fly—shot. Nicholas Bravo, his son, who had offered a thousand captives for his father's life—shot. Matamoras—shot. Mina—shot. Guerrera—shot. Then came the Republic—bloodier, bitterer, crueler. Victoria, its first president—shot. Mexia—shot. Pedraza—shot. Santmanet—shot by General Ampudia, who cut off his head, boiled it in oil, and stuck it up on a pole to blacken in the sun. Herrera—shot. Paredes—shot. All of them shot, these Mexican presidents, except Santa Anna, who lost a leg by the French and a country by the Americans. Among his game-cocks and his mistresses to-day in Havana, he will see never again, perhaps, the white brow of Orizava from the southern sea, and rest never again under the orange and the banana trees about Cordova.

It was a land old in the world's history that these men rode into, and a land stained in the world's crimes—a land filled full of the sun and the tropics. What wonder, then, that a deed was done on the fifth day's marching that had about it the splendid dash and bravado of medieval chivalry.

Keeping outermost guard one balmy evening far beyond the silent camp of the dreaming soldiers, James Wood and Yandell Blackwell did vigilant duty in front of the reserve. The fire had gone out when the cooking was done, and the earth smelt sweet with grasses, and the dew on the grasses. A low pulse of song broke on the bearded faces of the cacti, and sobbed in fading cadences as the waves that come in from the salt sea, seeking the south wind. This was the vesper strain of the katydids, sad, solacing, rhythmical.

Before the wary eyes of the sentinels a figure rose up, waving his blanket as a truce flag. Encouraged, he came into the lines, not fully assured of his bearings—frightened a little, and prone to be communicative by way of propitiation.

Had the Americans heard of Encarnacion?

No, they had not heard of Encarnacion. What was Encarnacion?

The Mexican, born robber and devout Catholic, crossed himself. Not to have heard of Encarnacion was next in infamy to have slaughtered a priest. Horror made him garrulous. Fear, if it does not paralyze, has been known to make the dumb speak.

Encarnacion was a *hacienda,* and a *hacienda,* literally translated, is a plantation with royal stables, and acres of corral, and abounding water, and long rows of male and female slave cabins, and a Don of an owner, who has music, and singing maidens, and pillars of silver dollars, and a passionate brief life wherein wine and women rise upon it at last and cut it short. Even if no ill luck intervenes, the pace to the devil is a terrible one, and superb riders though they are, the best sent in the saddle sways heavily at last, and the truest hand on the rein relaxes ere manhood reaches its noon and the shadows of the west.

Luis Enrico Rodriguez owned Encarnacion, a Spaniard born, and a patron saint of all the robbers who lived in the neighboring mountains, and of all the senoritas who plaited their hair by the banks of his *arroyos* and hid but charily their dusky bodies in the limpid waves. The hands of the French had been laid upon him lightly. For forage and foray, Dupin had never penetrated the mountain line which shut in his guarded dominions from the world beyond. When strangers came he gave them greeting; when soldiers came, he gave them of his flocks and herds, his wines and treasures.

There was one pearl, however, a pearl of great price, whom no stranger eyes had ever seen, whom no stranger tongue had ever spoken a fair good morning. The slaves called it a spirit, the confessor a sorceress, the lazy gossips a Gringo witch; the man who knew best of all called it wife, and yet no sprinkling of water or blessing of church had made the name a holy one.

Rodriguez owned Encarnacion, and Encarnacion owned a skeleton. This much James Wood and Yandell Blackwell knew when the half goat-herder and robber had told but half his story. When he had finished his other half, this much remained of it:

Years before in Sonora, a California hunter of gold had found his way to some streams where a beautiful Indian woman lived with her tribe. They were married, and a daughter was born to them, having her father's Saxon hair and her mother's eyes of tropical dusk. From youth to womanhood this daughter had been educated in San Francisco. When she returned she was an American, having nothing of her Indian ancestry but its color. Even her mother's language was unknown to her. One day in Guaymas, Rodriguez looked upon her as a vision. He was a Spaniard and a millionaire, and he believed all things possible. The wooing was long, but the web, like the web of Penelope, was never woven. He failed in his eloquence, in his money, in his passionate entreaties, in his stratagems, in his lyings-in-wait—in everything that savored of pleading or purchase. Some men come often to their last dollar—never to the end of their audacity. If fate should choose to back a lover against the world, fate would give long odds on a Spaniard.

At last, when everything else had been tried, Rodriguez determined upon abduction. This was a common Mexican custom, dangerous only in its failure. No matter what the risk, no matter how monstrous the circumstances, no matter how many corpses lay in the pathway leading up from plotting to fulfillment, so only in the end the lusts of the man triumphed over the virtue of the woman. Gathering together hastily a band of bravos whose devotion was in exact proportion to the dollars paid, Rodriguez seized upon the maiden, returning late one night from the opera, and bore her away with all speed toward Encarnacion. The Californian, born of a tiger race that invariably dies hard, mounted such few men as loved him and followed on furiously in pursuit. Bereft of his young, he had but one thing to do—*kill.*

Fixed as fate and as relentless, the race went on. Turning once fairly at bay, pursued and pursuers met in a death-grapple. The Californian died in the thick of the fight, leaving stern and stark traces behind of his terrible prowess. What cared Rodriguez, however, for a bravo more or less? The woman was safe, and on his own garments nowhere did the strife leave aught of crimson or dust. Once well in her chamber—a mistress, perhaps—a prisoner, certainly, she beat her wings in vain against the strong bars of her palace, for all that gold could give or passion suggest had been poured out at the feet of Inez Walker. Servants came and went at her bidding. The priest blessed and beamed upon her. The captor was fierce by turns, and in the dust at her shrine, by turns, but amid it all the face of a murdered father rose up in her memory, and prayers for vengeance upon her father's murderer broke ever from her unrelenting lips. At times fearful cries came out from the woman's chamber. The domestics heard them and crossed themselves. Once in a terrible storm she fled from her thraldom and wandered frantically about until she sank down insensible. She was found alone with her beauty and her agony. Rodriguez lifted her in his arms and bore her back to her chamber. A fever followed, scorching her wan face until it was pitiful, and shredding away her Saxon hair until all of its gloss was gone and all its silken rippling stranded. She lived on, however, and under the light of a Southern sky, and by the fitful embers of a soldier's bivouac, a robber goat-herd was telling the story of an American's daughter to an American's son.

"Was it far to Encarnacion?"

Jim Wood asked the question in his broken Spanish way, looking out to the front, musing.

"By to-morrow night, Senor, you will be there."

"Have you told the straight truth, Mexican?"

"As the Virgin is true, Senor."

"So be it. You will sleep this night at the outpost. To-morrow, we shall see."

The Mexican smoked a cigarrito and went to bed. Whether he slept or not, he made no sign. Full confidence very rarely lays hold of an Indian's heart.

Replenishing the fire, Wood and Blackwell sat an hour together in silence. Beyond the sweeping, untiring glances of the eyes, the men were as statues. Finally Blackwell spoke to Wood:

"Of what are you thinking?"

"Encarnacion. And you?"

"Inez Walker. It is the same."

The Mexican turned in his blanket, muttering. Wood's revolver covered him:

"Lie still," he said, "and muffle up your ears. You may not understand English, but you understand this," and he waved the pistol menacingly before his eyes. "One never does know when these yellow snakes are asleep."

"No matter," said Blackwell sententiously; "they never sleep."

It was daylight again, and although the two men had not unfolded their blankets, they were as fresh as the dew on the grasses—fresh enough to have planned an enterprise as daring and as desperate as anything ever dreamed of in romance or set forth in fable.

The to-morrow night of the Mexican had come, and there lay Encarnacion in plain view under the starlight. Rodriguez had kept aloft from the encampment. Through the last hours of the afternoon, wide-hatted rancheros had ridden up to the corral in unusual numbers, had dismounted and had entered in. Shelby, who took note of everything, took note also of this.

"They do not come out," he said. "There are some signs of preparation about, and some fears manifested against a night attack. By whom? Save our grass and goats, I know of no reason why foraging should be heavier now than formerly."

Twice Jim Wood had been on the point of telling him the whole story, and twice his heart had failed him. Shelby was getting sterner of late, and the reins were becoming to be drawn tighter and tighter. Perhaps it was necessary. Certainly since the last furious attack by the guerrillas over beyond Parras, those who had looked upon discipline as an ill-favored mistress, had ended by embracing her.

As the picquets were being told off for duty, Wood came close to Blackwell and whispered:

"The men will be ready by twelve. They are volunteers and splendid fellows. How many of them will be shot?"

"*Quien sabe?*[1] Those who take the sword shall perish by the sword."

"Bah! When you take a text, take one without a woman in it."

"I shall not preach to-night. Shelby will do that to-morrow to all who come forth scathless."

With all his gold and his leagues of cattle and land, Rodriguez had only for an eagle's nest an adobe eyrie. Hither his dove had been carried. On the right of this long row of cabins ran the quarters of his peons. Near to the gate were acres of corral. Within this, saddled steeds were in their stalls, lazily feeding. A Mexican loves his horse, but that is no reason why he does not starve him. This night, however, Rodriguez was bountiful. For fight and flight both men and animals must not go hungry. On the top of the main building a kind of tower lifted itself up. It was roomy and spacious and flanked by steps that clung to it tenaciously. In the tower a light shone, while all below and about it was hushed and impenetrable. High adobe walls encircled the mansion, the cabins, the corral, the acacia trees, the fountain that splashed plaintively, and the massive portal which had mystery written all over its rugged outlines.

It may have been twelve o'clock. The nearest piquet was beyond Encarnacion, and the camp guards were only for sentinel duty. Free to come and go, the men had no watchword for the night. None was needed.

Suddenly, and if one had looked up from his blankets, he might have seen a long, dark line standing out against the sky. This line did not move.

It may have been twelve o'clock. There was no moon, yet the stars gave light enough for the men to see each other's faces and to recognize one another. It was a quarter of a mile from the camp to the *hacienda,* and about the same distance to the picquet posts from where the soldiers had formed. In the ranks one might have seen such campaigners—stern and rugged and scant of speech in danger—as McDougall, Boswell, Armistead, Winship, Ras. Woods, Macey, Vines, Kirtley, Blackwell, Tom Rudd, Crockett, Collins, Jack Williams, Owens, Timberlake, Darnall, Johnson and the two Berrys, Richard and Ike. Jim Wood stood forward by right as leader. All knew he would carry them far enough; some may have thought, perhaps, that he would carry them too far.

The line, hushed now and ominous, stood still as a wall. From front to rear Wood walked the whole length, speaking some low and cheering words.

"Boys," he commenced, "none of us know what is waiting inside the corral. Mexicans fight well in the dark, it is said, and see better than wolves, but we must have that American woman safe out of their hands, or we must burn the buildings. If the hazard is too great for any of you, step out of the ranks. What we are about to do must needs be done quickly. Shelby sleeps little of late, and may be, even at this very moment, searching through the camp for some of us. Let him find even so much as one blanket empty, and from the heroes of a night attack we shall become its criminals."

Sweeny, a one-armed soldier who had served under Walker in Nicaragua, and who was in the front always in hours of enterprise or peril, replied to Wood:

"Since time is valuable, lead on."

The line put itself in motion. Two men sent forward to try the great gate returned rapidly. Wood met them.

"Well?" he said.

"It is dark all about there, and the gate itself is as strong as a mountain."

"We shall batter it down."

A beam was brought—a huge piece of timber wrenched from the upright fastenings of a large irrigating basin. Twenty men manned this and advanced upon the gate. In an instant thereafter, there were tremendous and resounding blows, shouts, cries, oaths, and musket shots. Before this gigantic battering-ram, adobe walls and iron fastenings gave way. The bars of the barrier were broken as reeds, the locks were crushed, the hinges were beaten in, and with a fierce yell and rush the Americans swarmed to the attack of the main building. The light in the tower guided them. A legion of devils seemed to have broken loose. The stabled steeds of the Mexicans reared and plunged in the infernal din of the fight, and dashed hither and thither, masterless and riderless.

The camp where Shelby rested was alarmed instantly. The shrill notes of the bugle were heard over all the tumult, and with them the encouraging voice of Wood.

"Make haste! make haste, men, for in twenty minutes we will be between two fires!"

Crouching in the stables, and pouring forth a murderous fire from their ambush in the darkness, some twenty *rancheros*[2] made sudden and desperate battle. Leading a dozen men against them, Macey and Ike Berry charged through the gloom and upon the unknown, guided only by the lurid and fitful flashes of the muskets. When the work was over the corral no longer vomited its flame. Silence reigned there—that fearful and ominous silence fit only for the dead who died suddenly.

The camp, no longer in sleep, had become menacing. Short words of command came out of it, and the tread of men forming rapidly for battle. Some skirmishers, even in the very first moments of the combat, had been thrown forward quite to the *hacienda*. These were almost nude, and stood out under the starlight as white spectres, threatening yet undefined. They had guns at least, and pistols, and in so much they were mortal. These spectres had reason, too. Close upon the fragments of the great gate, and looking in upon the waves of the fight as they rose and fell, they yet did not fire. They believed, at least, that some of their kindred and comrades were there.

For a brief ten minutes more the combat raged evenly. Cheered by the voice of Rodriguez, and stimulated by his example, his retainers clung bitterly to the fight. The doors were as redoubts. The windows were as miniature casements. Once on the steps of the tower, Rodriguez showed himself for a second. A dozen of the best shots in the attacking party fired at him. No answer save a curse of defiance so harsh and savage that it sounded unnatural even in the roar of a furious hurricane.

There was a lull. Every Mexican combatant outside the main building had been killed or wounded. Against the massive walls of the adobes the rifle bullets made no headway. It was murder longer to oppose flesh to masonry. Tom Rudd was killed, young and dauntless; Crockett, the hero of the Lampasas duel, was dead; Rogers was dead; the boy Provines was dead; Matterhorn, a stark giant of a German, shot four times, was breathing his last; and the wounded were on all sides, some hit hard, and some bleeding, yet fighting on.

"Once more to the beam!" shouted Wood.

Again the great battering-ram crashed against the great door leading into the main hall, and again there was a rending away of iron and wood and mortar. Through splintered timber and over crumbling and jagged masonry the besiegers poured. The building was gained. Once well withinside, the storm of revolver balls was terrible. There, personal prowess told, and there the killing was quick and desperate. At the head of his hunted following, Rodriguez fought like the Spaniard he was, stubbornly and to the last. No lamps lit the savage *melee*. While the Mexicans stood up to be shot at, they were shot where they stood. Most of them died there. Some few broke away toward the last and escaped, for no pursuit was attempted, and no man cared how many fled or how fast. It was the woman the Americans wanted. Gold and silver ornaments were everywhere, and precious tapestry work, and many rare and quaint and woven things, but the powder-blackened and blood-stained hands of the assailants touched not one of these. It was too dark to tell who killed Rodriguez. To the last his voice could be heard cheering on his men, and calling down God's vengeance on the Gringos. Those who fired at him specially fired at his voice, for the smoke was stifling and the sulphurous fumes of the gunpowder almost unbearable.

When the *hacienda* was won Shelby had arrived with the rest of the command. He had mistaken the cause of the attack, and his mood was of that kind which seldom came to him, but which, when it did come, had several times before made some of his most hardened and unruly followers tremble and turn pale. He had caused the *hacienda* to be surrounded closely, and he had come alone to the doorway, a look of wrathful menace on his usually placid face.

"Who among you have done this thing?" he asked, in tones that were calm yet full and vibrating.

No answer. The men put up their weapons.

"Speak, some of you. Let me not find cowards instead of plunderers, lest I finish the work upon you all that the Mexicans did so poorly upon a few."

Jim Wood came forward to the front. Covered with blood and powder-stains, he seemed in sorry plight to make much headway in defense of the night's doings, yet he told the tale as straight as the goat-herd had told it to him, and in such simple soldier fashion, taking all the sin upon his own head and hands, that even the stern features of his commander relaxed a little, and he fell to musing. It may have been that the desperate nature of the enterprise appealed more strongly to his own feelings than he was willing that his men should know, or it may have been that his set purpose softened a little when he saw many of his bravest and best soldiers come out from the darkness and stand in silence about Wood, their leader, some of them sorely wounded, and all of them covered with the signs of the desperate fight; but certain it is that when he spoke again his voice was more relenting and assuring:

"And where is the woman?"

Through all the terrible moments of the combat the light in the tower had burned as a beacon. Perhaps in those few seconds when Rodriguez stood alone upon the steps leading up to the doves' nest, in a tempest of fire and smoke, the old love might have been busy at his heart, and the old yearning strong within him to make at last some peace with her for whom he had so deeply sinned, and for whose sake he was soon to so dreadfully suffer. Death makes many a sad atonement, and though late in coming at times to the evil and the good alike, it may be that when the records of the heart are writ beyond the wonderful river, much that was dark on earth will be bright in eternity, and much that was cruel and fierce in finite judgment will be made fair and beautiful when it is known how *love* gathered up the threads of destiny, and how all the warp that was blood-stained, and all the woof that had bitterness and tears upon it, could be traced to a woman's hand.

Grief-stricken, prematurely old, yet beautiful even amid the loneliness of her situation, Inez Walker came into the presence of Shelby, a queen. Some strands of gray were in her glossy, golden hair. The liquid light of her large dark eyes had long ago been quenched in tears. The form that had once been so full and perfect was now bent and fragile; but there was such a look of mournful tenderness in her eager, questioning face that the men drew back from her presence instinctively and left her alone with their General. He received her commands as if she were bestowing a favor upon him, listening as a brother might until all her wishes were made known. These he promised to carry out to the letter, and how well he did so this narrative will further tell. For the rest of that night she was left alone with her dead. Recovered somewhat from the terrors of the wild attack, her womanly qualities came back to her, and she wept over the slain and prayed piteously for their souls.

When the dead had been buried, when the wounded had been cared for, and when Wood received a warning which he will remember to his dying day, the column started once more on its march to the south. With the guard of honor regularly detailed to protect the families of those who were traveling with the expedition, there was another carriage new to the men. None sought to know its occupant. The night's work had left upon all a sorrow that was never entirely obliterated—a memory that even now, through the lapse of long years, comes back to all who witnessed it as a memory that brings with it more of real regret than gladness.

CHAPTER XIII.

The great guns were roaring furiously at Matehuala when the expedition came within hearing distance of its outposts. Night had fallen over the city and its twenty thousand inhabitants before the advanced guard of the column had halted for further orders. The unknown was ahead. All day, amid the mountains, there had come upon the breeze the deep, prolonged rumbling of artillery firing; and as the column approached nearer and nearer to the city, there were mingled with the hoarse voices of the cannon the nearer and deadlier rattle of incessant musketry.

Shelby rode up to the head of the advance and inquired the cause of the heavy firing. No one could tell him.

"Then we will camp," he said. "Afterward a few scouts shall determine definitely."

The number of scouts detailed for the service was not large—probably sixty all told. These were divided into four detachments, each detachment being sent out in a direction different from the others. James Kirtley led one, Dick Collins another, Jo. Macey the third and Dorsey the fourth. They were to bring word back of the meaning of all that infernal noise and din that had been raging about Matehuala the whole day through.

Kirtley took the main road running down squarely into the city. A picquet post barred his further progress. Making a circuit cautiously, he gained the rear of this, and came upon a line of soldiers in bivouac. In the shadow himself, the light of the campfires revealed to him the great forms and the swarthy countenances of a battalion of guerrillas. Further beyond there were other fires at which other battalions were cooking and resting.

Collins was less fortunate in this that he had to fight a little. Warned against using weapons except in self-defense, he had drawn up his small detachment under the cover of a clump of mesquite bushes, watching the road along which men were riding to and fro. His ambush was discovered and a company of cavalry came galloping down to uncover his position. Halted twice, they still continued to advance. There was no help for it save a point-blank volley, and this was given with a will and in the darkness. Some saddles were emptied, and one riderless horse dashed into the midst of the Americans, this was secured and carried into camp.

Macey made a wide detour upon the left of the road, and across some cultivated fields in which there were a few huts filled with peons. Five of these peons were captured and brought back to Shelby. Questioned closely, they revealed the whole situation. Matehuala was held by a French garrison numbering five hundred of the Eighty-second Infantry of the line—a weak detachment enough for such an exposed outpost. These five hundred Frenchmen were commanded by Major Henry Pierron, an officer of extreme youth and dauntless enterprise.

Shelby called a council of his officers at once. The peons had further told him that the besieging force was composed of about two thousand guerrillas under Colonel Escobeda, brother of that other one who laughed and was glad exceedingly when Maximilian fell, butchered and betrayed, at Queretero. At daylight the garrison was to be attacked again, and so what was to be done had great need to be done quickly.

The officers came readily, and Shelby addressed them.

"We have marched far, we have but scant money, our horses are foot-sore and much in need of shoes, and Matehuala is across the only road for scores of miles in any direction that leads to the City of Mexico. Shall we turn back and take another?"

"No! no!" in a kind of angry murmur from the men.

"But there are two thousand Mexican soldiers, or robbers, who are next of kin, across this road, and we may have to fight a little. Are you tired of fighting?"

"Lead us on and see," was the cry, and this time his officers had begun to catch his meaning. They understood now that he was tempting them. Already determined in his own mind to attack the Mexicans at daylight, he simply wished to see how much of his own desire was in the bosoms of his subordinates.

"One other thing," said Shelby, "before we separate. From among you I want a couple of volunteers—two men who will take their lives in their hands and find an entrance into Matehuala. I must communicate with Pierron before daylight. It is necessary that he should know how near there is succor to him, and how furiously we mean to charge them in the morning. Who will go?"

All who were present volunteered, stepping one pace nearer to their commander in a body. He chose but two—James Cundiff and Elias Hodge—two men fit for any mission no matter how forlorn or desperate.

By this time they had learned enough Spanish to buy meat and bread—not enough to pass undetected an outlying guerrilla with an eye like a lynx and an ear keener than a coyote's. They started, however, just the same. Shelby would write nothing.

"A document might hang you," he said, "and besides, Pierron can not, in all probability, read my English. Go, and may God protect you."

These two dauntless men then shook hands with their commander, and with the few comrades nearest. After that they disappeared into the unknown. It was a cloudy night and some wind blew. In this they were greatly favored. The darkness hid the clear outlines of their forms, and the wind blended the tread of their footsteps with the rustling of the leaves and the grasses. Two revolvers and a Sharps' carbine each made up the equipment. Completely ignorant of the entire topography of the country, they yet had a kind of vague idea of the direction in which Matehuala lay. They knew that the main road was hard beset by guerrillas, and that upon the right a broken and precipitous chain of mountains encircled the city and made headway in that direction well nigh impossible. They chose the left, therefore, as the least of three evils.

It was about midnight, and it was two long miles to Matehuala. Shelby required them to enter into the city; about their coming back, he was not so particular. Cundiff led, Hodge followed in Indian fashion. At intervals both men would draw themselves up and listen, long and anxiously. At last after crossing a wide field, intersected by ditches and but recently plowed, they came to a road which had a mesquite hedge on one side, and a fence with a few straggling poles in it on the other. Gliding stealthily down this road, the glimmering of a light in front warned them of immediate danger. In avoiding this they came upon another house, and in going still further to the left to avoid this also, they found themselves in the midst of a kind of extended village, one of those interminable suburbs close to yet disconnected from all Mexican cities.

Wherever there was a *tienda*—that is to say, a place where the fiery native drink of the country is sold—two or three saddle horses might have been seen. In whispers, the men conferred together.

"They are here," said Hodge.

"They seem to be everywhere," answered Cundiff.

"What do you propose?"

"To glide quietly through. I have a strong belief that beyond this village we shall find Matehuala."

They struck out boldly again, passing near to a *tienda* in which there was music and dancing. When outside of the glare of the light which streamed from its open door, the sound of horses' feet coming down the road they had just traveled called for instant concealment. They crouched low behind a large maguey plant and waited. The horsemen came right onward, laughing loud and boisterously. They did not halt in the village, but rode on by the ambush and so close they could have touched the Americans with a saber.

"A scratch," said Hodge, breathing more freely.

"Hush," said Cundiff, crouching still closer in the shadow of the maguey, "the worst is yet to come."

And it was. From where the Americans had hidden to the *tienda* in which the Mexicans were carousing it was probably fifteen paces. The sudden galloping of the horsemen through the village had startled the revelers. If they were friends, they called out to each other, they would have tarried long enough for a stirrup cup; if they are enemies we shall pursue.

The Mexicans were a little drunk, yet not enough to make them negligent. After mounting their horses, they spread out in skirmishing order, with an interval, probably, of five feet between each man. Against the full glare that streamed out from the lighted doorway, the picturesque forms of five guerrillas outlined themselves. The silver ornaments on their bridles shone, the music of the spurs penetrated to the ambush, and the wide *sombreros* told all too well the calling of those mounted robbers who are wolves in pursuit and tigers in victory. None have ever been known to spare.

Hodge would talk, brave as he was, and imminent as was his peril. Even in this extremity his soldierly tactics came uppermost.

"There are five," he said, "and we are but two. We have fought worse odds."

"So we have," answered Cundiff, "and may do it again before this night's work is over. Lie low and wait."

The guerrillas came right onward. At a loss to understand fully the nature of the men who had just ridden through the village, they were maneuvering now as if they expected to meet them in hostile array at any moment. There were fifty chances to five that some one of the skirmishers would discover the ambush.

Although terrible, the suspense was brief. Between the maguey plant and the road, two of the guerrillas filled up the interval. This left the three others to the left and rear. They had their musquetoons in their hands, and were searching keenly every clump of grass or patch of underbrush. Those nearest the road had passed on, and those upon the left were just abreast of the ambush. The Americans did not breathe. Suddenly, and with a fierce shout, the third skirmisher in the line yelled out:

"What ho! comrades, close up—close up—here are two skulking Frenchmen. *Per Dios*,[1] but we will have their hearts' blood."

As he shouted he leveled his musket until its muzzle almost touched the quiet face of Cundiff, the rest of the Mexicans rushing up furiously to the spot.

CHAPTER XIV.

If it be true, that when a woman hesitates she is lost, the adage applies with a ten-fold greater degree of precision to a Mexican guerrilla, who has come suddenly upon an American in ambush and who, mistaking him for a French soldier, hesitates to fire until he has called around him his comrades. A revolver to a Frenchman is an unknown weapon. Skill in its use is something he never acquires. Rarely a favorite in his hands no matter how great the stress, nor how frightful the danger, it is the muzzle-loader that ever comes uppermost, favored above all other weapons that might have been had for the asking.

Cundiff, face to face with imminent death, meant to fight to the last. His orders were to go in Matehuala, and not to give up as a wolf that is taken in a trap. His revolver was in his hand, and the Mexican took one second too many to run his eye along the barrel of his musket. With a motion as instantaneous as it was unexpected, Cundiff fired fair at the Mexican's breast, the bullet speeding true and terrible to its mark. He fell forward over his horse's head with a ghastly cry, his four companions crowding around his prostrate body, frightened, it may be, but bent on vengeance. As they grouped themselves together, Hodge and Cundiff shot into the crowd, wounding another guerrilla and one of the horses, and then broke away from cover and rushed on toward Matehuala. The road ran directly through a village. This village was long and scattering and alive with soldiers. A great shout was raised; ten thousand dogs seemed to be on the alert, more furious than the men, and keener of sight and scent. The fight became a hunt. The houses sent armed men in pursuit. The five guerrillas, reduced now to three, led the rush, but not desperately. Made acquainted with the stern prowess of the Americans, they had no heart for a close grapple without heavy odds. At intervals Cundiff and Hodge would halt and fire back with their carbines, and then press forward again through the darkness. Two men were keeping two hundred at bay, and Cundiff spoke to Hodge:

"This pace is fearful. How long can you keep it up?"

"Not long. There seems, however, to be a light ahead."

And there was. A large fire, distance some five hundred yards, came suddenly in sight. The rapid fire coming from both pursuers and pursued had created a commotion in front. There were the rallying notes of a bugle, and the sudden forming of a line of men immediately in front of the camp-fire seen by the Americans. Was it a French outpost? Neither knew, but against this unforeseen danger now outlined fully in the front that in the rear was too near and too deadly to permit of preparation.

"We are surrounded," said Hodge.

"Rather say we are in the breakers, and that in trying to avoid Scylla we shall be wrecked upon Charybdis,"[1] replied Cundiff, turning coolly to his comrade, after firing deliberately upon the nearest of the pursuers, and halting long enough to reload his carbine. "It all depends upon a single chance."

"And what is that chance?"

"To escape the first close fusillade of the French."

"But are they French—those fellows in front of us?"

"Can't you swear to that? Did you not mark how accurately they fell into line, and how silent everything has been since? Keep your ears wide open, and when you hear a single voice call out, fall flat upon the ground. That single voice will be the leader's ordering a volley."

It would seem that the Mexicans also had begun to realize the situation. A last desperate rush had been determined upon, and twenty of the swiftest and boldest pursuers charged furiously down at a run, firing as they came on. There was no shelter, and Cundiff and Hodge stood openly at bay, holding, each, his fire, until the oncoming mass was only twenty yards away. Then the revolver volleys were incessant. At a distance they sounded as if a company were engaged; to the guerrillas the two men had multiplied themselves to a dozen.

The desperate stand made told well. The fierce charge expended itself. Those farthest in the front slackened their pace, halted, fell back, retreated a little, yet still kept up an incessant volley.

"Come," said Cundiff, "and let's try the unknown. These fellows in the rear have had enough."

Instead of advancing together now, one skirted the road on the left and the other on the right. The old skirmishing drill was beginning to re-assert itself again—a sure sign that the danger in the rear had transferred itself to the front. Of a sudden a clear, resonant voice came from the direction of the fire. Cundiff and Hodge fell forward instantly upon their faces, a hurricane of balls swept over and beyond them, and for reply the loud, calm shout of Hodge was heard in parley:

"Hold on, men, hold on. We are but two and we are friends. See, we come into your lines to make our words good. We are Americans, and we have tidings for Captain Pierron."

Four French soldiers came out to greet them. Explanations were mutually had, and it was long past midnight when the commander of the garrison had finished his conference with the daring scouts, and had been well assured of his timely and needed succor.

Pierron offered them food and lodging.

"We must return," said Cundiff.

The Frenchman opened his eyes wide with surprise.

"Return, the devil! You have not said your prayers yet for being permitted to get in."

"No matter. He prays best who fights the best, and Shelby gives no thanks for unfinished work. Am I right, Hodge?"

"Now as always; but surely Captain Pierron can send us by a nearer road."

The Frenchman thus appealed to gave the two men an escort of forty cuirassiers and sent them back to Shelby's camp by a road but slightly guarded, the Mexican picquets upon it firing but once at long range and then scampering away.

It was daylight, and the great guns were roaring again. The column got itself in motion at once and waited. Shelby's orders were repeated by each captain to his company, and in words so plain that he who ran might have understood. The attack was to be made in columns of fours, the men firing right and left from the two files as they dashed in among the Mexicans. It was the old way of doing deadly work, and not a man there was unfamiliar with the duty marked out for his hands to do.

Largely outnumbered, the French were fighting men who know that defeat means destruction. Many of them had been killed. Pierron was anxious, and through the rising mists of the morning, his eyes more than once and with an eagerness not usually there, looked away to the front where he knew the needed succor lay. It came as it always came, whether to friend or foe, *in time*. Not a throb of the laggard's pulse had Shelby ever felt, and upon this day of all days of his stormy career he meant to do a soldier's sacred duty. From a walk the column passed into a trot, Shelby leading. There was no advance guard ahead, and none was needed.

"We know what is before us," was his answer to Langhorne, "and it is my pleasure this morning to receive the fire first of you all. Take your place with your company, the fifth from the front."

"Gallop—march!"

The men gathered up the reins and straightened themselves in their stirrups. Some Mexicans were in the road before them and halted. The apparition came to them from the unknown. They might have been spectres, but they were armed, and armed spectres are terrible. The alarm of the night before had been attributed to the daring of two adventurous Frenchmen.

Not one of the besieging host had dreamed that a thousand Americans were within two miles of Matehuala, resolved to fight for the besieged, and take the investing lines in rear and at the gallop.

On one side of the road down which Shelby was advancing there ran a chain of broken and irregular hills; on the other, the long, straggling village in which Cundiff and Hodge had well-nigh sacrificed themselves. These the daylight revealed perfectly. Between the hills and the village was a plain, and in this plain the Mexican forces were drawn up, three lines deep, having as a *point d'appui* [2] a heavy six-gun battery.

Understanding at last that while the column coming down from the rear was not Frenchmen, it was not friendly, the Mexicans made some dispositions to resist it. Too late! Caught between two inexorable jaws, they were crushed before they were aware of the peril. Shelby's charge was like a thunder-cloud. Nothing could live before the storm of its revolver bullets. Lurid, canopied in smoke-wreaths, pitiless, keeping right onward, silent in all save the roar of the revolvers, there was first a line that fired upon it, and then a great upheaving and rending asunder. When the smoke rolled away the battery had no living thing to lift a hand in its defense, and the fugitives were in hopeless and helpless flight toward the mountains on the right and toward the village upon the left. Pursuit Shelby made none, but God pity all whom the French cuirassiers overtook, and who, cloven from *sombrero* to sword-belt, fell thick in all the streets of the village, and died hard among the dagger-trees and the precipices of the stony and unsheltering mountains.

Pierron came forth with his entire garrison to thank and welcome his preservers. The freedom of the city was extended to Shelby, the stores of the post were at his disposal, money was offered and refused, and for three long and delightful days the men rested and feasted. To get shoes for his horses Shelby had fought a battle, not bloodless, however, to him, but a battle treasured to-day in the military archives of France—a battle which won for him the gratitude of the whole French army, and which, in the end, turned from him the confidence of Maximilian and rendered abortive all his efforts to recruit for the Austrian a corps that would have kept him upon the throne. Verily, man proposes and God disposes. [3]

CHAPTER XV.

Pierron made Matehuala a paradise. There were days of feasting and mirth and minstrelsy, and in the balm of the fragrant nights the men dallied with the women. So when the southward march was resumed, many a bronzed face was set in a look of sadness, and many a grateful heart pined long and tenderly for the dusky hair that would never be plaited again, for the tropical lips that for them would never sing again the songs of the roses and the summer time.

Adventures grew thick along the road as cactus plants. Villages multiplied, and as the ride went on, larger towns and larger populations were daily entered into. The French held all the country. Everywhere could be seen the picturesque uniforms of the Zouaves, the soberer garments of the Voltigeurs, the gorgeous array of the Chasseurs, and the more somber and forbidding aspect of the Foot Artillery. The French held all the country, that is to say, wherever a French garrison had stationed itself, or wherever a French expeditionary force, or scouting force, or reconnoitering force had camped or was on the march, such force held all the country within the range of their cannon and their *chassepots*.[1] Otherwise not. Guerrillas abounded in the mountains; robbers fed and fattened by all the streams; spies swarmed upon the haciendas, and cruel and ruthless scourges from the marshes rode in under the full of the tropical moons and slew for a whole night through, and on many a night at intervals thereafter, whoever of Mexican or Punic faith had carried truth or tidings of Liberal movements to the French.

It was in Dolores, the home of Hidalgo—priest, butcher, revolutionist—that those wonderful blankets were made which blend the colors of the rainbow with the strength of the north wind. Soft, warm, gorgeous, flexible, two strong horses can not pull them asunder—two weeks of an east rain can not find a pore to penetrate. Marvels of an art that has never yet been analyzed or transferred; Dolores, a century old, has yet an older secret than itself, the secret of their weaving.

Shelby's discipline was now sensibly increasing. As the men marched into the south, and as the soft airs blew for them, and the odorous blossoms opened for them, and the dusky beauties were gay and gracious for them, they began to chafe under the iron rule of the camp, and the inexorable logic of guard and picquet duty. Once a detachment of ten, told off for the grand guards, refused to stir from the mess-fire about which an elegant supper was being prepared.

And in such guise did the word come to Shelby.

"They refuse?" he asked.

"Peremptorily, General."

"Ah! And for what reason?"

"They say it is unnecessary."

"And so, in addition to rank mutiny, they would justify themselves? Call out the guard."

The guard came, Jo. Macey at its head—twenty determined men, fit for any work a soldier might do. Shelby rose up and went with it to where the ten mutineers were feasting and singing. They knew what was coming, and their leader, brave even to desperation, laid his hand upon his revolver. There was murder in his eyes, that wicked and wanton murder which must have been in Sampson's heart when he laid hold of the pillar of the Temple and felt the throes of the crushing edifice as it swayed and toppled and buried all in a common ruin.

Jo. Macey halted his detachment within five feet of the mess fire. He had first whispered to Shelby:

"When you want me, speak. I shall kill nine of the ten with the first broadside."

It can do no good to write the name of the leader of the mutineers. He sleeps to-day in the golden sands of a Sonora stream; sleeps forgiven by all whose lives he might have given away—given away without cause or grievance. When he dared to disobey, either this man or the Expedition had to be sacrificed. Happily, both were saved.

Shelby walked into the midst of the mutineers, looking into the eyes of all. His voice was deep and very grave.

"Men, go back to your duty. I am among you all, an adventurer like yourself, but I have been charged to carry you through to Mexico City in safety, and this I will do, so surely as the good God rules the universe. I don't seek to know the cause of this thing. I ask no reason for it, no excuse for it, no regrets or apologies for it. I only want your soldierly promise to obey."

No man spoke. The leader mistook the drift of things and tried to advance a little. Shelby stopped him instantly.

"Not another word," he almost shouted; "but if within fifteen seconds by the watch you are not in line for duty, you shall be shot like the meanest Mexican dog in all the Empire. Cover these men, Macey, with your carbines."

Twenty gaping muzzles crept straight to the front, waiting. The seconds seemed as hours. In that supreme moment of unpitying danger the young mutineer, if left to himself, would have dared the worst, dying as he had lived; but the others could not look full into the face of the grim skeleton and take the venture for a cause so disgraceful. They yielded to the inevitable, and went forth to their duty bearing their leader with them. Thereafter, no more faithful and honorable soldiers could be found in the ranks of the Expedition.

The column had gone southward from Dolores a long day's journey. The whole earth smelt sweet with spring. In the air was the noise of many wings, on the trees the purple and pink of many blossoms. Summer lay with bare breast upon all the fields—a queen whose rule had never known an hour of storm or overthrow. It was a glorious land filled full of the sun and of the things that love the sun.

Late one afternoon, tired, hot and dusty, Dick Collins and Ike Berry halted by the wayside for a little rest and a little gossip. In violation of orders this thing had been done, and Mars is a jealous and vengeful god. They tarried long, smoking a bit and talking a bit, and finally fell asleep.

A sudden scout of guerrillas awoke the gentlemen, using upon Collins the back of a saber, and upon Berry, who was larger and sounder of slumber, the butt of a musquetoon. There were six of them—swart, soldierly fellows, who wore gilded spurs and bedecked *sombreros*.

"*Francaisces,* eh!" they muttered one to another.

Berry knew considerable Spanish—Collins not so much. To lie under the imputation of being French was to lie within the shadow of sudden death. Berry tried to keep away from that. He answered:

"No, no, Senors, not *Francaisces* but *Americanos.*"

The Mexicans looked at each other and shrugged their shoulders. Berry had revealed to them that he spoke Spanish enough to be dangerous.

Their pistols were taken from them; their carbines, their horses, and whatever else could be found, including a few pieces of silver in Berry's pocket. Then they felt of Collins' pantaloons. It had been so long since they echoed to the jingle of either silver or gold, that even the pockets issued a protest at the imputation. Afterward the two men were marched across the country to a group of adobe buildings among a range of hills, far enough removed from the route of travel to be safe from rescue. They were cast into a filthy room where there was neither bed nor blanket, and bade to rest there. Two of the guard, musquetoons in hand and revolvers at waist, occupied the same room. With them, the dirt and the fleas were congenial companions.

Collins fell a musing.

"What are you thinking about, Dick?" Berry asked.

"Escape. And you?"

"Of something to eat."

Here was a Hercules who was always hungry.

A Mexican in his normal condition must have drink. A stone ewer of fiery *catalan* was brought in, and as the night deepened, so did their potations. Before midnight the two guards were drunk. An hour later, and one of them was utterly oblivious to all earthly objects. The other amused himself by pointing his cocked gun at the Americans, laughing low and savagely when they would endeavor to screen themselves from his comic mirth.

His drunken comrade was lying on his back, with a scarf around his waist, in which a knife was sticking.

Collins looked at it until his eyes glittered. He found time to whisper to Berry:

"You are as strong as an ox. Stand by me when I seize that knife and plunge it into the other Mexican's breast. I may not kill him the first time, and if I do not, then grapple with him. The second stab shall be more fatal."

"Unto death," replied Berry. "Make haste."

For one instant the guard took his eyes from the movements of the Americans. Collins seized the knife and rose up—stealthy, menacing, terrible. They advanced upon the Mexican. He turned as they came across the room and threw up his gun. Too late. Aiming at the left side, Collins' blow swerved aside, the knife entering just below the breast bone and cutting a dreadful gash. With the spring of a tiger-cat, Berry leaped upon him and hurled him to the floor. Again the knife arose—there was a dull, penetrating thud, a quiver of relaxing limbs, a groan that sounded like a curse, and beside the drunken man there lay another who would never touch *catalan* again this side of eternity.

Instant flight was entered into. Stripping the arms from the living and the dead, the Americans hurried out. They found their horses unguarded; the wretched village was in unbroken sleep, and not anywhere did wakeful or vigilant sentinel rise up to question or restrain. By the noon of the next day they had reported to Shelby, and for many days thereafter a shadow was seen on Collins' face that told of the desperate blow struck in the name of self-defense and liberty. After that the two men never straggled again.

Crosses are common in Mexico. Lifting up their penitential arms, however, by the wayside, and in forlorn and gloomy places, if they do not affright one, they at least put one to thinking. There where they stand, ghastly and weather-beaten under the sky, and alone with the stars and the night, murder has been done. There at the feet of them—in the yellow dust of the roadway—innocent, it may be, and true, and too young to die—a dead man has lain with his face in a pool of blood. Sometimes flowers adorn the crosses, and votive offerings, and many a rare and quaint conceit to lighten the frown on the face of death, and fashion a few links in the chain of memory that shall make even the dead claim kinship with all the glad and sweet-growing things of the wonderful summer weather.

Over beyond Dolores Hidalgo, a pleasant two days' journey, there was a high hill that held a castle. On either side of this there were heavy masses of timber. Below the fall of the woodlands, a meadow stretched itself out, bounded on the hither side by a stream that was limpid and musical. Beyond this stream a broken way began, narrowing down at last to a rugged defile, and opening once more into a country as fruitful as Paradise and filled as full of the sun.

Just where the defile broke away from the shade of the great oaks a cross stood, whose history had a haunting memory that was sorrowful even in that sinful and sorrowful land. There was a young girl who lived in this castle, very fair for a Mexican and very steadfast and true. The interval is short between seedtime and harvest, and she ripened early. In the full glory of her beauty and her womanhood, she was plighted to a young *commandante* from Dolores, heir of many fertile acres, a soldier and an Imperialist. Maybe the wooing was sweet, for what came after had in it enough of bitterness and tears. The girl had a brother who was a guerrilla chief, devoted first to his profession and next to the fortunes of Juarez. Spies were everywhere, and even from his own household news was carried of the courtship and the approaching marriage.

For days and days he watched by the roadside, scanning all faces that hurried by, seeking alone for the face that might have been told for its happiness. One night there was a trampling of horsemen, and a low voice singing tenderly under the moon. The visit had been long, and the parting passionate and pure. Only a little ways with love at his heart and the future so near with its outstretched hands as to reach up almost to the marriage-ring. No murmur ran along the lips of the low-lying grasses, and no sentinel angel rose up betwixt fate and its victim. His uniform carried death in its yellow and gold. Not to his own alone had the fair-haired Austrian brought broken hearts and stained and sundered marriage vows. Only the clear, long ring of a sudden musket, and the dead Imperialist lay with his face in the dust and his spirit going the dark way all alone. From such an interview why ride to such an ending? No tenderness availed him, no caress consoled him, no fond farewell gave him staff and script for the journey. He died where the woods and the meadows met—for a love by manhood and faith anointed.

In the morning there had been lifted up a cross. It was standing there still in the glorious weather. The same flowers were blooming still, the same stream swept on by the castle gates, the same splendid sweep of woodland and meadow spread itself out as God's land loved of the sky—but the gallant Commandante, where was he? Ask of the masses that the pitying angels heard and carried on their wings to heaven.

One tall spire, like the mighty standard of a king, arose through the lances of the sunset. San Miguel was in sight, a city built upon a hill. Around its forbidding base the tide of battle had ebbed and flowed, and there had grim old Carterac called out, the cloud of the cannon's smoke and the cloud of his beard white together:

"My children, the Third know how to die. One more victory and one more cross for all of you. Forward!"

This to the Third Zouaves as they were fixing bayonets on the crest of a charge with which all the empire rang. Afterward, when Carterac was buried, shot foremost in the breach, the natives came to view the grave and turned away wondering what manner of a giant had been interred therein. He had gone but a little way in advance of his children. What San Miguel had spared, Gravelotte finished. Verily war has its patriarchs no less renowned than Israel's.

From out the gates of the town, and down the long paved way leading northward, a gallant regiment came gaily forth to welcome Shelby. The music of the sabers ran through the valley. Pennons floated wide and free, the burnished guns rose and fell in the dim, undulating swing of perfect horsemen, and the rays of the setting sun shone upon the gold of the epaulettes until, as with fire, they blazed in the delicious haze of the evening.

Some paces forward of all the goodly company rode one who looked like a soldier. Mark him well. That regiment there is known as the Empress' Own. The arms of Carlota are on the blue of the uniforms. That silken flag, though all unbaptized by blood or battle, was wrought by her gentle hands—hands that wove into the tapestry of time a warp and woof sadder than aught of any tragedy ever known before the king-craft or conquest. She was standing by a little altar in the palace of Chapultepec on an afternoon in May. The city of Montezuma was at her feet in the delicious sleep of its siesta.

"Swear," she said, putting forth the unfolded standard until the sweep of its heavy fringes canopied the long, lustrous hair of the Colonel, "swear to be true to king and country."

The man knelt down.

"To king and *queen* and country," he cried, "while a sword can be drawn or a squadron mustered."

She smiled upon him and gave him her hand as he arose. This he stooped low to kiss, repeating again his oath, and pledging again all a soldier's faith to the precious burden laid upon his honor.

Look at him once more as he rides up from the town through the sunset. At his back is the regiment of Carlota, and over this regiment the stainless banner of Carlota is floating. The face is very fair for a Mexican's, and a little Norman in its handsome outline. Some curls were in the lustrous hair, not masculine curls, but royal enough, perhaps, to recall the valorous deeds that were done at Flodden, when from over seas the beautiful Queen of France, beloved of all gallant gentlemen, sent to the Scottish monarch

> "A turquoise ring and glove,
> And charged him as her knight and love,
> To march three miles on English land,
> And strike three strokes with Scottish brand,
> And bid the banners of his band
> In English breezes dance."[2]

He gave Shelby cordial greeting, and made him welcome to San Miguel in the name of the Empire. His eyes, large and penetrating, wore yet a sinister look that marred somewhat the smile that should have come not so often to the face of a Spaniard. He spoke English well, talked much of New York which he had visited, predicted peace and prosperity to Maximilian and his reign after a few evil days, and bowed low in salute when he separated.

That man was Col. Leonardo Lopez, the traitor of Queretero, the spy of Escobedo, the wretch who sold his flag, the coward who betrayed his regiment, the false knight who denied his mistress, and the decorated and ennobled thing who gave up his emperor to a dog's death. And the price—thirty thousand dollars in gold. Is it any wonder that his wife forsook him, that his children turned their faces away from him, that the church refused him asylum, that a righteous soldier of the Liberal cause smote him upon either cheek in the presence of an army on parade, and that even the very *lazzaroni*[3] of the streets pointed at him as he passed, and shouted in voluble derision:

"The Traitor! the Traitor!"

And yet did all these things happen to the handsome horseman who rode up quietly to the Expedition in front of San Miguel, and bade it welcome in the name of hospitality and the Empire.

Gen. Felix Douay held San Luis Potosi, the great granary of Mexico.[4] It was the brother of this Douay who, surrounded and abandoned at Weissembourg, marched alone and on foot toward the enemy, until a Prussian bullet found his heart. Older and calmer and wiser, perhaps, than his brother, Gen. Felix Douay was the strong right arm of Bazaine and Maximilian. Past sixty, gray-bearded and gaunt, he knew war as the Indian knows a trail. After assigning quarters to the men, he sent at once for Shelby.

"You have come among us for an object," he commenced in perfect English, "and as I am a man of few words, please state to me frankly what that object is."

"To take service under Maximilian," was the prompt reply.

"What are your facilities for recruiting a corps of Americans?"

"So ample, general, that if authority is given me, I can pledge to you the services of fifty thousand in six months."

Some other discourse was had between them, and Douay fell to musing a little. When he was done he called an aide to his side, wrote a lengthy communication, bade the staff officer take it and ride rapidly to the City of Mexico, returning with the same speed when he had received his answer.

As he extended his hand to Shelby in parting, he said to him:

"You will remain here until further orders. It may be that there shall be work for your hands sooner than either of us expect."

Southward from San Luis Potosi, and running far down to the Gulf, even unto Tampico, was a low, level sweep of land, where marshes abounded and retreats that were almost unknown and well-nigh inaccessible. In the fever months, the fatal months of August and September, these dismal fens and swamps were alive with guerrillas. *Vomito* lurked in the long lagoons, and lassitude, emaciation and death peered out from behind every palm tree and cypress root.[5] Foreigners there were none who could abide that dull, greyish exhalation which wrought for the morning a winding sheet, and for the French it was not only the valley, but the Valley of the Shadow of Death. Bazaine's light troops, his Voltigeurs and his Chasseurs of Vincennes, had penetrated there and died. Most of the Foreign Legion had gone in there and perished. Two battalions of Zouaves—great, bearded, medaled fellows, bronzed by Syrian night winds and tempered to steel in the sap and siege of Sebastopol—had borne their eagles backward from the mist, famishing because a fever came with the morning and the fog.

No matter how, the guerrillas fattened. Reptiles need little beside the ooze and the foetid vegetation of the lowlands, and so when the rains came and the roads grew wearisome and long, they rose upon the convoys night after night, massacring all that fell into their hands, even the women and the live stock.

Figueroa was the fell spirit of the marshes—a Mexican past forty-five, one-eyed from the bullet of an American's revolver, tall for his race, and so bitter and unrelenting in his hatred of all foreigners, especially Americans, that when he dies he will be canonized. If in all his life he ever knew an hour of mercy or relenting, no record in story or tradition stands as its monument. Backward across the Rio Grande there have been borne many tales of Escobedo and Carabajal, Martinez and Cortina, Lozado the Indian and Rodriguez the renegade priest; but for deeds of desperate butchery and vengeance, the fame of all these is as the leaves that fell last autumn.

No matter his crimes, however, he fought as few of them do for his native land, and dreaded but two things on earth—Dupin and his Contre-Guerrillas. Twice they had brought him to bay, and twice he had retired deeper and deeper into his jungles, sacrificing all the flower of his following, and pressed so furiously and fast that at no time thereafter could he turn as a hunted tiger and rend the foremost of his pursuers.

Figueroa lay close to the high national road running from San Luis Potosi to Tampico, levying such tribute as he could collect by night and in a manner that left none on the morrow to demand recompense or reckoning. Because it was a post in possession of the French, it was necessary for Douay to have safe and constant intercourse with Tampico. This was impossible so long as Figueroa lived in the marshes and got fat on the fog that brought only fever and death to the Frenchman and the foreigner. Three expeditions had been sent down into the Valley of the Shadow of Death and had returned; those that were left of them soldiers no longer, but skeletons whose uniforms served only to make the contrast ghastly. The road was still covered with ambushments, and creeping and crawling forms that murdered when they should have slept.

With the arrival of Shelby, a sudden resolution had come to Douay. He meant to give him service in the French army, send him down first to fight the fog and Figueroa, and afterward—well, the future gives generally but small concern to a Frenchman—but afterward there could have been no doubt of Douay's good intentions, and of a desire to reward all liberally who did his bidding and who came out of the swamps alive. For permission to do this he had sent forward to consult Bazaine, and had halted Shelby long enough to know the Marshal's wishes.

The aide-de-camp returned speedily, but he brought with him only a short, curt order:

"Bid the Americans march immediately to Mexico."

There was no appeal. Douay marshaled the expedition, served it with rations and wine, spoke some friendly and soldierly words to all of its officers, and bade them a pleasant and a prosperous journey. Because he possessed no *baton* is no reason why he should not have interpreted aright the future, and seen that the auspicious hours were fast hastening away when it would be no longer possible to recruit an army and attach to the service of Maximilian a powerful corps of Americans. Bazaine had mistrusted their motives from the first, and had been more than misinformed of their movements and their numbers since the expedition had entered the Empire. As for the Emperor, his mind had been poisoned by his Mexican counselors, and he was too busy then with his botany and his butterflies to heed the sullen murmurings of the gathering storm in the north, and to understand all the harsh, indomitable depths of that stoical Indian character which was soon to rush down from Chihuahua and gratify its ferocious appetite in the blood of the uptorn and uprooted dynasty. They laughed at Juarez then, the low, squat Indian, his sinister face scarred with smallpox like Mirabeau's, and his sleuth-hound ways that followed the trail of the Republic, though in the scent there was pestilence and famine and death.

One day the French lines began to contract as a wave that is baffled and broken. The cliff followed up the wave, and mariners like Douay and Jeanningros, looking out from the quarter-deck, saw not only the granite, but the substance, the granite typified; they saw Juarez and his forty thousand ragged followers, hungry, brutal, speaking all dialects, grasping bright American muskets, having here and there an American officer in uniform, unappeasable, oncoming—murderous. Again the waves receded and again there was Juarez. From El Paso to Chihuahua, from Chihuahua to Matamoras, from Matamoras to Monterey, to Matehuala, to Dolores Hidalgo, to San Miguel, to the very spot on which Douay stood at parting, his bronzed face saddened and his white hair waving in the winds of the summer morning.

It was no war of his, however. What he was sent to do he did. Others planned. Douay executed. It might have been better if the fair-haired sovereign had thought more and asked more of the gray-haired subject.

It was on the third day's march from San Luis Potosi that an ambulance broke down, having in its keeping two wounded soldiers of the Expedition. The accident was near the summit of the Madre mountains—an extended range between San Luis Potosi and Penamason—and within a mile of the village of Sumapetla. The rear guard came within without it. In reporting, before being dismissed for the night, Shelby asked the officer of the ambulance.

"It is in Sumapetla," the Captain answered.

"And the wounded?"

"At a house with one attendant."

His face darkened. The whole Madre range was filled with robbers, and two of his best men, wounded and abandoned, were at the mercy of the murderers.

"If a hair of either head is touched," he cried out to the officer, "it will be better that you had never crossed the Rio Grande. What avails all the lessons you have learned of this treacherous and deceitful land that you should desert comrades in distress and ride up to tell me the pleasant story of your own arrival and safety? Order Kirtley to report instantly with twenty men."

Capt. James B. Kirtley came—a young, smooth-faced, dauntless officer, tried in the front of fifty battles, a veteran and yet a boy. The men had ridden thirty miles that day, but what mattered it? Had the miles been sixty, the same unquestioned obedience would have been yielded, the same soldierly spirit manifested of daring and adventure.

"Return to Sumapetla," Shelby said, "and find my wounded. Stay with them, wait for them, fight for them, get killed if need be, for them, but whatever you do, bring or send them back to me. I shall wait for you a day and a night."

A pale-faced man, with his eyes drooping and his form bent, rode up to Shelby. He plucked him by the sleeve and pleaded.

"General, let me go too. I did not think when I left them. I can fight. Try me, General. Tell Kirtley to take me. It is a little thing I am asking of you, but I have followed you for four years, and I think, small as it is, it will save me."

All Shelby's face lit up with a pity and tenderness that was absolutely winning. He grasped his poor, tired soldier's hand and spoke to him low and softly:

"Go, and come back again. I was harsh, I know, and over cruel, but between us two there is neither cloud nor shadow of feeling. I do forgive you from my soul."

There were tears in the man's eyes as he rode away, and a heart beneath his uniform that was worth a diadem.

It was ten long miles to Sumapetla, and the night had fallen. The long, swinging trot that Kirtley struck would carry them there in two hours at farthest, and if needs be, the trot would grow into a gallop.

He rode along his ranks and spoke to his men:

"Keep quiet, be ready, be loaded. You heard the orders. I shall obey them or be even beyond the need of the ambulance we have been sent back to succor."

Sumapetla was reached in safety. It was a miserable, squalid village, filled with Indians and beggars and dogs. In the largest house the wounded men were found—not well cared for, but comfortable from pain. Their attendant, a blacksmith, was busy with the broken ambulance. Kirtley threw forward picquets and set about seeking for supper. While active in its preparations a sudden volley came from the front—keen, dogged, vicious. From the roar of the guns Kirtley knew that his men had fired at close range and all together. It was a clear night, yet still quite dark in the mountains. Directly a picquet rode rapidly up, not the least excited, yet very positive.

"There is a large body in front of us and well armed. They tried a surprise and lost five. We did not think it well to charge, and I have come back for orders. Please say what they are quick, for the boys may need me before I can reach them again."

This was the volunteer who had commanded the rear guard of the day's march.

Skirmishing shots now broke out ominously. There were fifteen men in the village and five on outpost.

"Mount, all," cried Kirtley, "and follow me."

The relief took the road at a gallop.

The space between the robbers and their prey was scarcely large enough for Kirtley to array his men upon. From all sides there came the steady roar of musketry, telling how complete the ambuscade, and how serviceable the guns. Some fifty paces in the rear of the outpost the road made a sudden turn, leaving at the apex of the acute angle a broken zig-zag piece of rock-work capable of much sturdy defense, and not flanked without a rush and a moment or two of desperate in-fighting that is rarely the choice of guerrillas. This Kirtley had noticed with the eye of a soldier and the quickness of a man who meant to do a soldier's duty first and a comrade's duty afterward. Because the wounded men had to be saved was no reason why those who were unwounded should be sacrificed.

He fell back to the rocky ledge facing the robbers. Word sent to the blacksmith in the village to hurry, to make rapid and zealous haste, for the danger was pressing and dire, got for an answer in return:

"Captain Kirtley, I am doing my best. A Mexican's blacksmith shop is an anvil without a hammer, a forge without a bellows, a wheel without its felloes; and I have to make, instead of one thing, a dozen things. It will be two hours before the ambulance is mended."

Very laconic and very true. Kirtley never thought a second time, during all the long two hours, of the smithy in the village, and the swart, patient smith who, within full sound of the struggling musketry, wrought and delved and listened now and then in the intervals of his toil to the rising and falling of the fight, laughing, perhaps, low to himself, as his practiced ear caught the various volleys, and knew that neither backward nor forward did the Americans recede nor advance a stone's throw.

The low reach of rock, holding fast to the roots of the trees that grew up from it, and bristling with rugged and stunted shrubs, transformed itself into a citadel. The road ran by it like an arm that encircles a waist. Where the elbow was the Americans stood at bay. They had dismounted and led their horses still further to the rear—far enough to be safe, yet near at hand. From the unknown it was impossible to tell what spectres might issue forth. The robbers held on. From the volume of fire their numbers were known as two hundred—desperate odds, but it was night, and the night is always in league with the weakest.

Disposed among the rocks, about the roots and the trunks of the trees, the Americans fired in skirmishing order and at will. Three rapid and persistent times the rush of the guerrillas came as a great wave upon the little handful, a lurid wealth of light all along its front, and a noise that was appalling in the darkness. Nothing so terrifies as the oscillation and the roar of a hurricane that is invisible. Hard by the road, Kirtley kept his grasp upon the rock. Nothing shook that—nothing shook the tension of its grim endurance.

The last volley beat full into the faces of all. A soldier fell forward into the darkness.

"Who's hurt?" the clear voice of Kirtley rang out without a tremor.

"It's me, Jim; it's Walker. Hard hit in the shoulder; but thank God for the breech loader, a fellow can load and fire with one sound arm left."

Bleeding through the few rags stuffed into the wound, and faint from much weakness and pain, Walker mounted again to his post and fought on till the struggle was ended.

Time passed, but lengthily. Nine of the twenty were wounded, all slightly, however, save Walker—thanks to the darkness and the ledge that seemed planted there by a Providence that meant to succor steadfast courage and devotion. The ambulance was done, and the wounded were placed therein.

"It can travel but slowly in the night," said Kirtley to William Fell, who had stood by his side through all the bitter battle, "and we must paralyze pursuit a little."

"Paralyze it—how?"

"By a sudden blow, such as a prize fighter gives when he strikes below the belt. By a charge some good hundred paces in the midst of them."

Fell answered laconically:

"Desperate but reasonable. I have seen such things done. Will it take long?"

"Twenty minutes all told, and there will be but eleven of us. The nine who are wounded must go back."

The horses were brought and mounted. Walker could scarcely sit in his saddle. As he rode to the rear, two of his comrades supported him. The parting was ominous—the living, perhaps, taking leave of the dead.

Far into the night and the unknown the desperate venture held its way. Two deep the handful darted out from behind the barricade, firing at the invisible. Spectre answered spectre, and only the ringing of the revolvers was real. The impetus of the charge was such that the line of the robbers' fire was passed before, reined up and countermarching, the forlorn hope could recede as a wave that carried the undertow. The reckless gallop bore its planted fruit. Back through the pass unharmed the men rode, and on by the ledge, into Sumapetla. No pursuit came after. The fire of the guerrillas ceased ere the charge had been spent, and when the morning came there was the camp, and a thousand blessings for the bold young leader who had held his own so well, and kept his faith as he had kept the fort on its perch among the mountains.

It was a large city set upon a hill that loomed up through the mists of the evening—a city seen from afar and musical with many vesper bells. Peace stood in the ranks of the sentinel corn, and fed with the cattle that browsed by the streams in the meadows. Peace came on the wings of the twilight and peopled the grasses with songs that soothed, and many toned voices that made for the earth a symphony. Days of short parade and longer merry-making dawned for the happy soldierly. The sweet, unbroken south wind brought no dust of battle from the palms and the orange blossoms by the sea. Couriers came and went, and told of peace throughout the realm; of robber bands surrendering to the law; of railroads planned and parks adorned; of colonists arriving and foreign ships in all the ports; of roads made safe for travel, and public virtue placed at premium in the market lists; of prophecies that brightened all the future, and to the Empire promised an Augustan age.[6] The night and the sky were at peace as the city grew larger and larger on its hill, and a silence came to the ranks of the Expedition that was not broken until the camp became a bivouac with the goddess of plenty to make men sing of fealty and obeisance.

It was the City of Queretaro.

Yonder ruined convent, its gateway crumbling to decay, its fountains strewn with bits of broken shrubs and flowers, held the sleeping Emperor the night the traitor Lopez surrendered all to an Indian vengeance and compassion. When that Emperor awoke he had been dreaming. Was it of Miramar and "poor Carlota?"

The convent was at peace then, and the fountains were all at play. Two bearded Zouaves stood in its open door, looking out curiously upon the serried ranks of the Americans as they rode slowly by.

Yonder, on the left where a hill arises, the capture was made; yonder the Austrian cried out in the agony of this last desertion and betrayal:

"Is there then no bullet for me?"

Later, when the bullets found his heart, they found an image there that entered with his spirit into heaven—the image of "Poor Carlota."

CHAPTER XVI.

Quite a large concentration of Americans had taken place in the City of Mexico. Many of these were penniless; all of them were soldiers. As long as they believed in the luck, or the fortune, or the good destiny of Shelby—and that, being a born soldier, the Empire must needs see and recognize those qualities which even his enemies had described as magnificent—they were content to wait for Shelby's arrival, living no man knew how, hungry always, sometimes sad, frequently in want of a roll or a bed—but turning ever their faces fair to the sunrise, saying, it may be a little reproachfully, to the sun: "What hast thou in store for us this day, oh King?"

Maximilian was like a man who had a desperate race before him, and who started out to win it. The pace in the beginning was therefore terrible. So firm was the stride, so tense were the muscles, so far in the rear were all competitors, that opposition had well-nigh abandoned the contest and resistance had become so enfeebled as to be almost an absolute mockery.

In the noonday of the struggle a halt was had. There were so many sweet and odorous flowers, so many nights that were almost divine, so much of shade and luxury and ease, so much of music by the wayside, and so many hands that were held out to him for the grasping, that the young Austrian, schooled in the luxuries of literature and the pursuits of science, sat himself down just when the need was sorest and smoked and dreamed and planned and wrote and—died.

Maximilian was never a soldier. Perhaps he was no statesman as well. Most certainly all the elements of a politician were wanting in his character, which was singularly sweet, trusting and affectionate. To sign a death warrant gave him nights of solitude and remorse. Alone with his confessor he would beseech in prayer the merciful God to show him that mercy he had denied to others. On the eve of an execution he had been known to flee from his capital as if pursued by some horrible nightmare. He could not kill, when, to reign as a foreigner, it was necessary to kill, as said William the Conqueror, until the balance is about even between those who came over with you and those whom you found upon your arrival.

The Emperor had given shelter to some honored and august Americans. Commodore M. F. Maury, who had preceded the Expedition, and who had brought his great fame and his transcendent abilities to the support of the Empire, had been made the Imperial Commissioner of Immigration.[1] Entering at once upon an energetic discharge of his duties, he had secured a large and valuable grant of land near the city of Cordova, which, even as early as September, 1865, was being rapidly surveyed and opened up for civilization. Agents of colonization had been sent to the United States, and reports were constantly being received of their cordial and sometimes enthusiastic reception by the people, from New Orleans to Dubuque, Iowa, and from New York westward to San Antonio, Texas. There was a world of people ready to emigrate. One in five of all the thousands would have been a swart, strapping fellow, fit for any service but best for the service of a soldier.

Therefore, when these things were told to Shelby, riding down from the highlands about Queretero to the lowlands about Mexico, he rubbed his hands as one who feels a steady flame by the bivouac-fire of a winter's night, and spoke out gleefully to Langhorne:

"We can get forty thousand and take our pick. Young men for war, and only young men emigrate. This Commodore Maury seems to sail as well upon land as upon the water. It appears to me that we shall soon see the sky again. What do *you* say, Captain?"

Langhorne answered him laconically:

"The French are not friendly—that is to say, they want no soldiers from among us. You will not be permitted to recruit even so much as a front and a rear rank; and if this is what you mean by seeing the sky, then the sky is as far away as ever."

It was not long before the sequel proved which of the two was right.

Gen. John B. Magruder, who had also preceded the Expedition, and who had known Marshal Bazaine well in the Crimea, was commissioned Surveyor-General of the Empire through French influence, and assigned to duty with Commodore Maury. He had spoken twice to the Marshal in behalf of Shelby, and spoken frankly and boldly at that. He got in reply what Jeanningros had got and Depreuil and Douay and all of them. He got this sententious order:

"Bid Shelby march immediately to Mexico."

General Preston, who through much peril and imminent risk by night and day had penetrated to the Capital, even from Piedras Negras, had begged and pleaded for permission to return with such authority vouchsafed to Shelby as would enable him to recruit his corps. Preston fared like the rest. For answer he also got the order:

"Bid Shelby march immediately to Mexico."

And so he marched on into the glorious land between Queretero and the Capital, and into the glorious weather, no guerrillas now to keep watch against, no robbers anywhere about the hills or the fords. The French were everywhere in the sunshine. Their picquets were upon all the roads. The villages contained their cantonments. There was peace and prosperity and a great rest among all the people. The women laughed in this glad land, and the voices of the many children told of peaceful days and of the fatness of the field and the vine—of the streams that ran to the sea, and uplands green with leaf or gray with ripening grain.

Maybe Fate rests its head upon its two hands at times, and thinks of what little things it shall employ to make or mar a character—save or lose a life—banish beyond the light or enter into and possess forever a Paradise.

The march was running by meadow and river, and the swelling of billowy wheat, and great groves of orange trees wherein the sunshine hid itself at noon with the breeze and the mocking birds.

It was far into the evening that John Thrailkill sat by the fire of his mess, smoking and telling brave stories of the brave days that were dead. Others were grouped about in dreaming indolence or silent fancy—thinking, it may be, of the northern land with its pines and firs—of great rolling waves of prairie and plain, of forests where cabins were and white-haired children all at play.

Thrailkill was a guerrilla who never slept—that is to say, who never knew the length or breadth of a bed from Sumter to Appomattox. Some woman in Platte county had made him a little black flag, under which he fought. This, worked in the crown of his hat, satisfied him with his loyalty to his lady-love. In addition to all this, he was one among the best pistol shots in a command where all were excellent.

Perhaps neither before nor since the circumstance here related has anything so quaint in recklessness or bravado been recorded this side of the Crusades. Thrailkill talked much, but then he had fought much, and fighting men love to talk now and then. Some border story of broil or battle, wherein, at desperate odds, he had done a desperate deed, came uppermost as the night deepened, and the quaint and scarred guerrilla was overgenerous in the share he took of the killing and the plunder.

A comrade by his side, Anthony West, doubted the story and ridiculed its narration. Thrailkill was not swift to anger for one so thoroughly reckless, but on this night he arose, every hair in his bushy beard bristling.

"You disbelieve me, it seems," he said, bending over the other until he could look into his eyes, "and for the skeptic there is only the logic of a blow. Is this real, and this?" and Thrailkill smote West twice in the face with his open hand—once on either cheek. No insult could be more studied, open and unpardonable.

Comrades interfered instantly, or there would have been blood shed in the heart of the camp and by the flames of the bivouac fire. Each was very cool—each knew what the morrow would bring forth, without a miracle.

The camp was within easy reach of a town that was more of a village than a town. It had a church and a priest, and a regular Don of an Alcalde who owned leagues of arable land and two hundred game cocks besides. For Shelby's especial amusement a huge main was organized and a general invitation given to all who desired to attend.

The contest was to begin at noon. Before the sun had risen Capt. James H. Gillette came to Thrailkill, who was wrapped up in his blankets, and said to him:

"I have a message for you."

"It is not long, I hope."

"Not very long, but very plain."

"Yes, yes, they are all alike. I have seen such before. Wait for me a few minutes."

Thrailkill found Ike Berry, and Berry in turn soon found Gillette.

The note was a challenge, brief and peremptory. Some conferences followed, and the terms were agreed upon. These were savage enough for an Indian. Colt's pistols, dragoon size, were the weapons, but only one of them was to be loaded. The other, empty in every chamber, was to be placed alongside the loaded one. Then a blanket was to cover both, leaving the butt of each exposed. He who won the toss was to make the first selection, and Thrailkill won. The loaded and the unloaded pistol lay hidden beneath the blanket, the two handles so nearly alike that there was no appreciable difference. Thrailkill walked up to the tent whistling a tune. West stood behind him, watching with a face that was set as a flint. The first drew, cast his eyes along the cylinder, saw that it was loaded, and smiled. The last drew—every chamber was empty. Death was his portion as absolutely and as certainly as if death already stood by his side. Yet he made no sign other than to look up to the sky. Was it to be his last look?

The terms were ferocious, yet neither second had protested against them. It seemed as if one man was to murder another because one had been lucky in the toss of a silver dollar. As the case stood, Thrailkill had the right to fire *six shots* at West before West had the right to grasp even so much as a loaded pistol, and Thrailkill was known for his deadly skill throughout the ranks of the whole Expedition.

The two were to meet just at sunset, and the great cock main was at noon. To this each principal went, and each second, and before the main was over the life of a man stood as absolutely upon the prowess of a bird as the spring and its leaves upon the rain and the sunshine.

And thus it came about:

In Mexico cock fighting is a national recreation, perhaps it is a national blessing as well. Men engage in it when they would be robbing else, and waylaying couriers bearing specie, and haunting the mountain gorges until the heavy trains of merchandise entered slowly in to be swallowed up.

The priests fight there, and the fatter the *padre* the finer his chicken. From the prayer-book to the pit is an easy transition, and no matter the *aves* so only the odds are in favor of the church. It is upon the Sundays that all the pitched battles begin. After the matin bells, the matches. When it is vespers, for some there has been a stricken and for some a victorious field. No matter again—for all there is absolution.

The Alcalde of the town of Linares was a jolly, good-conditioned Mexican, who knew a bit of English, picked up in California, and who liked the Americans but for two things—their hard drinking and their hard swearing. Finding any ignorant of these accomplishments, there flowed never any more for them a stream of friendship from the Alcalde's fountain. It became dry as suddenly as a spring in a desert.

Shelby won his heart by sending him a case of elegant cognac—a present from Douay—and therefore was the main improvised which was to begin at noon.

The pit was a great circle in the midst of a series of seats that arose the one above the other. Over the entrance, which was a gateway opening like the lids of a book, was a chair of state, an official seat occupied by the Alcalde. Beside him sat a bugler in uniform. At the beginning and the end of a battle this bugler, watching the gestures of the Alcalde, blew triumphant or penitential strains accordingly as the Alcalde's favorite lost or won. As the main progressed, the notes of gladness outnumbered those of sorrow.

A born cavalryman is always suspicious. He looks askance at the woods, the fences, the ponds, the morning fogs, the road that forks and crosses, and the road that runs into the rear of a halted column, or into either flank at rest in bivouac. It tries one's nerves to fumble at uncertain girths in the darkness, a rain of bullets pouring down at the outposts and no shelter anywhere for a long week's marching.

And never at any time did Shelby put aught of faith in Mexican friendship, or aught of trust in Mexican welcome and politeness. His guard was perpetual, and his intercourse, like his marching, was always in skirmishing order. Hence one-half the forces of the expedition were required to remain in camp under arms, prepared for any emergency, while the other half, free of restraint, could accept the Alcalde's invitation or not as they saw fit. The most of them attended. With the crowd went Thrailkill and West, Gillette and Berry. All the village was there. The pit had no caste. Benevolent priests mingled with their congregations and bet their *pesos* on their favorites. Lords of many herds and acres, and mighty men of the country round about, the Dons of the *haciendas* pulled off their hats to the *peons,* and staked their gold against the greasy silver palm to palm. Fair *senoritas* shot furtive glances along the ranks of the soldiers—glances that lingered long upon the Saxon outline of their faces and retreated only when to the light of curiosity there had been added that of unmistakable admiration.

The bugle sounded and the weighing began. The sport was new to many of the spectators—to a few it was a sealed book. Twenty-five cocks were matched—all magnificent birds, not so large as those fought in America, but as pure in game and as rich in plumage. There, too, the fighting is more deadly, that is to say, it is more rapid and fatal. The heels used have been almost thrown aside here. In the north and west absolutely, in New Orleans very nearly so. These heels, wrought of the most perfect steel and curved like a scimitar, have an edge almost exquisite in its keenness. They cut asunder like a sword-blade. Failing in instant death, they inflict mortal wounds. Before there is mutilation, there is murder.

To the savage reality of combat there was added the atoning insincerities of music. These diverted the drama of its premeditation, and gave to it an air of surprise that, in the light of an accommodating conscience, passed unchallenged for innocence. In Mexico the natives rarely ask questions—the strangers never.

Shelby seated himself by the side of the Alcalde, the first five or six notes of a charge were sounded and the battle began. Thereafter with varying fortunes it ebbed and flowed through all the long afternoon. Aroused into instant championship, the Americans espoused the side of this or that bird, and lost or won as the fates decreed. There was but scant gold among them, all counted, but twenty dollars or twenty thousand, it would have been the same. A nation of born gamblers, it needed not a cock fight to bring all the old national traits uppermost. A dozen or more were on the eve of wagering their carbines and revolvers, when a sign from Shelby checked the unsoldierly impulse and brought them back instantly to a realization of duty.

Thrailkill had lost heavily—that is to say every dollar he owned on earth. West had won without cessation—won in spite of his judgment, which was often adverse to the wagers he laid. In this, maybe, Fate was but flattering him. Of what use would all his winnings be after the sunset?

It was the eighteenth battle, and a magnificent cock was brought forth who had the crest of an eagle and the eye of a basilisk.[2] More sonorous than the bugle, his voice had blended war and melody in it. The glossy ebony of his plumage needed only the sunlight to make it a mirror where courage might have arrayed itself. In an instant he was everybody's favorite—in his favor all the odds were laid. Some few clustered about his antagonist—among them a sturdy old priest who did what he could to stem the tide rising in favor of the bird of the beautiful plumage.

Infatuated like the rest, Thrailkill would have staked a crown upon the combat; he did not have even so much as one *real*.[3] The man was miserable. Once he walked to the door and looked out. If at that time he had gone forth, the life of West would have gone with him, but he did not go. As he returned he met Gillette, who spoke to him:

"You do not bet, and the battle is about to begin."

"I do not bet because I have not won. The pitcher that goes eternally to a well is certain to be broken at last."

"And yet you are fortunate."

Thrailkill shrugged his shoulders and looked at his watch. It wanted an hour yet of the sunset. The tempter still tempted him.

"You have no money, then. Would you like to borrow?"

"No."

Gillette mused awhile. They were tying on the last blades, and the old priest had cried out:

"A dubloon to a dubloon against the black cock!"

Thrailkill's eyes glistened. Gillette took him by the arm. He spoke rapidly, but so low and distinct that every word was a thrust:

"You do not want to kill West—the terms are murderous—you have been soldiers together—you can take the priest's bet—here is the money. But," he looked him fair in the face, "if you win you pay me—if you lose I have absolute disposal of your fire."

"Ah!" and the guerrilla straightened himself up all of a sudden, "what would you do with my fire?"

"Keep your hands clean from innocent blood, John Thrailkill. Is not that enough?"

The money was accepted, the wager with the priest was laid, and the battle began. When it was over the beautiful black cock lay dead on the sands of the arena, slain by the sweep of one terrific blow, while over him, in pitiless defiance, his antagonist, dun in plumage and ragged in crest and feather, stood a victor, conscious of his triumph and his prowess.

The sun was setting, and two men stood face to face in the glow of the crimson sky. On either flank of them a second took his place, a look of sorrow on the bold, bronzed face of Berry, the light of anticipation in the watchful eyes of the calm Gillette. Well kept, indeed, had been the secret of the tragedy. The group who stood alone on the golden edge of the evening were all who knew the ways and means of the work before them.

West took his place as a man who had shaken hands with life and knew how to die. Thrailkill had never been merciful, and this day of all days were the chances dead against a moment of pity or forgiveness.

The ground was a little patch of grass beside a stream, having trees in the rear of it, and trees over beyond the reach of the waters running musically to the sea. In the distance there were houses from which peaceful smoke ascended. Through the haze of the gathering twilight, the sound of bells came from the homeward-plodding herds, and from the fields the happy voices of the reapers.

West stood full front to his adversary—certain of death. He expected nothing beyond a quick and speedy bullet, one which would kill without inflicting needless pain.   The word was given. Thrailkill threw his pistol out, covered his antagonist once fairly, looked once into his eyes, and saw that they did not quail, and then, with a motion as instantaneous as it was unexpected, lifted it up overhead and fired in the air.

Gillette had won his wager.

CHAPTER XVII.

The city of all men's hopes and fears and aspirations; the city of the swart cavaliers of Cortez and the naked warriors of Montezuma, who rushed with bare bosom on lance and sword-blade; the city under the shadow of the old-world Huasco, that volcano, it may be, that was in its youth when Ararat bore aloft the ark as a propitiation to the God alike of the rainbow and the deluge, and that when the floods subsided sent its lava waves to the Pacific Ocean; the city which had seen the cold glitter of Northern steel flash along the broken way of Conteras, and wind itself up, striped thick with blood, into the heart of Chapultepec; the city filled now with Austrians and Belgians and Frenchmen and an Emperor newly crowned with manhood and valor, and an Empress, royal with an imperial youth and beauty—the city of Mexico was reached at last.

For many the long march was about to end, for others to begin again— longer, drearier, sterner than any march ever yet taken for king or country—the march down into the Valley of the Shadow, and over beyond the River and into the unknown and eternal.

Marshal Bazaine was a soldier who had seen service in Algeria, in the Crimea, in Italy—especially at Magenta—and he had won the *baton* at last in Mexico, that *baton* the First Napoleon declared might be in the knap-sack of every soldier.[1] The character of the man was a study some student of history may love to stumble upon in the future. Past fifty, white-haired where there was hair, bald over the forehead as one sees all Frenchmen who have served in Algeria, he made a fine figure on horseback, because from the waist up his body was long, lithe and perfectly trained; but not such a fine figure on foot, because the proportion was illy preserved between the two extremities. He was ambitious, brave to utter recklessness, crafty, yet outspoken and frank, a savage aristocrat who had married a fair-faced Spaniard and a million, merciless in discipline, beloved of his troops, adored by his military family, a gambler who had been known to win a thousand ounces on a single card, a speculator and the owner of ships, a husband whom even the French called true, a father and a judge who, after he had caressed his infant, voted death at the court-martial so often that one officer began to say to another:

"He shoots them all."

Bazaine was a skillful soldier. As long as it was war with Juarez, he kept Juarez starving and running—sometimes across the Rio Grande into Texas, where the Federals fed him, and sometimes in the mountains about El Paso, never despondent, it is true, yet never well-filled in either commissariat or cartridge-box. After the visit of General Castelneau, an aide-de-camp of Napoleon,[2] and the reception of positive orders of evacuation, the Marshal let the Liberals have pretty much their own way, so that they neither injured nor interrupted the French soldiers coming and going about the country at will. As the French waves receded, the waves of the Juaristas advanced. Bazaine sold them cannon and muskets and much ammunition, it is said, and even siege guns with which to batter down the very walls of Maximilian's palace itself. Those who have accused him of this have slandered and abused the man. He may have known much of many things, of ingratitude not one heart-throb. Not his the aggravation of evacuation, the sudden rending asunder of the whole frame-work of Imperialist society, the great fear that fell upon all, the patriotic uprisings that had infection and jubilee in them, the massacre of Mexicans who had favored the Austrian, the breaking up of all schemes for emigration and colonization, and the ending of a day that was to bring the cold, long night of Queretaro.

Rudolph, Emperor of Germany, who was born in 1218, and who was the son of Albert IV, Count of Hapsburg, was the founder of that family to which Maximilian belonged. In 1282 Rudolph placed his son Albert on the throne of Austria, and thus begins the history of that house which has swayed the destinies of a large portion of Europe for nearly eight hundred years, a house which, through many terrible struggles, has gained and lost and fought on and ruled on, sometimes wisely and sometimes not, yet ever ruling in the name of divine right and of the House of Hapsburg.

Through the force of marriage, purchase and inheritance, the State of Austria grew in extent beyond that of any other in the German Empire. In 1359 Rudolph IV assumed the title of Archduke Palatine, and in 1363 his reign was made notorious by the valuable acquisition of the Tyrol. This was the commencement of the history of the Archdukes, who were thereafter assigned to the high position of Emperor, the first taken from among them being Alfred II, who was chosen in 1438. The marriage of the bold, unscrupulous and ambitious Maximilian I, at the age of eighteen, to Mary, daughter of Charles the Bold, Duke of Burgundy, in 1477, added to Austria's territorial claim largely, and embraced Flanders, Franche Comte and all the Low Countries. In 1521 Ferdinand I married Ann, sister of Louis, King of Hungary and Bohemia, who was killed at the battle of Mohaez, in 1526, his empire being absorbed and incorporated with Austria. Upon the events of the fifteenth century, Charles V left an immortal impress, and the blood of this great Emperor was in the veins of Maximilian of Mexico.

In 1618 Europe, alarmed at the increasing territorial aggrandizement of Austria, and torn by feuds between Protestants and Catholics, saw the commencement of the thirty years' war. It terminated in the treaty of Westphalia in 1648, which accomplished the independence of the German states. In 1713 Austria gained the Italian provinces by the treaty of Utrecht, and in 1726, the last male of the House of Hapsburg, Charles II, died, the succession falling upon his daughter, Maria Theresa. She was succeeded by her son, Joseph II, and in 1792, at the age of twenty-two, Francis II succeeded his father, Leopold II, and became Emperor of Germany, King of Bohemia, Hungaria, etc. His reign was unusually stormy, and in three campaigns against the French he lost much of his territory and was forced into the unfortunate treaty of Presburg. In 1804 he assumed the title of Francis I, Emperor of Austria, and in 1806 yielded up that of Emperor of Germany. Thus, through an unbroken line, male and female, did the House of Hapsburg hold the title of Emperor of Germany from 1437 to 1806. Maria Louisa, the daughter of this Francis, was married to the great Napoleon in 1810, and in 1813 her father was in arms against France and in alliance with Russia, Prussia and England. In 1815 he had regained much of his lost territory, and had succeeded in cementing more firmly than ever the contending elements of the Austrian empire.

Francis I died in 1835, leaving the throne to his son Ferdinand I, who, in consequence of the political revolution of 1848, the fatigue of state affairs, and a wretched condition of health, abdicated in the same year in favor of his brother, Archduke Francis Charles, who, on the same day, transferred his right to the throne to his eldest son, the present Emperor, who was declared of age at eighteen. Hungary refused to recognize the new monarch, and constituted a republic under Kossuth, April 14, 1849. Bloody and short-lived, the republic was conquered and crushed under the feet of the Cossack and the Croat.

And in such guise is this history given of one who, inheriting many of the splendid virtues of his race, was to inherit some of its sorrows and tragedies as well.

Ferdinand Maximilian, Emperor of Mexico, was born in the palace of Schonbrun, near Vienna, on the 10th day of July, A.D. 1832. He was the second son of Francis Charles, Archduke of Austria, and of the Archduchess Frederica Sophia. His eldest brother was Francis Joseph I, the present Emperor of the Austrian Empire. Two younger brothers embraced the family—and among the whole there was a tenderness and affection so true and so rare in statecraft that in remarking it to the mother of the princes, Marshal McMahon is reported to have said:

"Madam, these are young men such as you seldom see, and princes such as you never see."

In height Maximilian was six feet two inches. His eyes were blue and penetrating, a little sad at times, and often introspective. Perhaps never in all his life had there ever come to them a look of craft or cruelty. His forehead was broad and high, prominent where ideality should abound, wanting a little in firmness, if phrenology is true, yet compact enough and well enough proportioned to indicate resources in reserve and abilities latent and easily aroused.[3] To a large mouth was given the Hapsburg lip, that thick, protruding, semi-cleft under lip, too heavy for beauty, too immobile for features that, under the iron destiny that ruled the hour, should have suggested Caesar or Napoleon. A great yellow beard fell in a wave to his waist. At times this was parted at the chin, and descended in two separate streams, as it were, silkier, glossier, heavier than any yellow beard of any yellow-haired Hun or Hungarian that had followed him from the Rhine and the Danube.

He said pleasant and courtly things in German, in English, Hungarian, Slavonic, French, Italian and Spanish. In natural kindness of temper, and in elegance and refinement of deportment, he surpassed all who surrounded him and all with whom he came in contact. Noblemen of great learning and cosmopolitan reputation were his teachers. Prince Esteraze taught him the Hungarian language; Count de Schnyder taught him mathematics; Thomas Zerman taught him naval tactics and the Italian language. A splendid horseman, he excelled also in athletic sports. With the broadsword or the rapier few men could break down his guard or touch him with the steel's point.

At the age of sixteen he visited Greece, Italy, Spain, Portugal, Madeira and Africa. He was a poet who wrote sonnets that were set to music, a botanist, a book-maker, the captain of a frigate, an admiral. He did not love to see men die. All his nature was tenderly human. He loved flowers and music and statuary and the repose of the home circle and the fireside. He had a palace called Miramar, which was a paradise. Here the messengers found him when they came bearing in their hands the crown of Mexico—a gentle, lovable prince—adored by the Italians over whom he had ruled, the friend of the Third Napoleon, a possible heir to the throne of Austria, a chivalrous, elegant, polished gentleman.

How he died the world knows—betrayed, butchered, shot by a dead wall, thinking of Carlota.

France never thoroughly understood the war between the States. Up to the evacuation of Richmond by Lee, Louis Napoleon believed religiously in the success of the Southern Confederacy. An alliance offensive and defensive with President Davis was proposed to him by Minister Slidell, an alliance which guaranteed him the absolute possession of Mexico and the undisturbed erection of an empire within its borders. For this he was asked to raise the blockade at Charleston and New Orleans, and furnish for offensive operations a corps of 75,000 French soldiers. He declined the alliance because he believed it unnecessary. Of what use to hasten a result, he argued, which in the end would be inevitable?

After Appomattox Court House he awoke to something like a realization of the drama in which he was the chief actor. The French nation clamored against the occupation. Its cost was enormous in blood and treasure. America, sullen and vicious, and victor in a gigantic war, looked across the Rio Grande with her hand upon her sword. Diplomacy could do nothing against a million of men in arms. It is probable that in this supreme moment Mr. Seward revenged on France the degradation forced upon him by the Trent affair,[4] and used language so plain to the Imperial minister that all ideas of further foothold or aggrandizement in the new world were abandoned at once and for ever.

When Shelby arrived in Mexico, the situation was peculiar. Ostensibly Emperor, Maximilian had scarcely any more real authority than the Grand Chamberlain of his household. Bazaine was the military autocrat. The mints, the mines and the custom houses were in his possession. His soldiers occupied all the ports where exporting and importing were done. Divided first into military departments, and next into civil departments, a French general, or colonel, or officer of the line of some grade, commanded each of the first, and an Imperial Mexican of some kind, generally half Juarista and half robber, commanded each of the last. For their allies the French had a most supreme and sovereign contempt—a contempt as natural as it was undisguised. Conflicts, therefore, necessarily occurred. Civil law, even in sections where civil law might have been made beneficial, rarely ever lifted its head above the barricade of bayonets, and its officers— finding the French supreme in everything, especially in their contempt— surrendered whatever of dignity or official appreciation belonged to them, and without resigning or resisting, were content to plunder their friends or traffic with the enemy.

Perhaps France had a reason or two for dealing thus harshly with the civil administration of affairs. Maximilian was one of the most unsuspecting and confiding of men. He actually believed in Mexican faith and devotion—in such things as Mexican patriotism and love of peace and order. He would listen to their promises and become enthusiastic; to their plans and grow convinced; to their oaths and their pledges, and take no thought for to-morrow, when the oaths were to become false and the pledges violated. France wished to arouse him from his unnatural dream of trusting goodness and gentleness, and put in lieu of the fatal narcotic more of iron and blood.

France had indeed scattered lives freely in Mexico. At first England and Spain had joined with France in an invasion for certain feasible and specified purposes, none of which purposes, however, were to establish an empire, enthrone a foreign prince, support him by a foreign army, seize possession of the whole Mexican country, govern it as part of the royal possessions, make of it in time, probably, a great menace, but certain— whatever the future might be—to ruffle the feathers pretty roughly upon that winged relation of the great American eagle, the Monroe Doctrine.

Before the occupation, however, Mexico was divided into two parties— that of the Liberals, led by Juarez, and that of the church, its political management in the hands of the Archbishop, its military management in the hands of Miramon. Comonfort, a Utopian dreamer and Socialist, yet a liberal for all that, renounced the presidency in 1858. Thereupon the Capital of the nation was seized by the church party, Miramon at its head, and much wrong was done to foreigners, so much wrong, indeed, that from it the alliance sprung that was to sow all over the country a terrible crop of armed men.

In 1861 England, France and Spain united to demand from Mexico the payment of all claims owed by her, and to demand still further and stronger some absolute guarantee against future murders and spoilations.[5]

England's demands were based upon the assertion that on the 16th day of November, 1860, Miramon unlawfully took from English residents one hundred and fifty thousand pounds sterling. This money was in the house of the British Legation. The house was attacked, stoned, fired into, some of its domestics killed and wounded, and the Minister himself saved with difficulty. Afterward, at Tacubaya, an outlying village of the capital, seventy-three Englishmen were brutally murdered—shot at midnight in a ditch, and to appease, it is thought, a moment of savage superstition and cruelty. To this day it is not known even in Mexico why Miramon gave his consent to this horrid butchery. In other portions of the country, and indeed in every portion of it where there were Englishmen, they were insulted with impunity, robbed of their possessions, often imprisoned, sometimes murdered, and frequently driven forth penniless from among their tormentors.

A treaty had been made in Paris, in 1859, between Spain and the Church party, which provided for the payment of the Spanish claims. This treaty was annulled when Juarez came into power, and the refusal was peremptory to pay a single dollar to Spain. The somewhat novel declaration was also made that the Republic of Mexico owed to its own citizens about as much as it could pay, and that when discriminations had to be made they should be made against the foreigner. Spain became furiously indignant, and joined in with England in the alliance.

France had also her grievances. A Swiss banker named Jecker, who had been living in Mexico a few years prior to the Expedition of the three great powers, had made a fortune high up among the millions. Miramon looked upon Jecker with awe and admiration, and from friends the two men soon became to be partners. A decree was issued by Miramon on the 29th of October, 1859, providing for the issuance of three million pounds sterling in bonds. These bonds were to be taken for taxes and import duties, were to bear six per cent interest and were to have the interest paid for five years by the house of Jecker. As this was considerably above the average life of the average Mexican Government, Miramon felt safe in taking no thought of the interest after Jecker had paid for the first five years. Certain regulations also provided that the holders of these bonds might transfer them and receive in their stead Jecker's bonds, paying a certain percentage for the privilege of the transfer. Jecker was to issue the bonds and to receive five per cent on the issue. He did not, however, consummate the arrangement as the provisions of the decree required, and at his own suggestion the contract was modified. At last the result narrowed itself down to this: the Church part stood bound for three millions seven hundred and twenty thousand pounds sterling, and Jecker found himself in a position where it was impossible to comply with his contract. In May, 1860, his house suspended payment. His creditors got the bonds, the Church party gave place to the Liberal party, and then a general repudiation came. This party refused to acknowledge any debt based upon the Miramon-Jecker transaction, just as it had refused to carry out the stipulations of a sovereign treaty made with Spain.

The most of Jecker's creditors were Frenchmen, and France resolved to collect not only this debt, but claims to the amount of twelve millions of dollars besides. Failing to obtain a peaceful settlement, late in the year 1860, the French Minister left the Capital after this significant speech:

"If there shall be a war between us, it shall be a war of destruction."

And it was.

CHAPTER XVIII.

The three complaining powers—England, France and Spain—met in London, October, 1861, and agreed that each should send upon the Expedition an equal naval force, and that the number of troops to be furnished by each should be regulated according to the number of subjects which the respective powers had in Mexico. It was further expressed and stipulated that the intervention should only be for the purpose of enforcing the payment of the claims assumed to be due, and that in no particular was any movement to be made looking to an occupation of the country. England, however, was dissatisfied with a portion of France's claim, and Spain coincided with England. Notwithstanding this fact, however, a joint fleet was sent to Vera Cruz, which reached its destination January 6, 1862. On the 7th, six thousand three hundred Spanish, two thousand eight hundred French, and eight hundred English troops were disembarked, and by a treaty made with Juarez at Soledad, and signed February 19, 1862, these troops were permitted to leave the fever marshes about Vera Cruz, and march to the glorious regions about Orizava.

Orizava, on the National Road midway between Cordova and Puebla,[1] is a city whose climate and whose surroundings might recall to any mind the Garden of Eden. Its skies are always blue, its air is always balmy, its women are always beautiful, its fruit is always ripe, and its sweet repose but rarely broken by the clamor of marauding bands, or the graver warfare of more ferocious revolutionists.

To admit the strangers into such a land, sick from the tossings of the sea, and weak from the poison of the low lagoons, was worse for Juarez than a pitched battle wherein the victory rested with the invaders. Some of them at least would lay hands upon it for its beauty alone, if other and more plausible reasons could not be found. At an early day, however, the ambitious designs of Napoleon began to manifest themselves. There were some protests made, some sharp correspondence had, not a few diplomatic quarrels indulged in, and at last, to cut a knot they could not untie, the English and Spanish troops were ordered back peremptorily to Vera Cruz, the two nations abandoning the alliance, and withdrawing their forces entirely from the country. This left the French alone and unsupported. The treaty of Soledad expired, and they were ordered by Juarez to return to their original position. For answer there was an immediate attack.

The city of Puebla, ninety miles north from Orizava, strong by nature, had been still more strongly fortified, and was held by a garrison of twenty thousand Liberals, under the command of Saragosa, an ardent and impassioned young Mexican, as brave as he was patriotic. General Lorencez, who commanded the French, without waiting for reinforcements, and being destitute of a siege train, dashed his two thousand soldiers against the ramparts of Puebla, and had them shattered and repulsed. The battle lasted a whole day through, and thrice the Third Zouaves passed the ditch, and thrice they were driven back. At nightfall a retreat was had, and after sore marching and fighting Lorencez regained Orizava, fortifying in turn, and waiting as best he could for succor from France.

It came speedily in the shape of General Forey and twelve thousand men. Puebla was besieged and captured, and without further resistance and without waiting to give Juarez time to repair his losses, he hurried on to the City of Mexico, meeting everywhere an enthusiastic reception from the Imperial Mexicans, who believed that the work of subjugation had been finished.

What the French do is generally done quickly. On the 17th of May, 1863, Puebla surrendered; on the 13th of May, Juarez evacuated the Capital; on the 10th of June, the French took possession, and on the 16th General Forey issued a decree for the formation of a provisional government.[2] This new government assembled with great solemnity on the 25th of June. On the 2nd of July, they published an edict containing a list of two hundred and fifteen persons who were declared to constitute the Assembly of Notables, entrusted with the duty of providing a plan for a permanent government. On the 8th of July, this body was installed in the presence of the French Commander-in-chief, and Count Dubois de Saligny, Minister Plenipotentiary of France. A committee was next appointed to draft a form of government, and on the 10th this committee submitted their plan to the Assembly, which was unanimously adopted.

These were its chief points:

1st—The Mexican Nation adopts for its form of government a limited, hereditary monarchy, with a Catholic Prince.

2d—The Sovereign will take the title of Emperor of Mexico.

3d—The Imperial Crown of Mexico is offered to His Imperial Highness, Prince Ferdinand Maximilian, Archduke of Austria, for him and his descendents.

4th—In case of any circumstances impossible to foresee, the Archduke Ferdinand Maximilian should not take possession of the throne which is offered him, the Mexican Nation submits to the benevolence of Napoleon III, Emperor of the French, to indicate to her another Catholic Prince.

And thus was that Government created, which was so soon to set in misery and tears.

It is not generally known, but it is true, however, that as early as October 30, 1861, Maximilian was offered the throne of Mexico and declined it. While expressing himself extremely grateful for the confidence reposed in his wisdom and moderation, and for the many sentiments of respect embraced in the letter containing the offer, he declared that he would first have to be assured of the will and co-operation of the country. And even when the French had conquered and occupied every important place in the Empire, and after the Assembly of Notables had created a government and sent its deputation to notify Maximilian of his unanimous election as Emperor, he still lingered as if unwilling to tempt the unknown. Did some good angel come to him in dreams and whisper of the future? Who knows? *He* at least deserved such a heavenly visit.

After he had accepted the second offer of the throne, and before his departure from Miramar, Maximilian sent a special messenger to Mexico, bearing a communication to Juarez, which was written by Baron de Pont, his counselor.[3] It was dated Bellevue Hotel, Brussels, March 16, 1864, and contained propositions to the effect that Maximilian did not wish to force himself upon the Mexicans by the aid of foreign troops, against the will of the people; that he did not wish to change or make for them any political system of government contrary to an express wish of a majority of the Mexicans; that he wished the bearer of the letter to say to President Juarez, that he, Maximilian, was willing to meet President Juarez in any convenient place, on Mexican soil, which President Juarez might designate, for the purpose of discussing the affairs of Mexico, in an amicable manner; and that doubtless an understanding and conclusion might be reached wholly in unison with the will of the people.

The gentleman bearing the letter went to Mexico, saw President Juarez, stated his mission, and gave him a copy of the communication. The President cooly answered that he could not consent to any meeting with Maximilian.

This was in March. In April, 1864, the newly chosen Emperor sailed away from Trieste, from his beautiful home by the blue Mediterranean; from the Old World with its luxury and its art; from a thousand memories fresh with the dawn of youth and sparkling in the sunshine of happiness; from the broad aegis of an Empire whose monarch he might have been; from a proud fleet created and made formidable by his genius; from the tombs of his ancestors and the graves of his kindred—and for what? To attempt an impossible thing. Instead of a civilized and Christian monarch, the Mexicans needed missionaries. Instead of the graces and virtues of

European culture and education, the barbarians required grape-shot and canister. Instead of plans for all kinds of improvements, for works of usefulness and adornment, the destroying vandals could be happy only with a despotism and the simple austerity of martial law. Poor Austrian and poor Emperor! Attempting to rule through justice and compassion, he seemed never to have known that for the work of regeneration he needed one hundred thousand foreign soldiers.

There can be no doubt of the enthusiasm with which Maximilian and his beautiful Empress were greeted when they landed at Vera Cruz. Indeed, from the sea to the great lakes about the Capital, it was an ovation such as one seldom sees in a country where all is treachery, stolidity, brutality and ignorance. The fires of a joyous welcome that were lit at Vera Cruz blazed all along the route, and flared up like a conflagration in Paso del Macho, in Cordova, in Puebla, smoking yet from the terrible bombardment, and on the lone mountain Rio Frio—where, looking away to the north, they for the first time might have almost seen the great cathedral spire of Mexico looming up through the mist—that hoary and august pile, as old as Cortez, and bearing high up, under the image of a saint, Montezuma's sacrificial stone, having yet upon it the blood of the foreigner.

The omen was unheeded.

When Shelby arrived in Mexico, Maximilian had been reigning over a year. The French held all the country that was worth holding—certainly all the cities, the large towns, the mining districts, and the seaports. Besides the French troops, the Emperor had in his service a corps of Imperial Mexicans, and a small body of Austrian and Belgian auxiliaries. The first was capable of infinite augmentation, but they were uncertain, unreliable, and apt at any time to desert in a body to the Liberals. The last were slowly wasting away—being worn out as it were by sickness and severe attrition. The treasury was empty. Brigandage, a plant of indigenous growth, still flourished and grew luxuriantly outside every garrisoned town or city. The French could not root it up, although the French shot everything upon which they got their hands that looked a little wild or startled. No matter for a trial. The order of an officer was as good as a decree from Bazaine. Thousands were thus offered up as a propitiation to the god of good order—many of them innocent—all of them shot without a hearing.

This displeased the Emperor greatly. His heart was really with his Mexicans, and he sorrowed over a fusillade for a whole week through. At times he remonstrated vigorously with Bazaine, but the imperturbable Marshal listened patiently and signed the death warrants as fast as they were presented. These futile discussions at last ended in an estrangement, and while Maximilian was Emperor in name, Bazaine was Emperor in reality.

With a soldier's quickness and power of analysis, Shelby saw and understood all these things and treasured them up against the day of interview. This was speedily arranged by Commodore Maury and General Magruder. Maximilian met him without ceremony, and with great sincerity and frankness. Marshal Bazaine was present. Count de Noue, the son-in-law of General Harney, and chief of Bazaine's civil staff, was the interpreter. The Emperor, while understanding English, yet preferred to converse in French and to hold all his intercourse with the Americans in that language.

Shelby laid his plans before him at once. These were to take immediate service in his Empire, recruit a corps of forty thousand Americans, supercede as far as possible the native troops in his army, consolidate the Government against the time of the withdrawal of the French soldiers, encourage emigration in every possible manner, develop the resources of the country, and hold it, until the people became reconciled to the change, with a strong and well-organized army.

Every proposition was faithfully rendered to the Emperor, who merely bowed and inclined his head forward as if he would hear more.

Shelby continued, in his straightforward, soldierly manner:

"It is only a question of time, Your Majesty, before the French soldiers are withdrawn."

Marshal Bazaine smiled a little sarcastically, it seemed, but said nothing.

"Why do you think so?" inquired the Emperor.

"Because the war between the States is at an end, and Mr. Seward will insist on the rigorous enforcement of the Monroe Doctrine. France does not desire a conflict with the United States. It would neither be popular nor profitable. I left behind me a million men in arms, not one of whom has yet been discharged from the service. The nation is sore over this occupation, and the presence of the French is a perpetual menace. I hope your Majesty will pardon me, but in order to speak the truth it is necessary to speak plainly."

"Go on," said the Emperor, greatly interested.

"The matter whereof I have spoken to you is perfectly feasible. I have authority for saying that the American Government would not be adverse to the enlistment of as many soldiers in your army as might wish to take service, and the number need only be limited by the exigencies of the Empire. Thrown upon your own resources, you would find no difficulty, I think, in establishing the most friendly relations with the United States. In order to put yourself in a position to do this, and in order to sustain yourself sufficiently long to consolidate your occupation of Mexico and make your Government a strong one, I think it absolutely necessary that you should have a corps of foreign soldiers devoted to you personally, and reliable in any emergency."

On being appealed to, Commodore Maury and General Magruder sustained his view of the case, and Shelby continued:

"I have under my command at present about 1,000 tried and experienced troops. All of them have seen much severe and actual service, and all of them are anxious to enlist in support of the Empire. With your permission, and authorized in your name to increase my forces, in a few months all the promises given here to day could be made good."

The Emperor still remained silent. It appeared as if Shelby was an enigma he was trying to make out—one which interested him at the same time that it puzzled him. In the habit of having full and free conversations with Commodore Maury, and of reposing in him the most unlimited confidence, he would look first at Shelby and then at Maury, as if appealing from the blunt frankness of the one to the polished sincerity and known sound judgment of the other. Perhaps Marshal Bazaine knew better than any man at the interview how keenly incisive had been Shelby's analysis of the situation; and how absolutely certain were events, neither he nor his master could control, to push the last of his soldiers beyond the ocean. At intervals the calm, immobile face would flush a little, and once or twice he folded and unfolded a printed despatch he held in his hands. Beyond these evidences of attention, it was not known that Bazaine was even listening. His own judgment was strongly in favor of the employment of the Americans, and had the bargain been left to him, the bargain would have been made before the end of the interview. He was a soldier, and reasoned from a soldier's standpoint. Maximilian was a Christian ruler, and shrank within himself, all his nature in revolt, when the talk was of bloodshed and provinces held by the bayonet. His mind was convinced from the first that Shelby's policy was the best for him, and he leant to it as to something he desired near him for support when the crisis came. He did not embrace it, however, and make it part and parcel of his heart and his affections. Therein began the descent that ended only at Queretaro. After the French left he had scarcely so much as a bundle of reeds to rest upon. Those of his Austrians and Belgians spared by pestilence and war died about him in dogged and desperate despair. They did not care to die, only they knew they could do no good, and as Lieutenant Karnak said, when speaking for all the little handful, they saw the end plainer, perhaps, than any removed yet a stone's throw further from the *finale*.

"This last charge will soon be over, boys, and there won't be many of us killed, because there are so few of us to kill; but (and he whispered it while the bugles were blowing) although we die with our Emperor to-day, he will die for us to-morrow."

When the rally sounded Karnak's squadron of seventy came back with six. Karnak was not among them.

The Emperor did not reply directly to Shelby. He rose up, beckoned De Noue to one side, spoke to him quietly and earnestly for some brief moments, dismissed his visitors pleasantly and withdrew. His mind, however, it appears, had been made up from the first. He was not willing to trust the Americans in an organization so large and so complete—an organization composed of forty thousand skilled and veteran soldiers, commanded by officers of known valor, and anxious for any enterprise, no matter how daring or desperate. Besides, he had other plans in view.

As De Noue passed out he spoke to Shelby:

"It's no use. The Emperor is firm on the point of diplomacy. He means to try negotiation and correspondence with the United States. He thinks Mr. Seward is favorably disposed toward him, and that the spirit of the dominant party will not be adverse to his experiment with the Mexicans. His sole desire is to give them a good government, lenient yet restraining laws, and to develop the country and educate the people. He believes that he can do this with native troops, and that it will be greatly to the interest of the American Government to recognize him, and to cultivate with him the most friendly relations. At any rate," and De Noue lowered his voice, "at any rate, His Majesty is an enthusiast, and you know that an enthusiast reasons ever from the heart instead of the head. He will not succeed. He does not understand the people over whom he rules, nor any of the dangers which beset him. You know he once governed in Lombardy and Venitia, when they were Austrian provinces, and he made so many friends there for a young prince that he might well suppose he had some divine right to reign successfully. There is no similarity, however, between the two positions. A powerful army was behind him when he was in Italy, and a singularly ferocious campaign, wherein the old Austrian, Marshal Radetsky, manifesting all the fire and vigor of his youth, had crushed Italian resistance to the earth. It was the season for the physician and the peace-maker, and the Emperor came in with his salves and his healing ointments. Singularly fitted for the part he had been called upon to perform, he won the hearts of all with whom he came in contact, and left at last universally loved and regretted. It is no use I say again, General, the Emperor will not give you employment."

"I knew it," replied Shelby.

"How?" and De Noue shrugged his shoulders.

"From his countenance. Not once could I bring the blood to his calm, benignant face. He has faith, but no enthusiasm, and enthusiasm such as he needs would be but another name for audacity. I say to you in all frankness, Count De Noue, Maximilian will fail in his diplomacy."

"Your reasons, General?"

"Because he will not have time to work the problem out. I have traveled slowly and in my own fashion from Piedras Negras to the City of Mexico— traveled by easy stages when the need was, and by forced marches when the need was, fighting a little at times and resting a little at ease at times, but always on guard, and watching upon the right hand and upon the left. Save the ground held by your cantonments and your garrisons, and the ground your cannon can hold in range, and your cavalry can patrol and scour, you have not one foot in sympathy with you, with the Emperor, with the Empire, with anything that promises to be respectable in government or reliable in administration. Juarez lives as surely in the hearts of the people as the snow is eternal on the brow of Popocatapetl, and ere an answer could come from Seward to the Emperor's Minister of State, the Emperor will have no Minister of State. That's all, Count. I thank you very much for your kind offices to-day, and would have given a good account of my Americans if king-craft had seen the wisdom of their employment. I must go back to my men now. They expect me early."

Thus terminated an interview that had more of destiny in it, perhaps, than the seeming indifference and disinclination to talk on the part of the Emperor might indicate. The future settled the question of policy that alone kept the ruler and his subject apart. When the struggle came that Shelby had so plainly and bluntly depicted, Maximilian was in the midst of eight million savages, without an army, with scarcely a guard, with none upon whom he could rely, abandoned, deserted and betrayed. Was it any wonder, therefore, that the end of the Empire should be the dead wall at Queretaro?

CHAPTER XIX.

The annunciation of Maximilian's emphatic resolution bore heavily upon the Americans for some brief hours, and they gathered about their barracks in squads and groups to talk over the matter as philosophers and look the future full in the face like men. A soldier is most generally a fatalist. Some few of them have presentiments, and some that abounding reverence for the Scriptures that makes them Christians even in the vengeful passions of pursuit; but to the masses rarely ever comes any thought of the invisible, any care for what lies out of sight, and out of reach, and under the shadows of the sunset world. Sufficient unto the day is indeed for them the evil thereof.

These Americans, however, of Shelby's, had moralized much about the future, and had dreamed, it may be, many useless and unprofitable dreams about the conquests that were to give to them a home, a flag, a country—a portion of a new land filled full of the richness of the mines and the tropics. And many times in dreaming these dreams they went hungry for bread. Silver had become almost invisible of late, and if all the purses of the men had been emptied into the lap of a woman, the dollars that might have been gathered up would scarcely have paid the price of a bridal veil. Still they were cheerful. When every other resource failed, they knew they were in a land of robbers, and that for horses and arms none surpassed them in all the Empire. Hence when Shelby called them around him after his interview with the Emperor, it was with something of apathy, or at least indifference that they listened to his report.

"We are not wanted," he commenced, "and perhaps it is best so. Those who have fought as you have for a principle have nothing more to gain in a war for occupation or conquest. Our necessities are grievous, it is true, and there is no work for us in the line of our profession; but to-day, as upon the first day I took command of you, I stand ready to abide your decision in the matter of our destiny. If you say we shall march to the headquarters of Juarez, then we shall march, although all of you will bear me witness that at Piedras Negras I counseled immediate and earnest service in his government. You refused then as you will refuse to-day. Why? Because you are all Imperialists at heart just as I am, and because, poor simpletons, you imagined that France and the United States might come to blows at last. Bah! the day for that has gone by. Louis Napoleon slept too long. The only foreigner who ever understood our war, who ever looked across the ocean with anything of a prophet's vision, whoever said yes when he meant yes and no when he said no, was Palmerston, and he was an Abolitionist *per se*."[1]

Here Shelby checked himself suddenly. The old ironical fit had taken possession of him, one which always came on him on the eve of the battle or the morning of the conflict.

"I find myself quoting Latin when I do not even understand Spanish. How many of you know enough Spanish to get you a Spanish wife with an acre of bread fruit, twenty-five tobacco plants and a handful of corn? We can not starve, boys."

The men laughed long and loud. They had been gloomy at first and a little resolved, some of them, to take to the highway. As poor as the poorest there, Shelby came among them with his badinage and his laughter, and in an hour the forces of the expedition were as a happy family again. Plans for the future were presented, discussed and abandoned. Perhaps there would be no longer any further unity of action. A great cohesive power had been suddenly taken away, and there was a danger of the band breaking up—a band that had been winnowed in the fierce winds of battle, and made to act as with one impulse by the iron influences of discipline and disaster. Many came solely for the service they expected to take. If they had to dig in the ground, or suffer chances in the raising of cotton or corn, they preferred to do it where it was not necessary to plow by day and stand guard over the mules and oxen at night—to get a bed at the end of the furrows instead of a fusillade.

To do anything, however, or to move in any direction, it was necessary first to have a little money. Governor Reynolds, with the same zeal and devotion that had always characterized his efforts in behalf of Missourians during the war in his own country, sought now to obtain a little favor for the men at the hands of Marshal Bazaine. In conjunction with General Magruder, he sought an interview with the Marshal and represented to him that at Parras the Expedition had been turned from its original course and forced to march to the interior by his own positive orders. This movement necessarily cut it off from all communication with friends at home, and rendered it impossible for those who composed it to receive either letters or supplies. Had it been otherwise, and had the march to the Pacific been permitted, in conformity with the original intention, access to California was easy, and the trips of the incoming and outgoing steamers to and from Guaymas and Mazatlan, regular and reliable. In their view, therefore, the Marshal, they thought, should at least take the matter under consideration, and act in the premises as one soldier should in dealing with another.

Bazaine was generous to extravagance, as most French officers are who hold power in their hands, and whose whole lives have been spent in barrack and field. He took from his military chest fifty dollars apiece for the men and the officers, share and share alike, and this amount came to each as a rain to a field that the sun is parching. It put into their hands in a moment, as it were, the choosing of their own destiny. Thereafter every man went the way that suited him best.

Commodore Maury had, several months before, been made Imperial Commissioner of Emigration, and was at work upon his duties with the ambition of a sailor and the intelligence of a *savant*. All who came in contact with him loved the simple, frugal, gentle Christian of the spiritual church and the church militant. Some of his family were with him. His son was there, Col. Richard H. Maury, and his son's wife, and other Americans who had families, and who were at work in his office. These formed a little society of themselves—a light, as it were, in the night of the exiles. The Commodore gave the entire energies of his massive mind to the work before him. He knew well the exhausted and discontented condition of the South, and he believed that a large emigration could be secured with but little exertion. He dispatched agents to the United States charged with the duty of representing properly the advantages and resources of the country, and of laying before the people the exact condition of Mexican affairs. This some of them did in a most satisfactory manner, and as a result a great excitement arose. By one mail from New York he received over seven hundred letters asking for circulars descriptive of the country, and of the way to reach it.

Maury's renown had filled the old world as well as the new. His "Physical Geography of the Sea" saw itself adorned in the graces of eleven separate languages. It also brought him fame, medals, crosses, broad ribbons of appreciation and purses well filled with gold, these last being the offerings sea captains and shippers made to the genius who laid his hand upon the ocean as upon a slate, and traced thereon the routes that the winds favored, and the routes that had in ambush upon them shipwreck and disaster. His calm, benevolent face, set in a framework of iron gray hair, was one which the women and the children loved—a picture that had over it the aureole of a saint. No gentler man ever broke bread at the table of a court. Much of the crispness and the sparkle of salt water ran through his conversation. He was epigrammatic to a degree only attained on board a man-of-war. His mind had the logic of instinct. He divined while other men delved. Always a student, the brilliance of his imagination required at his hands the most constant curbing. Who that has read that book of all sea books has forgotten his reference to the gulf stream when he says: "There is a river in the midst of the ocean." Destiny gave him a long life that he might combat against the treachery of the sea. When he died he was a conqueror.

General Magruder was the Imperial Commissioner of the Land Office, and he, too, had gathered his family around him, and taken into his service other Americans weary of degradation at home, and exiles in a land that might to-day have been Maximilian's. Magruder had once before entered Mexico as a conqueror. All its ways and its moods were known to him, and often in the sunshiny weather, when the blue air blessed the glad earth with its blessings of freshness and fragrance, those who were dreaming of the past followed him hour after hour about Chapultepec, and over the broken way of Cerro Gordo, and in amid the ruins of Molino de Rey, and there where the Belen gate stood yet in ghastly and scattered fragments, and yonder in its pedregral and under the shadow of Huasco, about the crest of Churubusco, green now in the garments of summer, and asleep so peacefully in the arms of the sunset that the young loiterers think the old man strange when he tells of the storm and the massacre, the wounded that were bayoneted and the dead that were butchered after all life had fled. There are no spectres there, and no graves among the ruins, and no splotches as of blood upon the velvet leaves. Yes, surely the old man wanders, for but yesterday, it seems to them, the battle was fought.

Soldiers never repine. Destiny with them has a name which is called April. One day it is gracious in sunshiny things, and the next ruinous with rainstorms and cloudy weather. As it comes they take it, laughing always and at peace with the world and things of the world. Some faces lengthened, it may be, and some hopes fell in the hey-day and the morning of their life, when Shelby told briefly the story of the interview, but beyond the expressions of a certain vague regret, no man went. Another separation was near at hand, one which, for the most of them there, would be the last and irrevocable.

In the vicinity of Cordova there was a large extent of uncultivated land which had once belonged to the church, and which had been rudely and unscrupulously confiscated by Juarez. When Maximilian came into possession of the Government, it was confidently believed that he would restore to the church its revenues and territory, and more especially that portion of the ecclesiastical domain so eminently valuable as that about Cordova. It embraced, probably, some half a million acres of cotton and sugar and coffee land, well-watered, and lying directly upon the great national road from Vera Cruz to the Capital, and upon the Mexican Imperial Railway, then finished, to Paso del Macho, twenty-five miles southward from Cordova.

Maximilian, however, confirmed the decree of confiscation issued by Juarez, and set all this land apart for the benefit of American emigrants who, as actual settlers, desired to locate upon it and begin at once the work of cultivation. Men having families received six hundred and forty acres of land, at the stipulated price of one dollar and a quarter per acre, and men without families three hundred and twenty acres at the same price. Commissioner Maury, remembering his schooling and the experience of his Washington days when he ruled the National Observatory so much to the glory of his country and the honor of science, adopted the American plan of division, and thereby secured the establishment of a system that was as familiar to the new comers as it was satisfactory.

Many settlers arrived and went at once to the colony, which in honor of the most perfect woman of the nineteenth century, was named Carlota. A village sprung up almost in a night. The men were happy and sang at their toil. Birds of beautiful plumage flew near and nearer to them while they plowed, and in the heat of the afternoons they reposed for comfort under orange trees that were white with bloom and golden with fruit at the same time. So impatient is life in that tropical land that there is no death. Before it is night over the eyes, the sun again has peopled all the groves with melody and perfume. The village had begun to put on the garments of a town. Emigration increased. The fame of Carlota went abroad, and what had before appeared only a thin stream of settlers, now took the form of an inundation.

Shelby told his men all he knew about Carlota, and advised them briefly to pre-empt the legal quantity of the land and give up at once any further idea of service in the ranks of Maximilian's army. Many accepted his advice and entered at once and heartily upon the duties of this new life. Others, unwilling to remain in the Empire as colonists, received permission from Bazaine to march to the Pacific. On the long and dangerous road some died, some were killed, and some took shipping for California, for China, for Japan, and for the Sandwich Islands.[2] A few, hearing wonderful stories of the treasures Kidd, the pirate, had buried on an island in the Pacific Ocean, got aboard a schooner at Mazatlan and sailed away in quest of gold. Those that survived the adventure returned starving, and for bread joined the Imperial army in Sonora. Perhaps fifty took service in the Third Zouaves. A singular incident determined the regiment of their choice. After authority had been received from the Marshal for the enlistment, a dozen or more strolled into the Almeda where, of evenings, the bands played and the soldiers of all arms promenaded. In each corps a certain standard of height had to be complied with. The grenadiers had need to be six feet, the artillery men six and an inch, the cuirassiers six feet, and the hussars six feet. Not all being of the same stature, and, not wishing to be separated, the choice of the Americans was reduced to the infantry regiments. It is further obligatory in the French service that when soldiers are on duty, the private in addressing an officer shall remove his cap and remain with it in his hand until the conversation is finished. This was a species of discipline the Americans had never learned, and they stood watching the various groups as they passed to and fro, complying scrupulously with the regulations of the service. At last a squad of Zouaves sauntered nonchalantly by—great bearded, medaled fellows, bronzed by African suns and swarthy of brow and cheek as any Arab of the desert. The picturesque uniform attracted all eyes. It was war dramatized—it was campaigning expressed in poetry. An officer called to one of the Zouaves, and he went forward saluting. This was done by bringing the right hand up against the turban, with the palm extended in token of respect, but the turban itself was not removed. The subordinate did not uncover to his superior, and therefore would the Americans put on turbans and make Zouaves of themselves. Captain Pierron, more of an American than a Frenchman, supervised the meta-morphosis, and when the *toilette* was complete even Shelby himself, with his accurate cavalry eyes, scarcely recognized his old Confederates of the four years' war. At daylight the next morning they were marching away to Monterey at the double quick.

General Sterling Price, of Missouri, with a remnant of his body guard and a few personal friends, built himself a bamboo house in the town of Carlota, and commenced in good earnest the life of a farmer. Emigration was active now both from Texas overland and by water from the gulf. General Slaughter and Captain Price established a large saw-mill at Orizava. General Bee engaged extensively in the raising of cotton, as, also did Captains Cundiff and Hodge. General Hindman, having mastered the Spanish language in the short space of three months, commenced the prac- tice of law in Cordova. General Stevens, the chief engineer of General Lee's staff, was made chief engineer of the Mexican Imperial Railway. Governor Reynolds was appointed superintendent of two short-line railroads run- ning out from the city. General Shelby and Major McMurty, with head- quarters at Cordova, became large freight contractors, and established a line of wagons from Paso del Macho to the Capital. Ex-Governor Allen, of Louisiana, assisted by the Emperor, founded the *Mexican Times,* a paper printed in English and devoted to the interests of colonization. Generals Lyon, of Kentucky, and McCausland, of Virginia, were appointed Government surveyors. General Watkins was taken into the diplomatic ser- vice and sent to Washington on a special mission. Everywhere the Americans were honored and promoted, but the army, to any considerable number of them, was a sealed book. Where they could have done the most good, they were forbidden to enter.

To the superficial observer the condition of affairs in Mexico in the latter part of the year 1865 seemed most favorable, indeed, to the ultimate and successful establishment of the Empire. The French troops occupied the entire country. M. Langlais, one of Napoleon's most favored ministers, had charge of the finances. Under his experienced hands, order was rapidly lifting itself above the waves of chaos. The Church party, always jealous and suspicious, still yielded a kind of sullen and ungracious allegiance. Maximilian was a devout Catholic, and his Empress was a devotee in all spiritual matters, but theirs was the enlightened Catholicism of Europe, which preferred to march with events and to develop instead of attempting to thwart and retard the inevitable advance of destiny. They desired to throw off the superstition of a century of ignorance and degradation and let a flood of light pour itself over the nation. An impoverished people had not only mortgaged their lands to the clergy, but their labor as well. The revenues were divided equally between the bishops and the *commandantes* of the districts. Among the Indians the influence of the monks was supreme. In their hands at any hour was peace or war. They began by asserting their right to control the Emperor; they ended in undisguised and open revolt. Desiring above all things the confidence and support of the church, Maximilian found himself suddenly in an unfortunate and embarrassing position. He was between two fires as it were, either of which was most formidable, and in avoiding the one he only made the accuracy of the other all the more deadly. Without the revenue derived from the sequestrated lands the church had owned in enormous quantities, he could not for a month have paid the expenses of his Government. Had he believed a restoration advisable, he would have found it simply impossible. The Archbishop was inexorable. Excommunication was threatened. For weeks and weeks there were conferences and attempted compromises. Bazaine, never very punctual in his religious duties, and over apt to cut knots that he could not untie, had always the same ultimatum.

"Our necessities are great," he would say, "and we must have money. You do not cultivate your lands, and will not sell them, you are opposed to railroads, to emigration, to public improvements, to education, to a new life of any kind, form or fashion, and we must advance somehow and build up as we go. Not a foot shall be returned while a French soldier can shoot a *chassepot*."

The blunt logic of the soldier bruised while it wounded. Maximilian, more conservative, tried entreaties and expostulations but with the same effect. A breach had been opened up which was to increase in width and destruction until the whole fabric fell in ruins. When in his direst extremity, the Emperor was abandoned by the party which of all others had the most to lose and expiate by his overthrow.

CHAPTER XX.

The Empress Charlotte was a woman who had been twice crowned—once with a crown of gold, earthly and perishable, and once with a crown of beauty as radiant as the morning. When she arrived in Mexico, this beauty, then in its youthful splendor, dazzled all beholders. Her dark auburn hair was heavy, long and silken. Her eyes were of that lustrous brown which were blue and dreamy at times, and at times full of a clear, penetrating light that revealed a thought almost before the thought was uttered. Her face was oval, although the forehead, a little high and projecting, was united at the temples by those fine curves which give so much delicacy and expression to the soul of women. Her mouth was large and firm, and her teeth were of the most perfect whiteness. About the lower face there were those lines of firmness which told of unbending will and great moral force and decision of character. Beneath the dignity of the Queen, however, she carried the ardor and the joyfulness of a school girl. Her nose was aquiline, the nostrils open and slightly projecting, recording, as if upon a page, the emotions of her heart and the dauntless courage which filled her whole being. At times her beautiful face wore an expression impossible to describe—an expression made up of smiles, divinations, questionings, the extreme and blended loveliness of the ideal and the real—the calmness and gravity which became the Queen—the softness and pensiveness which bespoke the woman.

The gallery that contained the portrait of Maximilian would be incomplete without that of his devoted and heroic wife. She was a descendant of Henry IV of France, the hero of Ivry, a ruler next in goodness and greatness to Louis IX, and the victim of the fanatical assassin Ravaillac. Her father was Leopold I, of Belgium, one of the wisest and most enlightened monarchs of Europe. An Englishman by naturalization, he married the Princess Charlotte Augusta, daughter of George IV, the 2d of May, 1816. His English wife dying in childbirth, in 1817, Leopold again married in 1832, uniting himself with Louise Maria Theresa Charlotte Isabella de Orleans, daughter of Louis Philippe, King of France. Of this marriage was the Empress Carlota born on the 7th of June, 1840, and who received at her christening the names of Maria Charlotte Amelia Auguste Victoire Clementine Leopoldino. Her father was called the Nestor of Kings, and her mother the Holy Queen, such being her charity, her purity and her religious devotion. The first died in 1865, while the Empress was in Mexico, and the last in 1850. At the time when she most needed the watchfulness and advice of a father, she was suddenly bereft of both his support and his protection.

No monarch on earth ever had a more ambitious or devoted consort. The daughter of a king, reared amid thrones and the intense personal loyalty of European subjects, she believed an empire might be established in the West greater than any ever founded, after long years of battle and statecraft, and she entered upon the struggle with all the impassioned ardor of her singularly hopeful and confiding nature. Her unrivaled beauty won the enthusiasm of cities, and her unostentatious and Christian charity erected for her a throne in the hearts of the suffering and unfortunate. When the yellow fever was at its height in Vera Cruz, and when all who were wealthy and well-to-do had fled to the higher and healthier uplands, she journeyed almost alone to the stricken seaport, visited the hospitals, ministered unto the plague-stricken, ordered physicians from the fleet, encouraged the timid, inspired the brave, paid for masses for the dead, and came away wan and weary, but safe and heaven-guarded. The fever touched not even the hem of her garments. Fate, that sent the east wind and the epidemic, may, like the stricken sufferers, have thought her an angel.

There were pestilence and famine and insurrection in Yucatan. The Indians there, naturally warlike and enterprising, rose upon the Government and cast off its authority. Tribes revolted and warred with one another. The French, holding the large towns, fortified and looked on in sullen apathy, sallying out at times to decimate a province or lay waste to a farming district. In a few weeks the insurrection would be civil war. It was decreed in council that the Emperor's presence was needed in Yucatan. His affairs at home, however, were not promising, and he tarried a little to arrange them better before leaving. Of a sudden the Empress besought leave to go in his stead. It was refused. She persevered day after day, and would not be denied. Inspired with more than a woman's faith, and heroic in all the grandeur of accepted sacrifice, she made the perilous journey, taking with her only an escort and a confessor. Her arrival at Merida was like a coronation. All the State arose to do her homage. She went among the tribes and pacified them. She redressed their wrongs, brought back the rebellious leaders to a strict allegiance, cast herself into the midst of pestilence, opened the churches, recalled the proscribed and scattered priests, and came away again an angel. Unto the end the faith she founded in her husband's empire remained unshaken. After Queretaro, Yucatan relapsed into barbarism.[1]

The year 1865 was spent by the Emperor and Marshal Bazaine in vigorous attempts to pacify the country and consolidate its power. The Liberal cause seemed hopeless. Nowhere did Juarez hold a seaport, an outlying mine, a foot of grain-growing territory, a ship, an arsenal, a field large enough to encamp an army. Yet he held on. That sluggish, tenacious, ferocious Indian nature of his was aroused at last, and while he starved he schemed. A sudden dash of cavalry upon his winter quarters at El Paso drove him into the United States. He went to San Antonio a fugitive President without a dollar or a regiment, and waited patiently until the force of the blow had spent itself. As the French retired he advanced. Scarcely had his adieu been forgotten in El Paso, when his good day greeted its good people again. Everywhere, also, were his guerrillas at work. Once in a speech upon the annexation of San Domingo, Carl Schurz exclaimed: "Beware of the tropics."[2] And why? Because the tropics breed guerrillas. They do not die in war times. Malaria does not kill them. To eradicate them it is first necessary to find and to capture them. They can not be found and fought. All nature is in league with them—the heat, the bread-fruit, the bananas, the orange-groves, the zepotas, the mangos, the coco-nuts, the monkeys. These last sentinels, through imitation, chatter volubly at the pursuers and cry out in soldier fashion and in words of warning: *"Quien vive!"*[3] Wherever the Spanish blood is found there is found also an obstinacy of purpose impossible to subdue—a singularly ferocious and untamable resolution that dies only with annihilation. It will never make peace, never cease from the trail, never let go its hold upon the roads, never spare a captive, never yield a life to mercy, never forgive the ruler who would rule as a Christian and make humanity the law of the land.

All the following that Juarez had now was of guerrillas. Porfino Diaz lived by his wits and his *prestamos.*[4] Escobedo, constitutionally a coward and nationally a robber, preyed alone upon his friends. Try how they would, the French found him always a runaway or a thief. Negrete, with six thousand blanketed *ladrones,*[5] abandoned a captured train and fled as a stampeded buffalo herd before a battalion of Zouaves. Lozado preserved in the mountains of Nayarit an armed neutrality. Corona, in the delightful possession of his beautiful American wife, sat himself down in Sonora and waited for the tide to turn. For his country he never so much as lifted his hand. Cortina prayed to the good Lord and the good devil, and went alternately to mass and the monte bank.

They all held on, however. An unorganized commune—the goods of other people were their goods, the money of other people was their money. As long as the rains fell, the crops matured, the cattle kept clear of the murrain, and bread-fruit got ripe, and the maguey made mescal, they were safe from pestilence or famine. The days with them meant so many belly fulls of *tortillas* and *frijoles.*

With the French it is different. Red tape has a dynasty of its own—a caste, a throne, an army of field and staff officers. Each day represented so many rations, so many bottles of wine, so many ounces of tobacco, so many cigars, so much soup and bread and meat. Failing in any of these, red tape stepped in with its money commutation in lieu of rations. Then for each decoration there was an annuity. Some Zouaves drew more pay than generals of brigade. The Malakoff medal so much, the Inkermann medal so much, the Chinese Emperor's Palace medal so much, the Fort Constantine medal so much, the Magenta and Solferino medals so much, the Puebla medal so much, and so much for all the rest of the medals these many laureled and magnificent soldiers wore. When they were paid off, they had monthly a saturnalia.

To make both ends meet, Napoleon's great finance minister, Langlais— loaned as an especial favor to Maximilian—did the work of a giant.[6] One day he died. Apoplexy, that ally and avenger of the best-abused brain, laid hands on him between the Palace of Chapultepec and the office of the treasury. In two hours he was dead. All that he had done died with him. Of his financial fabric, reared after so many nights of torture and trouble, there was left scarcely enough of pillar or post to drape with mourning for the single-minded, sincere and gifted architect. In the dearth of specie the church was called upon. The church had no money, at least none for the despoiler of its revenues and the colonizer of its lands. Excommunication was again threatened, and thus over the threshold of the altar as well as the treasury, there crept the appalling shadow of bankruptcy.

Bazaine threatened, the Emperor prayed, the Empress threw into the scale all her private fortune at her command. Outside the cabinet walls, however, everything appeared fair. Brilliant reviews made the capital gorgeous and enchanting. There were operas, and fetes, and bull-fights, and great games of monte in the public square, and duels at intervals, and one unbroken tide of French successes everywhere. Napoleon sent over in the supreme agony of the crisis two ship loads of specie, and there was a brief breathing time again. Meanwhile they would see, for when it is darkest it is the nearest to the morning.

Inez Walker, the rescued maiden of Encarnacion, was too beautiful to have been lightly forgotten. Free once more, and with the terrors of that terrible night attack all gone from her eager eyes, she had continued with the Expedition to the capital, courteously attended each day by an escort of honor furnished as regularly as the guards were furnished.

In the City of Mexico, at the time of her arrival, there was an American woman who had married a Prussian prince, and who was known as the Princess Salm Salm. Once when she was younger, she had ridden in a circus, several of them, and as Miss Agnes Le Clerc was noted for her accomplished equestrianism, her magnificent physique, a beauty that was dark and over-bold, a devil-may-care abandon which won well with those who sat low by the footlights and felt the glamour of the whirling music and the red flames that flashed on golden and gaudy trappings of acrobat or actor.

Miss Le Clerc had met the Prussian in Mobile after the American war was over. The Prince had been a Federal General of brigade whose reputation was none the best for soldierly deeds, although it is not recorded that he either shunned or shirked a fight. Still he was not what these *parvenu* Americans of ours think a prince should be—he did not clothe himself in silver, or gold, in purple or fine linen, and conquer armies as Rarey might have conquered a horse. There were some stories told, too, of unnecessary cruelty to prisoners whom the fortunes of war cast upon his hands helpless, but these did not follow him into Mexico with his American wife, who had married him in Mobile, and who had got thus far on her way in search of a coronet.

She was told the story of Inez Walker, and she was a brave, sympathetic, tender-hearted woman, who loved her sex as all women do whom the world looks upon as having already unsexed themselves. They became fast friends speedily, and were much together at the opera and upon the *passeo*[7] during those last brief yet brilliant days of the Empire.

The Prince Salm Salm was on duty with a brigade at Apam, in the mountains toward Tampico. Guerrillas had been at work there lately, a little more savage than usual, and Bazaine sent forward Salm Salm to shoot such as he could lay hands upon and disperse those that could not be caught. He acted with but little of energy, and with scarcely anything of ambition. He was recalled finally, but not until his wife had been grossly insulted and a Confederate had avenged her.

One day in a *cafe* several groups of Belgian officers were at the tables sipping their wine and jesting and talking of much that was bad and useless. At other places there were Austrians and French, and a few Spaniards, who even then were beginning to avoid the foreigners, and a single American, who was sitting alone and at his leisure.

Dr. Hazel was a young physician from South Carolina, who had gone through the siege of Sumter with a devotion and a constancy that had found their way into general orders, and that had returned in the shape of a rain more precious to a soldier than sunlight to flowers—the rain of official recognition. In addition to the compliments received, he was promoted. As he sipped his claret, several ladies entered, some attended and some unattended. French custom makes a *cafe* as cosmopolitan as the street.

All sexes congregate there, and all stratas of society; custom simply insists that the common laws of society shall be obeyed—that those of the *demi-monde*[8] shall not advertise their profession, that the gambler shall not display his cards, the guerrilla uncoil his lasso, the grand dame exhibit her prudery, the detective his insincerity and the priest his protests and his confessional. Appetite admits of no divided sovereignty, and hence, at meal time, the French recognize only one class in society, that of the superlatively hungry.

The Princess Salm Salm returned the salutation of several French officers as she entered, and bowed one or twice in acknowledgment of salutes rendered by the Austrians of her husband's brigade. Beyond these, she seemed to prefer isolation and privacy. Among the Belgians there was a Major who had a huge yellow beard, a great coarse voice, a depth of chest like an ox, a sword-belt whose extent would girth a hogshead. In French *cafes*, gentlemen very rarely speak above the low conversational tone of the drawing room. To be boisterous is to be either drunk or a blackguard. This Belgian, Major Medomark of the Foreign Legation, did not seem to be drunk, and yet as he looked at the Princess Salm Salm, his voice would change its intonation and deepen harshly and gratingly. If he meant to be offensive, he succeeded first rate.

The Princess pushed back her plate and arose as one who felt that she was the subject of conversation without understanding the words of it. As she passed through the door, Medomark boisterously and in great glee, called out a slang term of the circus, and shouted:

"Hoop la!"

The Agnes Le Clerc that was of the sawdust and tights, the Princess Salm Salm that is now of the titles and diamonds, heard the brutal cry and felt to her heart the studied insult. Turning instantly, she came again half into the *cafe*—her eyes full and discolored with passion, and her face so white that it appeared as if the woman was in mortal pain. She could not speak, though she tried hard, poor thing, but she looked once at Medomark as if to crush him where he sat, and once to Hazel, who understood it all now and arose as she again retired.

He went straight to his American countrywoman. At the cowardly inference of the Belgian, the French officers had laughed and the Austrians had applauded. Even those of her husband's own brigade had not uttered protest or demanded apology. Hazel found her in tears.

"You have been insulted," he said. "I know it, or rather, may I say I saw it. Not understanding German, if, indeed, the Belgians speak German, I have to rely for my opinion more upon the manner than the matter of the insult. Your husband is away, you are an American lady, you are a countrywoman of mine, you are in trouble, and you need a protector. Will you trust your honor in my hands?"

This actress was a brave, proud woman, born, perhaps, to rule men as much by the force of her will as the bizarre style of her beauty and her physical development. She took Hazel's hand and thanked him, and bade him chastise the insolent bully. She knew very well what chastisement meant in the language of a soldier, and she was a soldier's wife. She never referred to the future, however. She did not even evince interest enough to be curious. Perhaps her passion kept her from this—at least her champion bowed low to her as he entered, thinking her the coldest woman a man ever put his life in jeopardy for. Cold she was not. She simply considered what was done for her as being done because of her inalienable right to have it done. She was not familiar, she only tolerated.

Hazel, in stature, was very slight. As he stood up before Medomark, the huge Belgian glowered upon him as Goliath of Gath might have done upon David.

"Do you speak English?" he asked of the Major.

"A little."

"Enough to understand the truth when I tell it to you?"

"Perhaps, if it is not so plain that for the telling I will have to break every bone in your body."

Medomark's voice was one of that uncontrollable kind that ran away with a subject in spite of itself. He meant to be quiet so as not to attract attention, but he was so rude that many of the spectators quit eating to look on.

"That lady," Hazel continued, "who has just gone out is a country-woman of mine. She may have been an actress just as you may have been a hangman's son, but whatever she has been she is a woman. We do not insult women in the country where I once lived, nor do we permit it to be done elsewhere. Will you apologize to her?"

"I will not."

"Will you accept this card and let me send a friend to you?"

"I will with pleasure."

"Then I wish you a good day, gentlemen." Hazel bowed to all as he went out, like a man who had just finished his dinner.

Medomark was brave, besides, he was an officer. There were, therefore, but two courses left to him, but two things to do—to accept Hazel's cartel or to refuse it. In preference to disgrace he chose the duello. Hazel found his second speedily. He, too, was a soldier—one of Shelby's best, James Wood—who would go to any extreme on earth for a friend.

When two men mean business, the final arrangements are simply matters of form. On the morning after Medomark's insult in the *cafe,* Wood called upon him early. During the day the preliminaries were all amicably agreed upon, and at sunrise the next morning, about a quarter of a mile southeast of the American burying ground, Hazel and Medomark met at ten paces with duelling pistols. The Belgian's second was a young French Lieutenant named Massac, who won both the position and the word. When the men took their places, Hazel had the sun in his eyes, and this annoyed him at first, for it was very hot and penetrating. They fired twice at each other. The first time both missed, the second time Hazel struck Medomark upon the outside point of the right shoulder, injuring the bone greatly and severing an artery that bled as if the man would bleed to death. Prompt and efficient surgical skill, however, saved his life. The duel ended after the second fire, and the Princess Salm Salm, so splendidly vindicated at the hands of her young countryman, was the toast thereafter of the officers of the garrison. The Prince on his return could not render thanks enough, nor seek to show his appreciation of the chivalrous act by too many evidences of a more substantial gratitude. The city being under martial law, a court-martial was soon convened for the trial of all who were engaged in the duel. A sentence, however, was never reached. Upon the request of Bazaine, the court was dismissed and the prisoners set at liberty. Medomark recovered fully, only to be desperately wounded again at Queretaro, where, after long and devoted attention on the part of Dr. Hazel, a surgeon in the Republican army, he was restored to both health and liberty. From this little episode a friendship sprung up which has remained unbroken to this day.

The colony at Carlota grew apace and prospered. The men began to cultivate coffee and sugar, and from a jungle the plantations soon bloomed and blossomed like another Paradise. As an especial favor from Maximilian, Shelby was permitted to pre-empt the *hacienda* of Santa Anna, not a *hacienda,* however, that had belonged to this prince and chief of conspirators, but one that had been named for him. Spaniards once owned it, but in the massacres of the revolution, all had perished. About the ruins of the fortress which still abounded, there were signs which told of the fury of the onslaught and the scorching of the flames that followed when the rapine and ravishments were done. Situated two miles from Cordova, and in the very purple heart of the tropics, it might have been made at once into a farm and a flower garden. Twelve acres were put in coffee, and coffee well cultivated and permitted to grow in a land where there is a law and protection pays to the raiser a minimum price per acre of $1,500. It seems, however, that nature is never perfect in the equilibrium of her gifts. There, where the soil is so deep, the air so soft, the climate so delicious, the trade winds so cool and delightful, the men alone are idle, and come in the night to the plantations of the foreigners to break down their coffee trees, poison their spring water, wound their dumb stock, and damage everything that can be damaged and that comes in their way.

In the mountains in the rear of Shelby's plantation a robber band rendezvoused. Its chief, Don Manuel Rodriguez, was a daring leader, who descended to the plains at intervals with a reckless following, and made headway for hours at a time in his work of gathering up supplies and levying *prestamos*. In a month after Shelby's arrival a friendly relationship was established, and thereafter, until the end, Rodriguez protected Santa Anna and lived at peace with all who were settled round about. Just how the negotiations were commenced and consummated which led to a truce so satisfactory and so necessary, none ever knew, but true it is that in the cool of the evenings, and when the French drums had beaten tattoo at the fort only half a mile away, Rodriguez would come down from his fastnesses as a peaceful visitor, and sit for hours among the Americans, asking of the Yankee country, and the ups and downs of the Yankee war, for, to a Mexican, everything is Yankee which is American.

Ex-Governor Isham G. Harris, of Tennessee, also a settler, might have been designated the Alcalde of Carlota.[9] The Confederates looked upon him with a kind of reverence. By the side of Albert Sidney Johnston when he got his death wound, he had taken him in his arms and held him there until the mist came into his sad, prophetic eyes, and until the brave, fond heart, broken by his country's ingratitude and the clamor of despicable and cowardly politicians, had ceased to beat. Brownlow especially wanted Harris, and so Harris had come to Mexico.[10] He knew Brownlow well—a bitter, unrelenting, merciless fanatic, and a fanatic, too, who had come in on the crest of the wave that had drowned the cause for which Harris fought. He believed that if the old Pagan failed to find a law for his capital punishment, he would succeed certainly through the influence of gold and political power over an assassin. Unwilling at all events to risk the tyrant, he found penniless asylum at Cordova, poor only in pocket, however, and courageous and proud to the last. He was a cool, silent, contemplative man, with a heavy lower jaw, projecting forehead, and iron gray hair. In his principles he was an Ironside of the Cromwellian type.[11] Perhaps the intense faith of his devotion gave to his character a touch of fatalism, for when the ship stranded he was cast adrift utterly wrecked in everything but his undying confidence in the success of the Confederacy. He believed in Providence as an ally, and rejected constantly the idea that

Providence takes very little hand in wars that come about between families or States, if, indeed, in wars of any kind. With his great energy, his calm courage, his shrewd, practical intercourse with the natives, his record as a governor and a soldier, he exerted immense influence for good with the soldier-settlers and added much to the strength and stability of the colony.

Colonel Perkins, of Louisiana, a judge of great fame and ability, and a lawyer as rich in triumphs at the bar as he was possessed of slaves and cotton bales upon his plantation, abandoned everything at home but his honor, and isolated himself among his coffee-trees and bananas.[12] When the war closed, he took a week to speak his farewells and burn his dwelling house, his cotton presses, his stables, barns, out-houses, and to make in fact of his vast possessions a desert. He had a residence rich in everything that could amuse, instruct, delight, gratify. Painting, statuary, flowers, curiosities, rare plants, elegant objects of vertu[13] and art were there in abundance, and when from the war he returned crushed in spirit and broken in health, he rested one night brooding amid all the luxury and magnificence of his home. He arose the next morning a stoic. With a torch in his hand he fired everything that would burn, leaving nowhere one stone upon another to tell of what had once been the habitation of elegance and refinement. In his Mexican solitude he was an aristocratic philosopher, complaining of nothing and looking back with regret upon nothing. Sufficient unto the day for him had been the evil thereof.

General Sterling Price was another settler. Many of his escort company had taken lands around him. The patriarch chief in a new country, he sat much in the shade about his tent, telling the stories of the war and hoping in his heart for the tide of persecution and proscription in Missouri to run itself out. Politics was as necessary to his mental equilibrium as sleep to his physical. In the old days he had succeeded well. Nature gave him a fine voice, a portly frame, a commanding front, a graceful and dignified carriage, an *aplomb* that never descended into nervousness, and hence as the speaker of a legislative body he was unexcelled. He dreamed of a speakership again, of a governorship, of a senatorship, and he, therefore cultivated more corn than he did coffee, for it takes three years for coffee to grow and bear, and three years might—well, he did not choose to put himself in the hands of three years and wait.

It would be at least curious, if it were not interesting, to go in among these colonists in Carlota and learn their histories while displaying the individuality of each. A common misfortune bound them all together in the strength of a recognized and yet unwritten covenant. The pressure of circumstances from without kept them indissolubly united. Poverty, that dangerous drug which stimulates when its does not stupefy, lost its narcotism over men whom war had chastised and discipline made strong and reflective. They strove for but one purpose—to get a home and occupy it.

The privateer *Shenandoah,* that mysterious cruiser which was seen rarely at sea, yet which left upon the waves of the South Pacific a monstrous trail of fire and smoke, sent her officers into the colony with their ship money and their cosmopolitan hardihood.[14] Lieutenants Chew and Scales took valuable land and went enthusiastically to work. Around the *hacienda* of Santa Anna there was a cordon of strange pioneers who had histories written in characters impossible to decipher. The hieroglyphics were their scars.

And so affairs prospered about Carlota, and the long, sunshiny days went on, in which the trade winds blew and the orange blossoms scented all the air. It was near three days' long journey to the Capital, but rumors travel fast when every ear is listening for them, and a report deepened all along the route from the city of Mexico to Vera Cruz that a staff officer of the French Emperor had left Paris for the headquarters of Marshal Bazaine. A multitude of reasons were assigned for the visit. Napoleon might desire, for the purposes of information, the direct observations of one who was intimately acquainted with his views and intentions. It might be, again, with a view to increasing the forces of the Expedition, or to the employment of more active and rigorous measures in the pacification of the country. Accordingly, as men were hopeful or depressed, they reasoned concerning this visit of the French staff officer, even before the officer himself was half across the Atlantic.

From first to last, the treasury of Maximilian had been comparatively empty. He curtailed his own personal expenses, abandoned the civil list, lived like a plain and frugal farmer, set everywhere an example of retrenchment and economy, but it availed nothing. Mexico, with all of her immense mineral resources, is, and has been, usually poverty stricken. There is no agriculture, and, consequently, no middle class. At one extreme is immense wealth, at the other immense misery. Ignorance and superstition do the rest.

His exertions to pay his soldiers and carry forward a few vitally necessary internal improvements were gigantic. Pending the arrival of the French envoy extraordinary, he had negotiated a loan at home, which was taken by patriotism—a strange word for a Mexican—and which had already begun to flow into his empty coffers.

Things, therefore, were not so dark as they had been when General Castelnau, personal aide-de-camp of the Emperor Napoleon, arrived at Vera Cruz.

General Castelnau kept his own secret well, which was also the secret of his master, Napoleon III. A magnificent review was held in the city of Mexico at which he was present. Soldiers of all arms were there, and a great outpouring of the people. Everything looked like war, nothing like evacuation, and yet General Castelnau brought with him definite and final orders for the absolute and unconditional withdrawal of the French troops.

The Empress penetrated the purpose of his mission first, and again came forward to demand a last supreme effort in behalf of the tottering throne. She would go to Europe and appeal to its chivalry. The daughter of a king, it would be to monarchs to whom she would address herself face to face. She was young, and beautiful, and pleading for her crown, and why would not armies arise at her bidding and march either to avenge or reinstate her? Poor, heroic woman, she tried as never woman tried before to stem the tide of fate, but fate was against her. First the heart and then the head, until with hope, faith, ambition, reason all gone, she staggered out from the presence of Napoleon dead in all things but a love that even yet comes to her fitfully in the night time as dreams come, bringing images of the trees about the Alameda, of the palace where she dwelt, of Miramar and Maximilian.

In the summer of 1866 she sailed for Europe. She knew Castelnau's mission, and she determined to thwart it. There was yellow fever at Vera Cruz and pestilence on the ocean. Some of her attendants were stricken down by her side and died at Cordova, others on board the ship that carried her from port. She bore up wonderfully while the mind held out. Nothing affrighted her. The escort marching in the rear of her carriage was attacked by guerrillas. She alighted from it, bade a soldier dismount, got upon the back of his horse and galloped into the fight. Here was an Amazon of the nineteenth century who had a waist like a willow wand, who painted rare pictures, who had a husband whom she adored, who sang the ballads of her own exquisite making, who was struggling for a kingdom and a crown, and who never in all her life saw a drop of blood or a man die.[15]

The fight was simply a guerrilla fight, however, and from an Amazon the woman was transformed into an Empress again—tender, considerate, desperate in the wild emergency upon her, and joyous with the fierce eagerness of her longings and her despair.

Never any more in life did the blue eyes of her husband and her lover gaze upon that fair Norman face, almost colorless now and set as flint in the stormy sunset of the night when she sailed away to her destiny.

Bazaine took his time to obey his orders—indeed, he had margin enough and leisure enough to contract his lines pleasantly. Not always overbold in retreat, the French had learned well the nature of Mexican warfare and would turn sometimes viciously when galled to wincing on flank or rear, and deal a few parting blows that unto this day are recalled with shudderings or impotent vows of vengeance.

One at Matamoras is worth a mention. The Sixty-second of the line did garrison duty there under Colonel Lascolat. He was to Dupin what the needle-gun is to the smooth-bore. Dupin destroyed singly, at short range, in ambushments, by lonesome roads, in sudden and unmerciful hours— from the depths of isolation and the unknown. Lascolat, an Algerian offi- cer of singular ferocity, hunted in regiments. Even the physique of his men was angular, rakish, undulatory like the movements of a greyhound. They would march thirty miles a day fighting, bivouac anywhere, sleep if they could; very well, if they could not, still very well. With them was a priest who wore the five medals he had won in battle. When he had time he shrived all alike. In his hands the cross was good enough for the dying who spoke Spanish and the dying who spoke French. In the presence of the specter he took no thought of nationality.

As Lascolat came out from Matamoras, a portion of Escobedo's forces pressed him inconveniently. His orders from Bazaine were to take his time, fight only when forced, be dignified, patient and discreet, but to make sure of his egress out with everything that belonged to him or his. Lascolat had under him two battalions of 1,000 men each. The third battalion com- posing the regiment of the Sixty-second had already been sent forward to Jeanningros at Monterey. Escobedo attacked with 5,000. He knew of Lascolat's ferocity, of his terrible doings about and along the Rio Grande, and he meant to take a farewell, the memories of which would last even unto Algeria again.

One afternoon late the line of Lascolat's march led through a ravine, which commenced like the mouth of a funnel and tapered down to a point, as a funnel would taper. Near the outlet Escobedo fortified the road with loose boulders. Behind these and upon the sides of the acclivities on either side he placed his men in ambush. He had no artillery, for he so shaped the fight as to make it face to face and deadly. Lascolat entered into the trap listlessly. If he knew what had been prepared for him, he made no sign. Suddenly the loose, disjointed, impassive wall outlined itself. Some sharp skirmishing shots came from the front. The shadows of the twilight had begun to gather. It looked ugly and ominous where the stones were.

Lascolat called a halt and rode back along the ranks of his men. They were weary and they had seated themselves upon the ground to rest. His presence fired them as a torch passing across a line of ready gas-lights. He spoke to them pleasantly in his Algerian vernacular:

"The Arabs are ahead. We are hungry, we are tired; we want to go into camp; we have no time to make a flank movement. Shall we make quick work of the job that we may get some supper and some sleep?"

The men answered him with a shout. The charge commenced. It was a hurricane. The barricade of rocks was not even so much as a fringe of bulrushes. Those who held it died there. The hill slopes, covered with prickly pear and dagger-trees, hid a massacre. The Sixty-second swarmed to the attack like bees about a hive in danger. Paralyzed, routed, decimated, torn as a tempest, Escobedo's forces fired but one fair volley and fled as shadows flee when the wind pursues. The dead were never counted. Lascolat's farewell was taken, but those who came out well from the hand-shaking slackened march not a step until the route had passed into Matamoras, and over against a river that might be crossed for the wading. Thereafter the Sixty-second foraged as it pleased, and took its own time toward the coast.

Colonel Depreuil was in danger—Shelby's old antagonist of Parras—and it remained for Shelby to save him. In the marchings and countermarchings of the evacuation, Depreuil, commanding six hundred men of the Foreign Legion, was holding a post twenty leagues northwest of San Luis Potosi. Douay, with inadequate cavalry, was keeping fast hold upon this most important strategical point, awaiting the detachments from the extreme north. Shelby was a freighter now, and had come from the City of Mexico with a strong guard of Americans, and eighty wagons laden with supplies for the French. After reporting to Douay he was sent forward with twenty men and ten wagons to Cesnola, the outlying post garrisoned by Depreuil. The guerrillas, emboldened by the absence of cavalry, had risen up some two thousand strong and were between San Luis Potosi and Cesnola. As Shelby marched on into the open country, his advance, under James Kirtley, was fired upon, and two soldiers, James Ward and Sandy Jones, severely wounded. He countermarched to an abandoned *hacienda*, encamped his wagons within the walls, fortified as best he could, and sent Kirtley back with two men to report the condition of affairs to General Douay. Kirtley was not well mounted, he had served awhile in the Third Zouaves, the hostile Mexicans were swarming about all the roads, it looked like death to go on, it certainly was death to be taken, and so he started when the night fell, having with him two comrades, tried and true—George Hall and Thomas Boswell.

It was a good thirty miles to San Luis Potosi, and those who waylaid the roads had eyes that saw in the night and were not baffled.

Captain James Kirtley, burnt almost brown by exposure, and by four long years of struggle with the wind and sun, had the face of a Mexican and the heart of an English lancer who rode down to the guns with Cardigan and the Light Brigade.[16] Peril affected his spirits as wine might. Ambition and adventure with him were twin mistresses—blonde to his eyes, beautiful, full of all passionate love, fit to be worshipped, and they were worshipped. Always brave, he had need to be always generous. Danger, when it does not deter, sometimes gives to those who fear it least a certain kind of pensiveness that is often mistaken for indifference. When aroused, however, this kind of pensive man rides harder and faster, fights longer and more desperately, will hold and hang on under greater stress, reach out his life in his open hand oftener, and die, if so the fates desire, with less of murmur and regret than a regiment of great roistering soldiers whose voices are heard in songs in the night with the mighty roll and volume of the wind among the pines.

Kirtley, even under the tawny paint the sun had put upon his face, would blush like a girl when, to some noted deed of soldierly daring, public attention directed the eyes of appreciation. Praise only made him more reticent and retired. As he never talked of himself, one could not hear aught of his valorous deeds from his own lips, for these were a part of himself. To compliment him was to give him pain—to flatter was to offend; and yet this young hero, not yet a man, surrounded by all things that were hostile, even to the language, known to have been a soldier in the Third Zouaves, the terror of the Empire, badly mounted for pursuit or escape, came with a smile upon his face for the perilous venture, and rode away into the night and the unknown, in quest of succor for Depreuil and his beleaguered garrison.

It was a long thirty miles he had to go, the three men, Kirtley, Hall and Boswell. On every side there were guerrillas. The night was dark, although the road was plain, for it was the great national highway which ran from Monterey to the Capital. The danger, however, came from the fact that it was too plain. Others knew of it, and rode along it, and crouched in ambushment upon it, and made a torment for small parties by day as well as by night.

Kirtley, even in the darkness, advanced in skirmishing order. First, he of the three went alone in advance, behind him was Hall, in the rear of Hall, Boswell. Between each was the distance of twenty yards. It was necessary to get word through to Douay, and Kirtley argued the less risk taken the greater chance there would be for one of the party getting through.

"We must keep apart," he said, "just far enough to succor each other, but not too close to be killed by the discharge of a shot-gun, as out of a flock of partridges one might kill a bag full."

The ride was a silent and grimly tenacious one. Three times they turned from the high road to avoid a scouting party of guerrillas, and once, in going past a little group of four or five huts by the wayside—a place, indeed, where *mescal*[17] is sold, and where, upon all the roads in Mexico, huts are concentrated for this purpose alone—Kirtley, who had kept his position fixedly in front the whole night through, was fired upon from an angle of a house. The bullet missed his left thigh barely, and imbedded itself in the flank of his poor, tired horse that had borne himself staunchly through it all. One drop of blood was more really than the weary animal could afford to give up, but this wound bled freely and the horse staggered as he went. It was yet three leagues to San Luis Potosi, and the night had turned. By dint of much coaxing and walking to relieve him, Kirtley managed to get over some further ground slowly. He felt for his horse, as all cavalry soldiers do, and from the wound to his abandonment he never struck him once with the spur, though it might be that his life hung upon the gait the horse went, weak and crippled as it was. The wound was deeper than any one of the three thought, and so, when nearer the bottom of an abrupt descent, the gallant steed lurched forward suddenly, caught as it were by his fore feet, reeled blindly, and fell forward, too helpless to rise again, too far gone for leech or surgeon-craft.

Kirtley murmured not. Looking once at his faithful companion, as if in infinite pity, he strode on under the stars on foot, keeping his place still in the advance, and keeping his pensive face fixed in the iron mold of its energy and determination.

It was daylight when the three dauntless scouts reached the outposts at San Luis Potosi—tired, safe, proud of the perils passed, ready to return at a word and to carry back the succor Shelby so much needed at this time, and the succor Depreuil had needed, without knowing it, for a week.

Douay gave to the three soldiers a soldier's welcome. His old gray head, inclined a little forward, heard all the report that Shelby had sent, and it was brief enough even for him who dealt mostly in gestures or monosyllables.

"You have ridden all night," he said, "and you need food, sleep, brandy, horses. Captain."

An aide came.

"Your pardon one moment, General," said Kirtley, "while I correct you. We do not need any sleep. As we return we can sleep as we ride. That was once part of our drill. We left our General in danger, and he in turn sent us forward to notify you of the danger to your Colonel. We will take the food, the brandy and the horses, but the sleep, no, General, with many thanks."

Douay's keen brown eyes opened wide at this frank and ingenuous speech. It pleased him more than he cared to say, more than he admitted then. Afterward, when a soldier led up a magnificent Arab stallion to the *meson*[18] where Kirtley was eating and presented it to him in the name of

Douay, the young American felt in his heart the gratified pride of one whose perils and frankness had merited recognition at the hands of him who had fought in the four quarters of the world, and who had grown up from childhood to old age a hero beloved by the army and revered by a nation.

Before the sun rose three squadrons of Chasseurs, a section of flying artillery, with the three Americans thrown forward as guides, were galloping back toward the *hacienda* at which Shelby was fortified and fighting. Each American had been supplied with a splendid horse by Douay, and although they had ridden ten leagues the night before, they pressed on, indifferent to fatigue and impervious to the demands of sleep.

It was time. Shelby, of his whole force of twenty men, had only fifteen left. Two had been wounded, and three had been sent back to San Luis Potosi for succor. Of the wagons he had formed a corral. Between the wheels and in front and rear he had piled up sand-bags. Among the freight destined for Depreuil's outpost were several hundred sacks of corn. These were emptied, filled up again with sand, and laid two deep all about the wagons. No musket ball could penetrate them, and the guerrillas had no artillery.

A summons came for him to surrender.

Shelby parlayed all he could. He dreaded a charge where, from sheer momentum, five hundred sheep might overrun and crush fifteen men. A renegade priest named Ramon Guitierrez, having the name of a blood-thirsty priest and the fame of a cowardly one, commanded the besiegers. Before Shelby would talk of surrender, he wanted to see some show of force. His honor would not permit a capitulation unless his reason was convinced that to resist would be madness. In other words, he wanted on his side the logic and reasonableness of war.

Guitierrez took a look at the sand bags, and thought Shelby's proposition very fair. He took another and a closer look, having in his vision this time the gleaming of fifteen rifle barrels and the rising and falling of rough, hairy faces above the parapets of the hastily constructed fort, and he concluded to accept it. To be very certain of passing in review all the men he had, he marched about in various directions and in the most conspicuous places for several hours—precious hours they were, too, and worth a week of ordinary time to those who never meant to surrender, but who expected to fight desperately, maybe unavailingly, before the friendly succor came.

When the parade was over, Guitierrez sent word to ask if Shelby would surrender.

No, he would not. He had counted some five hundred illy armed *rancheros*, and he meant to fight them to the death. Firing at long range commenced. The Americans did not reply to it. The sun was too hot for the kind of work that did not pay in corpses. Emboldened by this silence, the Mexicans crept closer and closer. Here and there a bullet found its way into the fort. Volley answered volley now, and then the noise died out into calm, cold, cautious skirmishing. Shelby had mounted two dark looking logs at either angle of the *corral*, and these, from a distance, looked like cannon. It might not be best to charge them, and so Guitierrez crept backward and forward until the day wore well on its way. Suddenly he gathered together his followers and made a little speech to them. It was about four o'clock in the afternoon. Both Ward and Jones, who had been wounded the day before, had insisted on holding an embrasure between them. They had strength enough to load and fire their breech-loaders, and they were not refused. Every bullet counted in the desperate melee.

With a shrill, short yell the Mexicans dashed forward to the attack. Had the wave held on its course it would have inundated the earthwork. It broke, however, before it reached half way across the open space behind which it had gathered for the onset. Those in front began to fire too soon, and those in the rear, not seeing from the smoke what was really in front, fired too, without aim or object. With unloaded guns they dared not go on—the fire of the Americans was distressing beyond endurance—the wave broke itself into fragments, and the sun sunk lower and lower.

"Nearly out of the wilderness, boys," Shelby said; as his wary and experienced eyes took in the outline of the spent charge as it made itself clear against the range of hills in the rear of it.

"We need water greatly," Ras. Woods ejaculated, his mouth parched and his face black with powder smoke.

"In an hour you shall drink your fill," replied Shelby, "for in an hour the French will be here."

"But if Kirtley has fallen."

"He will not fall. Luck goes with him everywhere. What's that?"

He pointed as he spoke to a sudden agitation and fluttering among the masses of the besiegers, who were now galloping furiously to and fro, utterly without a head and heedless of all threat or command.

"Ah!" and Shelby's face cleared up all at once, as he returned to Woods, "you can go out for water now, the fight is over."

Before he had finished, the full, ringing notes of the French bugles were heard, and in a moment more the squadrons emerged from the trees, galloping straight and in beautiful order toward the guerrillas.

There was no combat after the French appeared. What killing was done was done solely upon those who were too slow in the race, and who could not reach the rocks in time that rose up on three sides as a series of walls that had once been laid with much symmetry and had fallen in rugged yet regular masses in some great convulsion or upheaval of nature. Nowhere in fair fight was a Mexican cut down, nor at no single time did even a squad rally among the rocks and fire back upon the pursuing cavalry. The panic at last degenerated into a stampede, while the impenetrable groves of cactus shrubs and the broken and uninhabitable country swallowed up the fugitives. The chase soon ended and the French returned.

These two rescuing squadrons were led by Captain Mesillon, whose orders were very full and explicit. He was first to cut Shelby out from the hostile forces which surrounded him, and next to report to Shelby and march withersoever Shelby directed.

The French rarely put faith in foreign officers. Their vanity—a kind of national inheritance—recognized no merit like French merit, no superiority in war, politics, diplomacy, love or religion like French superiority. Hence, where Frenchmen are concerned, they invariably insist that Frenchmen shall alone be responsible. In this instance, however, Douay wrote this manner of a note to Shelby:

"To complete the conquest of Colonel Depreuil, of whose bearing toward you at Parras I have been duly informed by General Jeanningros, I choose that he shall owe his life to you. Captain Mesillon awaits your orders. I need not advise you to be circumspect, and to tell you to take your own time and way to reach Cesnola and bring my Frenchmen back to me, for whom, I imagine, there is no great love in the hearts of its inhabitants."

Mesillon reported, and Shelby put himself at the head of the Cuirassiers.

"Since Depreuil has to come out from Cesnola," Shelby remarked to the young French Captain, "and since General Douay expects us to make haste and bring him out, there is no need to take our wagons further. Guitierrez has been too badly frightened to return here much under a month, and beyond his forces I can hear of no others in the mountains round about. We will let the wagons, therefore, remain where they are, forage and rest here until the night falls, and then—strengthened and refreshed—cut through, ride down or ride around everything that opposes us. So make these resolutions known, Captain."

The Frenchman bowed and retired. He saw in a moment that the soldier who was talking to him knew more of the warfare ahead in a moment than he had ever seen in his life. He knew, furthermore, that if the worst came to worst, it would not be the fault of the commander if Depreuil was not rescued.

The night came and the column started. Between the road where the wagons were left and Cesnola, the entire country was alive with guerrillas. Beyond Cesnola there were no Imperial troops of any kind, and between

Cesnola and San Luis Potosi there was neither garrisoned town nor fortified village. It was a stretch of ambush sixty miles long.

When the night came Shelby put himself at the head of his detachment and never drew rein until Cesnola was reached. The column was ambushed seven separate and distinct times, and fired upon from hedge-rows, from behind houses in villages through which it passed, and from a variety of places that were inaccessible to the sudden dash of cavalry. Twenty-eight French soldiers were killed and wounded. Twice the Captain solicited the privilege of making a charge upon the unseen enemy crouching by the roadside, and twice he was refused.

"You lay too much heart to these mosquito bites," Shelby said to him kindly, "when there is danger of centipedes and tarantulas before we are done with it. A man is bound to fall out here and there, hard hit and may be killed, but the balance will be enough to get through. When one gets surrounded as Depreuil has done, one must expect to pay the penalty of the rescue. Sometimes it is extremely costly, but the night favors us, and there is no moon. Keep with your men, Captain, encourage them, expose yourself freely in front of them, talk to them calmly, and my word for it you shall reach Cesnola with fewer depletions in your ranks than if you charged into the unknown every time a musket volley came from it."

Depreuil did not know of his danger. The succoring party appeared to him as an apparition. Well fortified at Cesnola, and having at his command no cavalry with which to ascertain what existed beyond the range of his cannon, he ate and slept and drank absinthe with the same *nonchalance* his life in Parras manifested. Safe for the day, he took no thought of the morrow. He was one of those officers who believed that one French battalion was stronger than destiny—more powerful than fate.

Mesillon awoke his reverie rudely. When there had been explained to him all the risk Shelby had run in getting cavalry to him, how he had fought and marched and planned and endured solely for his sake and for the sake of humanity, Depreuil's heart quickly softened. He came to Shelby as one who felt that he had a great debt of gratitude to repay, and took his hands in both of his.

"Never mind the past," he commenced, "nor the rude things said and done in Parras. I see it all now. Perhaps I owe my life to you—certainly the lives of many of my soldiers, for whom I am responsible. In the future let us remember each other only as brave men and soldiers. I, too, like Captain Mesillon, put myself under your orders. When shall we evacuate Cesnola?"

Shelby had his revenge at last—that kind of revenge which is always sweet to noble minds—the revenge of returning good for evil. He answered him:

"Would you take your heavy cannon with you?"

"I don't know. Would you?"

"In my military life I never left a trophy in the hands of my enemies. Were I a Frenchman, I would surely carry off my French guns."

"Then in a day we can march."

"Let it be so, but make haste, Colonel. This country breeds guerrillas as the marshes do miasma."

Still leading, Shelby came away from Cesnola in command of the whole French force. Depreuil's men wondered a little, but Depreuil, in the height of his gratitude, thought no compliment sufficiently high to pay the rough-clad, quiet American fighter, who did not even have so much as a red sash around him as an insignia of rank or authority.

Fighting commenced almost as soon as the evacuation of Cesnola took place. Heading always the Americans and the Cuirassiers in person, however, Shelby was enabled by several sudden and bloody repulses to put such a wholesome fear of punishment in the minds of the pursuers that they gave him ample time to carve out for the train a safe road in front while protecting amply the perilous road in the rear.

For three days and nights he held on his course, fighting constantly and caring alike for his dead and his wounded. The morning of the fourth day brought him to the French lines of San Luis Potosi and to an ovation. General Douay turned out the whole garrison under arms, and, as the detachment which had been doing garrison duty at Cesnola marched in— worn by much fighting—weary from long marching—dusty and faint, yet safe and victorious—it was saluted with sloping standards, presented arms, and the long exultant roll of triumphant music.

In the evening Douay called upon Shelby.

"I have come to reward you," he said in his usual bluff and sententious manner, "and would be glad to know your price."

"Your friendship, simply," was the reply of the proud American.

"That you already have," the good old General continued, "but you are poor, you are an exile, you can have no refuge more in this country when it is known that you rescued a French garrison, you have been turned aside from your business as freighter, and I demand the privilege of paying you at least for your time, and for your losses in mules and wagons."

"Very well, General," Shelby replied, "but as you are leaving the country you must wait until we meet again in the City of Mexico. Until then, remember your promise."

CHAPTER XXI.

In the short space of time accorded to him between the reception of the orders brought for the withdrawal of the French troops and their actual accomplishment, Maximilian did the work of one who meant to fight a good fight for his kingdom and his cause. And yet for the great super-structure he tried so hard to rear and decorate, the poor man had never considered a moment about its foundation. He had no standing army—nothing to rely upon when the French left that was real and tangible—nothing that was frank and manly and that would take him boldly by the hand and say: "Sire, we are here; trust us as you would yourself."

When that sudden dash of cavalry, which drove Juarez across the Rio Grande and into Texas, had spent itself, and when it was believed that there was no longer in the land either a regularly armed or regularly organized force of Liberal soldiers, the celebrated black flag order was promulgated. This law—based upon the declaration that Juarez had left the country, and that consequently there could be no longer in existence any regularly con-stituted government—required all Mexicans captured with arms in their hands after the date of the decree—October 3d, 1865—to be summarily put to death. Maximilian resisted its passage to the last, but Bazaine was inexorable. He appeared before the Council of State and declared upon his official honor that Juarez had left the territory of Mexico. He complained of the leniency shown to the guerrillas, and cited numerous instances to prove how French soldiers, captured on detached service, had been first tortured and then most brutally murdered, while those Mexican prisoners tried under the ordinary forms of a court-martial had either been punished lightly or suffered to escape altogether.

Bazaine triumphed, as he always did when brought in contact with the soft, pliable nature of the Emperor, and almost immediately after the decree was issued, there was enacted under it a fearful obedience. General Mendez, one of the few Mexicans really and sincerely devoted to Maximilian, was holding the enemy in awe in the State of Morelia. Of a sudden he turned upon a guerrilla force, routed it, captured well on to a hundred, shot them all, and proclaimed in triumphant language that such should be the fate of all who came within reach of his hands. Among the slain were General Arteaga and Colonel Salasa. Arteaga was what was rare in Mexico, a genu-ine humorist. Corpulent, fair though born in the tropics, fond of laughter and wine, in no wise cruel or vindictive, a soldier from necessity rather than inclination, a judge whose decisions were always in favor of the guilty, it did seem a sin to shoot the great, harmless, laughing gourmand,[1] who told his jokes much oftener than his beads, and had a whole regiment of friends in the very ranks of the French army itself. Other executions took place in other portions of the Empire, and when the Emperor found that he could no longer resist the tide of blood that had set in, he quarreled with Bazaine. The Marshal was firm, however, and the Emperor fled to Cuernavaca. This was a small town forty miles southwest from the City of Mexico. It had the deliciously blended climate of the tropical and the temperate latitudes. It was summer in the day, and autumn in the night-time. Maximilian had a retreat here, and thither he would go when State cares pressed too heavily from without, and little spites and pitiful envies and jealousies from within. He had a house there and a garden, and among his books and his flowers he held loving converse with the past and the present—the great who had passed away from earth and the beautiful which still remained. From these communions and reveries he would return a more patient and more gentle man.

The shooting went on, however, and Mendez and Miramon obeyed the decree with a persistence characteristic solely of the Spanish blood.

As the French lines contracted, the skeleton regiments and brigades of Juarez were fully recruited. In many places those Mexican troops who were in the service of the Empire were turned upon and beaten. At other times they ran without a fight, throwing away their arms and disbanding in hopeless and helpless confusion. Nowhere in the whole Imperial army was there an organization worth its uniform save and alone those few Austrians and Hungarians personally devoted to the Emperor and calmly resolved to die. If at any time Shelby's conversation ever recurred to him, he made no sign. He saw probably, and felt more keenly than any one there, the need of the American corps Shelby could and would have recruited for the asking, but even in the death hour, and in front of the ruined wall at Queretaro, he died as he had lived—a martyr to his belief in the sincerity of Mexican professions.

Of a sudden, and at one merciless blow, Sonora was wrenched from the grasp of the Empire. The French had already abandoned it, but an Austrian, devoted to the Empire, General Landberg, held it for his Majesty. The forces under his command were composed almost exclusively of Mexicans. Some few companies of these had American officers. One in particular was commanded by a young Confederate, Captain W. M. Burwell, who was from the Valley of Virginia, and who had won high honor in Pelham's memorable artillery.[2] He was only twenty, and had a face like a school girl. Tall, gentle in aspect and manner, with deep blue eyes and raven hair that curled and shone, he came into the Empire a boy adventurer, seeking fame and service in a foreign land. The Princess Iturbide,[3] when the Valley of Virginia was a Paradise, had visited at his father's house and had looked in admiration into the blue eyes of the beautiful boy. This boy, not yet a man and the smoke of Virginia battle-fields not yet gone from his long black hair, came to the country of the Princess, and to her palace by the Alameda. When he came out from her presence he was a Captain. He put on his uniform and came among his comrades in those few brief days, before the marching, a young Adonis—lithe, superb, a little Norman in feature, having red in his cheeks and dark in his hair.

All day had the battle ebbed and flowed about the port of Guaymas. A swart, fierce southern sun, coming in red from the ocean, got hotter and hotter, and by high noon it was blistering in among the foothills that held the thin handful of Landberg's dissolving army. Beautiful on the crest of the darkening conflict stood the young Virginian, no air brave enough anywhere to blow out the curls of his clustering hair, no succor anywhere near enough to save the flushed cheeks from the gray and the pallor of the death that was near. Landberg fell in the thick of the fight, cheering on his men who had fought well for Mexicans, but who had fought for all that as men who had no hope. A Frenchman, Colonel De Marsang, rode to the front. The army was falling to pieces. On watch in the port of Guaymas, two French frigates had been waiting since the sunrise. There stood safety and refuge for the shivered remnants when once well extricated from the coil that Landberg had failed to break, but how to get through? De Marsang spoke to Burwell, saluting:

"Will your men charge?"

"It may be, Colonel. Your orders."

"Yonder is a battery on a hill," pointing as he spoke to four sixteen-pounders massed upon an eminence that commanded the only road of retreat to Guaymas, "and it is scant of supporters. Silence it for a brief half hour and what is left of Landberg's loyal followers shall be saved."

Burwell drew his sword. He spoke to his men very gently. He put himself at their head. There was a sudden rush of some fifty or sixty desperate soldiers—a mass of blue and flame and dust and fury—the great roar of the guns broke hoarse and loud above the shrill, fierce cheer of the men, and the road was clear.

They brought him back from the rout of the cannoneers with a film on the blue eyes and white on the pallid cheeks. He spoke not, neither did he make moan. To-day in Guaymas there are yet those who cross themselves and tell with bated breath about the charge of the *muy bonita Americano.*[4]

Sonora was thus lost to Maximilian, and all the coast bordering upon the

Pacific. In the north, department after department was abandoned by the French, and at Matamoras, after a bloody siege and a desperate combat at the end, Mejia—an Indian of pure blood and truer and braver than all the multitude of Castilian flatteries who blessed the Emperor and fled from him when the darkness came—cut his way out from environment and fell back wearily and hard bestead toward Monterey.[5] In the passage out through the lines of Escobedo's army, an American squadron died nearly to a man. It had been recruited upon the Rio Grande, and was composed equally of those who had served in either the Federal or the Confederate army. Its Captain, Hardcastle, was one of Hooker's best scouts; one Lieutenant, Inge, had made himself a name with Mosby; another, Sarsfield, an Irishman from Memphis, had killed a comrade in a duel in Georgia, and had fled as it were from a spectre which pursued him; seven of the privates had but an arm apiece; all had seen long and desperate service—all were soldiers who seemed to have no home and no country.

Children of the war, what a life history many of them had. It is related of the little band that, the night before Mejia began the work that had need to be ended speedily, they exchanged with one another the secret of each heart. Sorrows had come to the most of them, and memories that were too sad for repining, too bitter for tenderness or tears. A boy was there not yet twenty. He had been a soldier under Lee and had loved a woman older and wiser than himself. One day he told her all and she laughed in his beardless face, a laugh that went deeper than any word of cold contempt or stern refusal. He was too young, she said. He knew she meant too poor. The morning after the interview, while it was yet dusky and dim in the east, a firm, set face was turned fair to the south, and James Randolph had left his native land forever. Among the foremost in the charge, and when the force of the squadron had spent itself, he was taken up dead from among the feet of the horses, happier than he had been, perhaps, since the parting months agone.

One was there because a life of peace had become intolerable. Hardcastle, a born soldier, fought for the love of the strife; Inge, to better his fortune; Sarsfield, to exorcise a memory that made his sensitive life a burden; a few for greed and gain; not any one for hatred or revenge.

Mejia loved his Americans, and had done a General's part by them. None rode finer horses, none displayed more serviceable arms. What they had to do they did, so terribly that none ever rose up to question the act. On guard they were never surprised; on their honor, they never betrayed; on duty, they never knew an hour of rest; on the foray, they kept a rank no stress had ever yet destroyed; and in the fight, when others halted or went forward, as those who grope, these—grim, silent, impassible as fate—rode straight on; resisted, very well; overpowered, still very well; cut to pieces—that might be. Having shaken hands with life, what meant a few days more or less to all who saw the end approaching.

Escobedo[6] had surrounded Matamoras with about 25,000 troops, not good troops, however, but hard to dislodge from the fortifications in which they had encased themselves. To get out, Mejia had to cut his way through. The American squadron went first. There was a heavy fog that had blown in from the gulf on the morning of the venture, so heavy, indeed, that the first files could not see the third files, nor the third the fifth, nor the Captain his Lieutenants in their places behind him.

No matter; a squadron like this did not need the sunlight in which to die.

It took an hour of furious work to open the only road between Mejia and Monterey—between a massacre as ferocious as the nature of the bandit, Escobedo, and the succor of Jeanningros' Zouaves marching twenty leagues in twenty hours to the rescue. Out of seventy-two, rank and file, only eleven escaped free and scathless. Afterward, in relating the story of the escape, General Mejia remarked sententiously to Governor Reynolds:

"To maintain an empire it is necessary only for a score of regiments, such as the squadron that charged at my command nine separate times, losing always and always closing up."

To-day it is doubtful if any man knows where even one of the heroes lies buried, nor aught of his inner life, nor anything of why or how he died.

"So much the leaden dice of war
Do make or mar of character."

In the height of the tide of evacuation, Maximilian turned his eyes once more in the direction of the colonists. A French Baron, Sauvage by name,[7] and an Englishman in finance and education, obtained from the Emperor a grant of land as large about as the State of Delaware. It was rare and valuable land. It grew India-rubber trees and mahogany trees. It was in the tropics, and it was fertile beyond all comparison. The Tuxpan river ran through the grant diagonally from northwest to southeast.[8] It had a seaport—Tampico—where the largest vessels might ride at anchor, and where only in the unusually sickly years did the yellow fever come at all.

Several tribes of Indians inhabited this section of the Empire, mostly ignorant and unknown Indians, yet supposed to be friendly and well disposed. At least the death of no white man had been laid at the door of any of the tribes, probably from the fact that no white man had ever been among them.

Sauvage dreaded Indians because he had never dealt with them. He was a cultivated and elegant gentleman. He loved to linger long at dinner and late over the wine, to take his ease in his own way and to protect his person. He wanted a partner who, accustomed to peril and privation, would not object to the life of a pioneer. Shelby was recommended. Freighting was no longer pleasant or profitable. Concentrated now principally in the cities, the French did not attempt to patrol the roads nor to afford protection to those who lived away from the garrisoned towns and who needed protection. As a consequence, Shelby and his partner, Major McMurty,[9] disposed of such stock as was left to them after the rigors of the rainy season and cast about for other work neither so difficult nor so uncertain.

Shelby met Sauvage, and when the interview was over a scheme of colonization was formed which needed only time to have added to the Empire a bulwark that might have proven impregnable. Surveyors under the charge of Major R. J. Lawrence, once a resident of Kansas City, were dispatched immediately to the granted lands. A railroad from Tampico to Vera Cruz was projected and a subsidy at the rate of $20,000 per mile was pledged by the Emperor. With Shelby to plan was to execute. Two hundred men were employed before the ink of the alliance between himself and Sauvage was scarcely dry. Taking passage in a rickety schooner to Havana, Shelby bought a seaworthy sail-boat there and loaded the boat at once with American plows, harrows, railroad tools of all kinds, and staple provisions enough for a summer's campaign. At the same time he also flooded Texas and Arkansas with his circulars setting forth the advantages of the Tuxpan country, its immense resources, the benefits a colonist might receive from a location there, and giving also the nature and quality of the soil, its products and the average price per acre under the Imperial decree confirming the grant. The circular soon begot an interest that was intense. Twenty families in a neighborhood would unite and send an agent forward to investigate the prospects of the colony. Meanwhile, the railroad was commenced. From Havana Shelby went to Vera Cruz, where he purchased another schooner belonging to the French fleet of observation in the harbor. Bazaine was in the city when he arrived in port. He went straight up to his hotel and spoke to him thus:

"Marshal, we have taken upon our hands much work. We have farming implements of all kinds, but we have no guns. Give us arms and ammunition. Your army of occupation has recently been supplied with *chassepots,* and it is not your intention to take your old muskets back to France. Some you will sell, some you will destroy, and some you will give away. Give me, therefore, five hundred of your most serviceable, and ball cartridges enough for a six month's siege, and when you hear of our colony again you will hear of a place as promising as the scheme of your Emperor in Africa."

Bazaine listened to this frank volubility as one does to something he has but rarely heard in his life, smiled, shrugged his shoulders, but gave the order just the same. Before the sun set, Shelby was sailing out from the harbor and past the dark battlements of San Juan d'Ulloa, the owner of half a thousand elegant guns, a great store of ammunition, and a faith in the future that amounted with him to an inspiration.

The Americans flocked to him from every direction. His name and his fame seemed a talisman. As fast as they arrived he armed them, and it was well that he did so. A tribe of Indians, the Tolucas, owning lands directly on the northern boundary of the grant, grew jealous of a sudden at the growing colony, and sought to exterminate it.[10] There were bad Mexicans among them who did the scheming and the plotting, and one rainy night a foray of eleven hundred dashed down upon the outposts. Shelby was with his surveying party at the time, a little detachment scarcely thirty strong. These fortified themselves behind a breastwork of logs, and fought until the settlement could be aroused. When the reinforcements were all up, Shelby massed them compactly together, and dashed down upon the invaders. They fought badly, and soon broke and fled. For thirty long and weary miles he followed them through swamp and chaparral, over ravines and rivers, by day and by night, killing what came to him, sparing naught that fell in his way. Weary, the men declared the work done well enough. He ordered them forward fiercely.

"What," he cried out, "is the necessity of doing to-morrow or the next day what could be done so well to-day? The colony is young, it is hated, it has been in perpetual ambush; it must have over it a mantle of blood. Forward, and spare not."

The blow dealt the Tolucas was a terrible one, but it was necessary. Thereafter they traded in peace with the whites, and maintained the alliance unbroken until the colony itself was destroyed, and the Americans driven out from all part or lot in the country.

Through no fault of any American there, however, the colony did not live. Shelby did the work of a giant. He was alcalde, magistrate, patriarch, contractor, surveyor, physician, interpreter, soldier, lawgiver, mediator, benefactor, autocrat, everything. All things that were possible were accomplished. Settlers came in and had lands given them. The schooners were loaded with tropical fruits and sent to New Orleans. When they returned they were filled with emigrants. The railroad took unto itself length and breadth and crept slowly through morass and jungle toward Vera Cruz. Disease also decimated. The rank forests, the tropical sun, the hardships and exposures of the new and laborious life told heavily against the men, and many whom the bullet had spared the fever finished. The living, however, took the place of the dead, and the work went on.

One day news came that the French garrison at Correzetla had marched at sunset for the Capital. Of all the good five hundred foot and horse not even so much as a saber or a sabertash[11] remained to hold the mountain line between the guerrillas of the south and the little handful of pioneers hewing away in the wilderness of mahogany, toiling by day and standing guard by night. It could not be far to the end. A sudden irruption of robbers, quite two thousand strong, poured through the gaps in the broken and higher country, and drove rapidly in all the outlying posts along the frontier. If any settler there, tarrying late to save from the wreck whatever was valuable or dear to him, fell into their hands, it was a rope, a dog's death, and a grave that hid in it neither coffin nor shroud. Death to the Gringo came on every breeze that swept to the sea.

Shelby knew that the beginning of the end was at hand, and that he had great need to bring back from the overthrow all that was worth a stroke for rescue. He met this last danger as he had met all others, with arms in his hand. He massed once more his movable columns and fought as he fell back in front of his sick and his helpless, dealing such blows as became one who felt that the sun had been turned away from him, and that thereafter it would be neither a cloudless sky nor a peaceful twilight.

The citizens rose in the town of Tampico when it was known that the French had retired, and seized upon the schooners at anchor off the bar. Some among their crew made battle and died in vain and in discharge of a duty that had neither country nor cause to remember and reward it. When the vessels were burned their corpses were thrown headlong into the sea. Nothing survived the inundation. The fields were all laid waste, the habitations were all pillaged and destroyed, what remained of the farming implements were broken to pieces, the luxuriant growth of the tropics sprang up in a night as it were, and hid the work of the devoted colonists. There was a moment of savage exultation over the wreck and the ruin of the beautiful valley, and to-day all the magnificent land watered by the Tuxpan river lies out under the sun, a waste place and a wilderness. Worn by long marching and fighting, the survivors found refuge at last in Cordova, homeless, penniless, and strangers in a strange land.

And death came, too, to one among the exiles who had cast his lot in their midst as a Christian hero, and who had fought the fight the hero always fights. Henry Watkins Allen, ex-Governor of Louisiana, and a general of brigade in the Confederate army, was carried up from the lowlands of the Gulf to die. Shattered by wounds, and broken in health and fortune, he bore so bravely up that none knew, not even those who knew him best, how weak was the poor, tired frame, and how clearly outlined to his own vision was the invisible angel of the somber wings.

Selected by the Emperor to publish a newspaper in the English language and in the interest of the Empire and colonization, he had founded the *Mexican Times,* and had labored faithfully for the stability of the Government and the development of its mineral resources.[12] Singularly gentle and lovable for one so desperately brave, he gave his whole time to the labors of his position, and toiled faithfully on in the work taken upon his hands to do. The Americans looked upon him as an adviser and friend. Marshal Bazaine counseled with him and bestowed upon him his confidence, and Maximilian trusted him as he would a household officer or aide. His charities were unostentatious and manifold. He delighted in giving his scanty means, and in keeping from his left hand what his right hand contributed. He wrote boldly and to the point. In the army his record had been one of extraordinary daring in a corps where all had been brave. Badly wounded at Shiloh, he kept his saddle until the battle was over, and led his troops the long day through, as though impervious to human weakness or physical pain. Later, at Baton Rouge, under Breckenridge, he had made a charge upon a battery, the fame of which filled the West. The guns were taken in the terrible contest, but Allen was lifted up from among his horse's feet, maimed, inert, speechless, almost dead. Three bullets from a canister shot had penetrated both legs, shattered the bones of one of them, and wounded him so desperately that for five months it was an almost hopeless struggle for life. To the last he was a sufferer and an invalid.

Having occasion to visit Vera Cruz on business during the height of the yellow fever, the hand of death was laid gently and silently upon him, and he returned to the City of Mexico to die. The conflict did not last long. What could the emaciated soldier do in the grasp of one so relentless and so fierce? The old wound bled afresh, and the old weakness had never left him. Bazaine sent to him his own physician. All that skill could do was done; all that tenderness or affection could suggest was performed. In vain. The good man died as he had lived, in peace with the world and with the good God who had afflicted him sorely in His own wise way, and who carried his soul straight to heaven.

The work of evacuation went steadily on. As the French retired, city after city received the Liberals with many demonstrations of joy. In some of these, also, those Mexicans who had sympathized with the Empire were cruelly treated; in others they were imprisoned or shot. The armies of Juarez were recruited by a levy *en masse* of all capable of bearing arms in the territory overrun by his ragamuffins. American sympathy was not wanting. Whatever in the way of arms, ammunition, supplies or clothing was needed, was bountifully supplied. A picked detachment of Californians, three squadrons strong, formed a desperate bodyguard for the President.

Unquestioning as fate, they did his bidding even to torture and to massacre. They were feared and hated of the nation.

A blow fell now, and fell suddenly, upon the colony of Carlota. The name itself, of all names, was the most fatal, and it appeased somewhat the fierce hatred of the born robbers and traitors, who hated everything noble or true, to plunder all who were unresisting or defenseless, and who had over them the blessing of the stricken woman of Miramar.[13]

In a night the labor and toil of a long year were utterly broken up and destroyed. A band of freebooters from the mountains, nearly two thousand strong, poured down through the gap the French had left unprotected, and the pillage was utter and complete. Quite a hundred colonists, males all of them, were captured in the night and marched into the gloomy places and recesses of the mountains. Their sufferings were terrible. Bare-footed, days without food, beaten with sabers and pricked with lances, some few died and the rest, after a month of barbarous captivity, made their way back to the French lines, scarcely more than alive. All had been robbed, many had been stripped. Those who survived the blow and the thrust were but few—those who were naked were the most numerous.

The blow finished the colony. The farming implements were destroyed, the stock was slaughtered in the fields, the cabins were burnt, the growing crops beaten down under the feet of the horses, and what the hurrying cavalry spared the winds and the torches finished. Nobody pitied the Americans. In the upheaval of all stable things, and in the ever-increasing contraction of the Imperial circle, what mattered a robbery more or less. The days of the colonists were numbered when the French vessel that bore Castelnau anchored off the mole at Vera Cruz.

Still, however, the Americans were here and there in demand. An English company owning valuable silver mines in Pachuca felt the terror of the French withdrawal, and sought for something stronger to rely upon than Mexican manhood. Colonel Robert C. Wood was in the City of Mexico at the time and was called upon to take command of the Company's forces.[14] These were peons and miners. He recruited in addition a dozen Americans and went down to Pachuca to look after the silver deposits entrusted to his keeping. Vast masses of enormously rich ore, cut off from the seaports because of the revolution going on in the land, were piled up in huge heaps awaiting shipment. Wood took a look at it all and turned to its owner, an old Englishman, nervous but brave:

"How much is it all worth?"

"Well on to a million."

"They will come for it strong, then—the robbers?"

"No, not for the silver ore, but for a ransom. I could stand one, or two, or three among the chiefs and pay them all well, but up among the hundreds it is impossible."

Wood took command and went to fortifying. The third day he found himself surrounded. A summons to surrender came. Before firing a gun a Mexican always seeks to arrange a capitulation. Palaver, from his own strong term *palabres,* means after all nothing but words, words, words, in the rugged old Spanish. Since the commander was influenced to surrender, he had but one thing to do—he fought like a tiger. In the end the first robber chief was driven away, for the Englishman's habitation was a fort, an arsenal, a storehouse, and a silver mine. Others advanced to the attack, but Wood held on for three weeks, fighting every day, and keeping his own right royally. The siege might have lasted longer, but Mendez, an Imperial Mexican, swept down from the Capitol and drove before him like chaff the robber bands, preying alike upon the innocent and the guilty. Colonel Wood marched out with the honors of war, the Englishman made his voyage sure to Vera Cruz; there was no more fighting about Pachuca, but there was no more silver ore as well.

As the news of reverse after reverse came to Maximilian, he turned once more his despairing eyes toward the Americans, and sought among them for the nucleus of a corps. He sent for Shelby, who was at Cordova, and had him to come post haste. Feeling that it was too late, Shelby yet answered the summons with alacrity, and presented himself to the Emperor.

The interview was brief, but, brief as it was, it was almost sad.

"How many Americans are yet in the country?" the Emperor inquired.

"Not enough for a corporal's guard," was Shelby's frank reply; "and the few who are left can not be utilized. Your Majesty has put off too long the inauguration of a plan which, while it might not have given you as many soldiers as France, would at least have restored a formidable rallying point, and stayed for a time the tide of reverses that is rising all over Mexico. I don't know of 200 effective men among my countrymen who could be got together before the evacuation is complete."

"I need 20,000," the Emperor rejoined, as one who talked mechanically.

"Yes, 40,000. Of all the Imperial regiments in your service, you can not count upon one that will stand fast to the end. What are the tidings? In Guadalajara, desertion; in Colima, desertion; in Durango, Zacatecas, San Luis Potosi, Matehuala—it is nothing but desertion, desertion. As I came in I saw the Regiment of the Empress marching out. You will pardon me if I speak the truth, but as devoted as that Regiment should be, I would call upon your Majesty to beware of it. When the need is greatest its loyalty will be most in doubt. Keep with you constantly all the household troops that yet belong to the Empire. Do not waste them in doubtful battles. Do not divide them among important towns. The hour is at hand when instead of numbers you will have to rely upon devotion. I am but as one man, but whatever a single subject can do that thing shall be done to the utmost."

The Emperor mused some little time in silence. When he spoke again it was in a voice so sad as to be almost pitiful.

"It is so refreshing to hear the truth," he said, "and I feel that you have told it to me as one who neither fears nor flatters. Take this in parting, and remember that circumstances never render impossible the right to die for a great principle."

As the Emperor spoke he detached the golden cross of the Order of Guadalupe from his breast and gave it into the hands of Shelby.

He has it yet, a precious souvenir—the sole momento of a parting that for both was the last on earth.

CHAPTER XXII.

It was in these last days of the Empire that General J. A. Early, a noble Southern Tacitus, came over from Havana to Mexico.[1] His journey from the United States had been a romantic one. After Lee's surrender at Appomattox Court House, General Early, with the keen eye of a thorough sportsman, had selected a horse in Virginia that in every way suited his ideas of a horse. Above all things he wanted one full of action and endurance. The ride before him was from ocean to ocean, as it were, from the Atlantic to the Pacific. Having on nothing that would stand in the shape of the uniform of a soldier, and a good enough looking citizen in all except the bronze of his rough campaigning, he rode through Virginia and North Carolina, through Tennessee and Mississippi, into Arkansas and across it into Texas, and on through outlying bands of guerrillas and robbers to the port of Matamoras. Sometimes he went hungry for bread. For days together he had no shelter. He spoke but two words of Spanish, and those contemptuously, because the words themselves expressed so aptly the Mexican's idea of eternal procrastination. He got along somehow, however, and made his appearance to the few who were left among the Mexicans, as full of the fire of war, and as indifferent to either extreme of fortune as when amid echoes of the long and perilous battle he had seen victory come and go, at one time his hand maiden, at another his Delilah.

General Early, even then, had written his book reviewing the military campaigns of Sheridan in the Valley of Virginia. Some articles had appeared in the American press not exactly between them, but about them. Each had written freely of each. Each was a man who followed up his words, if need be, with blows. He disliked skirmishing very much that was only skirmishing, so he concluded to go over to Havana and challenge Sheridan. He argued that Sheridan was an Irishman, that he probably would not be averse to the operations of the code, that he was personally brave and that a shot or two between them, while it might not settle a single point at issue, would at least clear up the atmosphere of the correspondence a little, and round off some of the angularities of the two antagonistic natures. He was over-persuaded, however, and did not send the challenge. He returned to Canada, published his book, told some very necessary yet unpalatable truths, and has remained on duty ever since, a watchful sentinel over Southern honor as amplified and exemplified by Southern history.

Foreigners of all nations now began to put each his house in order. None had faith in the Empire, none believed that it could survive the shock of the French withdrawal beyond three months. Maximilian had no money. He was suspicioned of the church. The Archbishop was his enemy. His wife, really and truly his better half, his noble, self-sacrificing, heroic Carlota, was dead to him, to his love, to whatever of triumph or despair the future had in store for him. The dark hour was upon Saul.[2] Shrouded in the mental blackness of a great darkness, Maximilian, as he always did when he was hard hunted, fled to Cuernavaca. He remained three days, the prey of conflicting emotions, and the one isolated and desolate figure in a land that had in it the birds and the odors of Paradise.

When he returned he had taken upon himself a sudden resolution. He would leave the country, too, he had said to some of his nearest followers. The Emperor Napoleon had urged him to retire with the French. The Emperor of Austria had done the same, so had the Queen of England, so had Bazaine, so had everybody who knew how the scholar and the gentleman would at last be destroyed in a contact with brute force, ignorance and cupidity. There can be no doubt whatever of the Emperor's intention at this time to abandon Mexico. The condition of his wife's health, the attitude of the Catholic Church, his empty treasury, the mutiny and disaffection among his native regiments, the baseness, corruption and falsehood on every hand so impressed him at last that a great reaction came and a great disgust for the people whose cause he had espoused and whose country he had endeavored to pacify and redeem. He retired suddenly to Orizaba, a city two days' journey toward Vera Cruz. The movement was ominous, and a great fear fell upon those among the Imperialists who had yet the manhood and the decency to thus preserve the semblance of affection. Generals Miramon and Marquez went to him at once.[3] Long consultations followed, and the result arrived at was a decree on the part of the Emperor convoking a national Congress, on the most ample and liberal basis, wherein all political parties might participate. On the 12th of October, 1866, the Emperor returned to Puebla, one day's journey toward the Capital, one day's journey farther from the sea-coast. The Imperialists again took courage. On the 5th of January, 1867, the Emperor returned again to the City of Mexico.

During his stay in Orizaba, his Majesty had a long and confidential interview with Governor Thomas C. Reynolds. He had been in the habit of consulting him upon various occasions, and had in more than one instance followed the advice given by this remarkable, clear-headed and conscientious man. To Reynolds he unbosomed himself fully and without reserve. He dwelt upon the condition of the country and the apparent hopelessness of the effort he was making to maintain himself. He complained that he had no advisers who understood the nature of the surroundings, and who could give a sensible and patriotic reason for anything. He wanted sympathy really as much as he did advice, and Reynolds gave him both. He urged upon him the necessity of remaining in Mexico and of dying, if needs be, for his kingdom and his crown. Reynolds also recalled briefly the history of his ancestors, the names great among the greatest of his race, and reminded him as delicately as possible, yet very firmly, that, Hapsburg as he was, he had need but of two things—to perish or succeed. There was a sacred duty he owed, first to his name, and then to those other young and dauntless spirits who had followed him across the ocean and who could not be abandoned to be destroyed. Men of the Hapsburg race either conquered destiny or were conquered by it in war harness and in front of the fight. Standing or falling, he should head his armies and trust himself, as his ancestors had done before him, to the God of battles and the sword.

Maximilian returned to the City of Mexico, as has been already stated, on the 5th of January, 1867. On the 6th of February, of the same year, the French troops left the Capital. The Congress provided for at the Council of Orizava, owing to the deplorable condition of the country, did not meet. War was at hand in the land, and rapine, and the slaughter of those who did not resist, nor yet had any arms in their hands. Bazaine, the night before the evacuation of the city, sought a private interview with the Emperor, and had it granted far into the morning. As a soldier he reasoned with the Emperor simply as a soldier. Treating the whole question at issue as one of men and means entirely, he demonstrated how futile all resistance would be, and how utterly impossible it was to maintain an alien government without an army. Having his mind made up, however, with the fixedness of desperation, Maximilian took no heed of Bazaine's inexorable logic. The two parted coldly, never to meet again, but not as enemies. The Marshal pitied the Emperor, the Emperor smiled upon the Marshal. In the presence of death, the man who can smile and forgive upon earth, is already forgiven in heaven.

If there were any Mexicans now in the Empire really devoted to Maximilian, they made no effort to sustain him. As the French lines receded, the lines of Juarez moved up and occupied everything. Regiments deserted in a body, garrisoned towns were given up, the native troops would not fight against native troops—all cohesiveness was gone. There was no discipline; it was dark in every quarter, and the time for giants to arise was near at hand. In this condition of the country Maximilian took the field.

From the first he led a forlorn hope. The whole Imperial fabric, unsupported by French bayonets, literally fell to pieces. Miramon was defeated in Durango; Mendez had to retreat from the South; Marquez lost in Puebla and the outlying towns about the Capital; from a force amounting to fifty thousand men on paper, Maximilian, all told, and when every General and every detachment was in at Queretaro, could not, if he had tried, have counted nine thousand soldiers, who had faith in the destiny of the Empire and who knew how to die for it.

On the 13th of February, 1867, the Emperor, leaving Marquez in command of the City of Mexico, concluded to take command of the army in the field. Accordingly, on that day he marched northward. The force under him numbered barely eighteen hundred, and was composed equally of the three arms—infantry, cavalry and artillery.

The first day's march brought skirmishing; on the fourth day the skirmishing grew suddenly heavy and hot; the Hungarians of his body guard made a splendid charge, the road was tolerably well cleared, and on the morning of the 19th, amid the ringing of innumerable bells and the noisy demonstrations of a vast multitude, the Emperor entered the city of Queretaro.

It was an historical city, this of Queretaro. Fifty-seven leagues from the Capital, it had been founded about the year 1445, and was a part of the empire of Montezuma I. A Spaniard, Fernando de Tapia, conquered it in 1531, and conferred upon it the name of Santiago de Queretaro—or, in the Tarasco idiom, a place where ball was played.

Ominous christening! The ball now about to be played was with those iron ones men play with death when death must win.

The population of Queretaro was fully fifty thousand, and during the war with the United States the Mexican Congress held its sessions there. Afterward, in 1848, the commissioners of peace assembled there and signed the famous treaty of Hidalgo.

The Emperor was no soldier, and yet he believed some fortifications were necessary to protect his inferior force from the greatly superior force he knew was rushing to overwhelm him from every portion of the Empire. From the 1st of March to the 16th, he worked like a grenadier. He rarely slept. He ate as the men did, fared alike with his soldiers, he appealed to them as a comrade, led them forward as a king, and was beloved beyond all.

On the 14th of March, General Escobedo, at the head of thirty thousand Mexicans, moved down from the north and invested the city. Here was one who had never known an hour of mercy; who had iron gray hair; who was angular and gaunt; who lived much alone, suspicioned all men; who had been known to have rivals poisoned; who hated the French worse than the Austrians, the Americans worse than the French, and who was a coward.

On the 14th of March the city was attacked—thirty thousand against nine thousand. All day long the Emperor was under fire. At night he took no rest. Brave, modest, gentle, no exposure was too great for him—no personal hazard accounted a feather's weight in the scale of the day's doubtful fortunes.

Not yet satisfied of his grip upon the town, Escobedo retired worsted. The grim lines of circumvallation, however, grew stronger day by day, and to the siege of the place a tide of soldiers poured constantly in, armed in all fashions, ragged, hungry for food, ravenous. It mattered not for guns. They had strength, and they could dig to keep well at bay those who, sooner or later, had to come out or starve.

Succor was needed, and on the 22d of March, at the head of one thousand mounted men, General Marquez, at the command of the Emperor, started to the Capital. He was to procure men, provisions and munitions of war, and he was to return within fifteen days. All his orders were explicit. If he had not men enough to garrison and defend the City of Mexico, and also to increase his force sufficiently for the defense of Queretaro, then he was to abandon Mexico and return with every soldier and every round of ammunition he could raise to the headquarters of the Emperor. The Emperor also conferred upon Marquez the title of *Lugar Teniente,* or what is usually translated as meaning Lieutenant General. It does mean this, and much more. Such an officer, in the absence of the sovereign, takes his place, and is recognized and obeyed accordingly. He has the absolute power of life and death in his hands, can declare war, appropriate money, make treaties, act, in short, as an absolute and unquestioning autocrat, and then in the end explain nothing.

Marquez never returned to Queretaro. Was he a traitor? In the peculiarly expressive language of the race to which he belonged, the answer is only a shrug of the shoulders and a *quien sabe.* In a nation of traitors, what matters one or two more or less? Marquez not only did not report, but such were the infamies of his reign in Mexico, and such the outrages and oppressions he put upon the people, that many, even in the last sad days of the Empire—many, indeed, who were faithful and pure of heart—rose up to curse Maximilian, and to rejoice when the couriers came riding southward, telling of how the work was done.

On the 27th of March a passable sortie was made. Two hundred Austrian Hussars, of the household troops, and a squadron or so of Hungarians, dashed across an open field at the charge, capturing two pieces of artillery and two hundred men.

No succor came from the Capital. Marquez reached the City of Mexico in safety and increased his forces to four thousand soldiers, eight hundred of whom were Europeans. Instead of marching immediately northward to Queretaro, he marched directly southward to Puebla, then held by an Imperial garrison, but closely besieged by General Porfirio Diaz. As Marquez approached, Diaz stormed the city, enlisted a large proportion of its defenders in his own ranks and turned savagely upon Marquez. He retreated at first without a battle. Diaz pressed him fiercely, some heavy skirmishing ensued, but in the end all opposition ceased, and the remnant of Maximilian's army cooped itself up within the walls of the City of Mexico and surrendered later at discretion.

On the 14th of April, at Queretaro, the Emperor's forces made another sortie, taking nineteen guns and six hundred prisoners. It was then his intention to abandon this position and reach Mexico by forced and incessant marches. But upon ascertaining fully the results of the victory, and becoming thoroughly acquainted with its magnitude and effect, he countermanded the order of execution and tarried yet a while longer, hoping to hear something that would reassure him from other quarters. Finally abandoning all idea of succor from the movements of Marquez, he ordered Prince Salm Salm, on the night of the 17th, to go in quest of him, ascertain exactly his intentions, arrest and iron him if the need was, and bring back with him every available soldier possible under his command.

Prince Salm Salm, at the head of five hundred cavalry, sallied out precisely at midnight and advanced probably half a league. Suddenly a tremendous fire was opened upon him from artillery and infantry. Severely wounded in the foot himself, and satisfied from the force in position across his only road of exit that he could not get through, he returned within the lines, baffled and demoralized.

On the 1st of May still another sortie was attempted. Miramon led this, and led it badly. Two hours of desperate fighting gave him no advantage, and when at last he was forced back, it was with a precipitancy so great as to appear like a rout.

The cloud of disaster now became darker and nearer. Maximilian bore up bravely. As long as his private funds lasted, he divided them among the sick and the wounded. Constantly in the front of the fight, and dauntless in the discharge of every duty, he commanded, inspired, toiled and faced the inevitable as became the greatness of his nature and the magnitude of the interests at stake. He commanded scarcely nine thousand men. Foremost in the sorties, forming all the forlorn hopes, looking forward to the future only as those who had no future, his Europeans died and made no moan. Many near and dear to him had fallen. Some who had followed his fortunes in other lands and on seas full of wonder and peril fell where neither friendly hand nor sepulchre could come to them. Those the enemy got they mutilated—those who dragged themselves back from the battle's wreck, slowly and painfully, had the prayer of the priest and the last warm grasp of a kingly hand. These were all—but to these poor, faithful, simple-minded soldiers, these were a great deal.

On the morning of the 13th of May, Maximilian determined when the night came to abandon the city of Queretaro. Having yet, however, to arm some three thousand citizens, the evacuation was postponed. On the evening of the 14th, Miramon came to the Emperor and suggested to him the importance of calling a council composed of all the Generals of the army. Above all things it was necessary to have unity of action, and this could best be done after a full and free interchange of opinion was indulged in. The Emperor consented, and in consenting signed his death warrant.

Before the consultation was had, the Emperor turned his honest, clear blue eyes upon the face of Colonel Lopez, commander of the Empress' Regiment, and said to him very gently, as he laid his hand, comrade fashion, upon his shoulder, decorated with the epaulettes the Empress herself had braided:

"*You* need take no concern about the march. Your regiment has been detailed as my especial escort."

The Judas smiled as all Judases have done for six thousand years, and went his way to betray him.

The Generals met during the day of the 14th, and resolved to march out from Queretaro at eleven o'clock that night. When the time came the volunteers were still unarmed, and some of the Generals asked the delay of another day. General Mendez, also, a gallant and devoted officer, being quite unwell and unable to ride, sent Colonel Redonet to the Emperor with a petition asking for further time that he might conquer his malady and lead his old brigade in person.

Maximilian yielded to these urgent solicitations and fixed at last positively upon the night of the 15th.

Full fifty thousand men now invested Queretaro. Corona, a General of more than ordinary Mexican ability, came down from Durango and joined his forces to those Escobedo. The lines of investment were complete—fifty thousand besieging nine thousand.

About the headquarters of Maximilian all was silence and expectancy. General Castillo, of the Imperial staff, conveyed to the various officers, secretly and verbally, the orders for the night. Nowhere did the gleaming of camp fires appear. The infantry were to carry their cartridges and blankets, the cannon upon the fortifications were to be spiked and the magazines flooded. Some eight and ten-pounders, dismounted and packed on mules, together with light supplies of grape and canister, completed the arm of resistance in the way of artillery.

On the west and directly in front of the lines held by Corona the entire garrison was to be concentrated. Thence pouring out through the night—surprising, stabbing, bayoneting, gaining the rugged defiles of the Sierra Gorda—there was slight work thereafter in laying hands upon succor and safety.

Twelve hundred armed citizens of Queretaro were to remain behind and protect the people and the property of the city as far as might be. These, after twenty-four hours had passed, were to surrender to General Escobedo. The Emperor retired at eight o'clock and slept until one. Prince Salm Salm, until twelve o'clock, was busy in arranging the private papers of Maximilian and in packing them in small canvas sacks that might be strapped to the saddles of the escort company. Many were busy in writing words of tenderness and farewell. As there were no lights, the staff officers assisted each other by smoking cigarettes close to the paper that a few words might be scribbled by the fleeting and uncertain light.

The sortie might have won. It was the last and only resort of nine thousand desperate men who had been starving, who in eleven days had only scant allowances of mule or horse meat, and who had been under fire long enough to be acclimated.

It was not to be, however. Between one and two o'clock the traitor Lopez, having previously communicated with Escobedo, crept silently from his quarters and took his way through the dark and narrow streets of Queretaro. Colonel Garza, commanding the advance outposts of the investing army, met him first. Garza was an honorable soldier who despised the work he was engaged in, and the man who came to him in the midnight, a coward and a traitor. As he advanced to meet him he did not extend his hand, but said curtly:

"You are expected. Such work as this needs to be done quickly."

Garza reported with Lopez to General Veliz, a division commander. The three together visited Escobedo and returned almost directly, Garza having been ordered to follow the traitor with his command and do as he was bidden.

There was a large church on the south called La Cruz, and near this church a hole in the wall of defense. Thither went Lopez, Veliz and Garza. Here Veliz halted, but Garza and Lopez went on. Be it remembered, also, that Lopez had been the officer of the day, that he was the highest just then in authority in the city, and that having the pass word, he could arrange the forces at pleasure, and transpose or withdraw posts and outposts as the exigencies of his terrible treason might demand.

When the nearest station of Imperial troops was reached, Garza halted his command. Lopez rode forward and asked of the officer on duty if there was any news.

"None," was the reply.

"Then parade your men and call the roll."

This was done with military accuracy and speed. Afterward, the detachment was marched to the rear of Garza, leaving him in possession of the fort. The Liberals were in Queretaro. The beginning of the end was at hand. Other Liberal officers were put in possession of other posts, and before an hour had passed the treachery was complete. As the Liberal forces entered the city, quite a number of the Imperial officers were awake. As they saw Colonel Rincon's regiment—a Liberal regiment of some celebrity—march by their barracks, they looked out carelessly and took no note. Some of their own troops, they imagined, were going by or getting ready for the sortie.

By half past three o'clock, fully two-thirds of the city was in possession of the Liberals. Suddenly and with great force all the church bells began to ring. The streets were filled with bodies of armed men. Aides galloped hither and thither. Skirmishing shots broke out in every direction. There were cries, shouts, the blare of bugles, and from afar the heavy rumbling and dragging of artillery.

Great confusion fell upon the Imperialists. Some thought that Marquez had returned, and had attacked and defeated Escobedo. Others, that it was only a fight at the outposts—many, that the short, hot work of the sortie had actually begun. And so it had, with the lines reversed. Lopez had an adjutant, a Pole named Yablonski, who was with him in his treasonable plot, but who yet sought to save the Emperor. Feigning sleep, he had not yet closed his eyes in slumber. All his senses were on the *qui vive*[4] for the ringing of the bells that were to usher in the tragedy. The first echo brought him to his feet—erect, nervous, vigorous.

Maximilian occupied the convent of La Cruz, and next to the room of the Emperor was that of his private secretary, Jose Blasio. Yablonski went up close to Blasio and whispered:

"The enemy are in the garden; get up!"

Half dressed and heavy with the deep sleep of exhaustion, Blasio staggered into the apartment of the Emperor. In a few moments Maximilian knew all. He was the coolest man there, and so sad and so gentle that it seemed as if he did not care to live. The convent was surrounded. Castillo,

Guzman, Salm Salm and Padillo, all officers who were quartered near the Emperor, walked into his presence. Padillo informed him that the enemy were in possession of the convent; that ten pieces of artillery had been taken in its very plaza, and that all defense of the mere building itself was useless. Maximilian very quietly took up a brace of revolvers, handed one to Padillo, and went to the door of his room, followed by Padillo, Blasio and Salm Salm. "To go out here or to die is the only way," he said, and they crossed the corridor.

A sentinel at the head of the steps halted them. Maximilian leveled his revolver. An officer of the Liberal army—a brave, chivalrous and heroic Mexican, supposed to be Col. Rincon—struck with a strange and generous pity, cried out to the sentinel:

"Let them pass; they are citizens."

In the Plaza a line of leveled muskets again came up in front of them. Capture was imminent—or death unknown and ignominious. Again Rincon spoke to the soldiers:

"Let them pass; they are civilians."

The lines opened and the Emperor, followed by his little escort, reached the regiment of the Empress. Lopez, its Colonel and its betrayer, was at its head, mounted and ready for orders. A huge hill, El Cerro de las Campanas, was the rallying point now of Maximilian's confused, scattered and demoralized forces. Thither he hurried with what was left of this chosen body of his very household's troops. On the way Castillo was met, who cried out:

"All is lost. See, your Majesty, the enemy's force is coming very near."

Just then a body of infantry was entering the Plaza. Mistaken in their uniforms, and not aware of the extent and nature of the surprise, Maximilian exclaimed:

"Thank God, our battalion of Municipal Guards are coming."

The error, however, was soon discovered and the little party started again for the hill, El Cerro. Maximilian was on foot. A horse, however, was brought to him which he mounted, reigning it in and keeping pace with his companions. Lopez remained close to his side. Passing the house of one Rubio, a rich Mexican, though not an Imperialist, Lopez said to the Emperor:

"Your majesty should enter here. In this way alone can you save yourself."

Maximilian refused peremptorily, and issued his orders with singular calmness and clearness. Meeting Captain Jenero, General Castillo's adjutant, he bade him seek Miramon at once and order him to concentrate every available soldier upon El Cerro de las Campanas. To another officer he cried out:

"Go among your men and talk to them. Expose your person and teach them how to die."

On the summit of the hill there were only about one hundred and fifty men gathered. These, belonging principally to the infantry regiments, had strayed there more because of the observation the elevation afforded than of a knowledge that it was the rallying point. Not all of them had ammunition. Some, roused suddenly from sleep, had snatched up only their guns and rushed out alarmed into the night. Soon the cavalry of the Empress arrived, and, recognizing the Emperor, cheered for him bravely. This devotion touched him, and under the light of the stars he was seen to lift up his hat and bow his head.

Was he thinking of Carlota?

Miramon did not come. The firing grew heavier in every direction. Mejia rallying a few men in the Plaza del Ayuntamiento followed the regiment of the Empress. As they approached, Maximilian spoke to Salm Salm.

"Ride forward and see if Miramon can not be distinguished among those who are coming up."

General Mendez, a lion in combat, and so weak from illness as to be put with difficulty upon his horse, was surprised in the Alameda and surrounded. Would he surrender? Never: and the battle began. It was a carnage—a massacre. His men fell fearfully fast—shot down, helpless, by an unseen and protected foe. A ball broke his left arm. He swayed in the saddle, but he held fast.

"Bring here a strap!" he shouted, "and strap me fast. I want to die in the harness."

He tried to cut through to El Cerro. Met half way and caught in a dreadful ambuscade, the slaughter was renewed. Another ball carried away the point of his chin, and yet a third disabled his right shoulder, and yet a fourth killed his horse. Scarcely alive, he was dragged out insensible. Reviving a little toward daylight, at six in the morning a fusillade finished him. Among all the soldiers of Maximilian, he was the noblest, the bravest and the best.

How fared it with Miramon, sound asleep when the traitor Lopez stole in through the battered wall at the head of an insatiable tide swallowing up the tottering and dissolving fabric of Imperialism?

CHAPTER XXIII.

Awakened by the ringing of bells, the broken rattle of irregular musketry and now and then a cannon shot, Miramon half arose in his bed, cleared his eyes from the heaviness of sleep, and spoke calmly to his aide-de-camp.

"I fear that we are lost. Inside the walls a traitor has surely been at work."

He dressed himself speedily, and descended into the street. It was full of soldiers. He imagined that they were his own. He spoke to them and announced his name and rank. An officer on horseback rushed upon him, put a carbine to his cheek and fired. Miramon, his jaw-bone shattered and his flesh blackened and powder burnt, swayed backward nearly off his feet, caught himself, lifted himself upright, and killed the officer dead in the saddle who had shot him.

Miramon had a devoted body-guard, and it rallied around him. In the darkness the fight became furious. Striving in vain to reach the hill where he supposed the Emperor was making a desperate stand, and weak from the loss of blood, Miramon staggered upon an open door and entered a house. It was the house of Dr. Samaniegos, who hid him and kissed him, and, Mexican-like, went out into the streets to give his life away. He proclaimed aloud to the Liberals that Miramon was alone in his house, and that the time was opportune to lay hands upon him. A band rushed in and bound and gagged him, and dragged him away—suffering excruciating torture—to the convent of Terrecitas.

The Emperor, therefore, waited in vain for Miramon—waited in agony and uncertainty until two batteries of San Gregorio and Celaya opened a tremendous fire upon his position. Turning to Prince Salm Salm, he was heard to exclaim from the depths of his despair:

"Oh, my friend, would that one of these shells would end it all now, and speedily."

Alas! he was reserved for Mexican bullets.

Directly, Colonel Gonzales galloped up with a portion of a regiment, saluted, and reported the condition of Miramon. Maximilian sighed heavily, rested his head upon his hands for a few moments, and then demanded suddenly of Castillo and Mejia if it were possible to break through the lines of the enemy.

Old Mejia, the small, cool, devoted Indian fatalist and fighter, turned his glass toward the enemy and surveyed them accurately through the night. When he had finished, he merely shrugged and replied:

"Sire, it is impossible. If you order it, we will try it. For my part, I am ready to die. For fifty years I have waited for this."

Maximilian then took Padillo by the arm and spoke to him briefly:

"It is necessary to make a quick determination in order to avoid greater misfortunes. Is it surrender?"

"Yes, sire," said Castillo, Padillo, Gonzales, and "Yes, sire," said Mejia in a sad whisper, his head drooping upon his breast.

Immediately a white flag was lifted up from the top of the hill, and messengers were sent at once to Escobedo asking an interview upon the following basis:

First—To make Maximilian alone the victim of the war.

Second—The men of the army to be treated with the soldierly consideration merited by their valor and devotion.

Third—The lives and liberty of those who were immediately in the Emperor's personal services.

Before an answer was returned, Maximilian saw in the distance a small squadron of soldiers, dressed in scarlet, and riding at rapid speed toward the Campanas. He mistook them for his own Hussars and cried out, his voice heavy with emotion:

"It is too late—they come too late, but see what a fearful risk they run to reach me. Look how they endure the fire of the batteries. Who would not be proud of such soldiers?"

Alas! they were not even a portion of his own decimated yet devoted foreign followers. They were the advance of Trevina's robber cavalry, coming to hunt the Emperor.

As they drew near, the fire slackened and suddenly ceased altogether. An officer, a captain, rode forward, and with a vulgar and cowardly epithet, demanded Maximilian. His Majesty, calm as a grenadier on guard, stepped outside the fortification and replied with much sweetness and dignity:

"I am he."

"Mendez has been shot," this officer continued brutally, "and Miramon, and by and by it will come Maximilian's and Mejia's turn."

The Emperor did not answer. He pitied the coward who did not know how to treat misfortune. Sternly bidding his subordinate to go to the rear, General Echegarry, a Liberal officer of some humanity, rode to the front and demanded courteously the surrender of Maximilian and his officers. This was at once accorded, the Emperor again exclaiming, "If you should require anybody's life, take mine, but do not harm my officers. I am willing to die if you require it, but intercede with General Escobedo for the life of my officers."

Presently General Corona rode up, and again the Emperor interceded for his personal adherents:

"If you want another victim, I am prepared to go. Do not harm those whose only crime in your eyes is their devotion to me."

Corona replied coldly:

"It does not belong to me to make promises. Until you are delivered to the General-in-chief in person, your own life and that of your officers will be safe."

Horses were furnished, and the Imperialist Generals, Costello, Mejia and Salm Salm, together with the Emperor and the Liberal Generals, Corona and Echegarry, mounted and rode down the hill toward the city. It was not long before General Escobedo was met, when a countermarch was had, and they all returned to the hill again, and into the fort where they dismounted.

After dismounting, Maximilian extended his hand to Escobedo. His own safety never, for a single instant, seemed to have entered his mind. His talk was ever of his followers.

"If you wish more blood," he remarked to Escobedo, "take mine. I ask at your hands good treatment for the officers who have been true to me. Do not let them be insulted or maltreated."

"All shall be treated as prisoners of war, even your Majesty," was the significant reply of the Mexican butcher.

In an hour, with a heavy guard over him—homeless, crownless, sceptreless—Maximilian was a close prisoner in the convent La Cruz. At his special request the officers of his household—Prince Salm Salm, Colonel Guzman, Minister Aguirre, Colonel Padillo, Dr. Basch, and Don Jose Blasio, his Secretary, were permitted to be imprisoned in the same building. They remained four days there—three of which the Emperor remained in bed, seriously sick with dysentery. On the fifth day they were removed to the Convent of Terrecitas. After enduring seven days of rigorous captivity in this gloomy abode, they were taken to the Convent of Capuchinas, where were also imprisoned all the Generals of the Imperial army. For four days they all remained together on the first floor. On the fifth, Maximilian, Mejia and Miramon were separated from the rest and imprisoned in the second story. The work of winnowing had already commenced—so soon and yet so ominous.

Here the Emperor had leisure to review the past, and answer to his own heart the question: Had he done his duty? In his conscience, perhaps, there was little of upbraiding. True, he had committed mistakes here and grievous errors of judgment yonder; but who is infallible? He had tried to do right, and he had nothing to reproach himself with. No form of speech could express his astonishment at the betrayal of Lopez. He had trusted him in all things, confided in him, leaned upon him, lifted him up and promoted him, brought him to the flattery and friendship of his beautiful Empress—and in the one supreme moment of his destiny, in the very hour of the desperate crisis of his life and his reign, this Lopez, this tawny, fawning, creeping, cowardly thing, surrendered himself without so much as a quickened pulse-beat, or a guilty and accusing blush. He had been the godfather to Lopez's child. He had laid bare to Lopez the innermost recesses of his heart, and in his last and most terrible hour to be betrayed when the struggle he was making was not for himself, was too bad.

Nor did Lopez lay himself down on a bed of roses when the black treachery was done. His beautiful wife deserted him, and published to all Mexico the story of his infamy and ingratitude. His children abandoned his household and sought shelter and protection with the mother. On dress parade one day, when an army was on review, a Juarista Colonel smote him upon either cheek, the *lazzaroni* hooted at him and cried out, *"el triador! el triador!"* as he passed along, the very beggars turned away their eyes from him without asking for alms, and nowhere could he find pity and charity except in the bosom of that church which, no matter how dark are the stains of the blood upon the hands of the sinners, prays always that they may be made white as snow.

The captivity of Maximilian continued. It was rigid, gloomy, foreboding—a little darker than Spanish captivity generally, because to the cruelty of the original Spaniard, there had been added the cunning and selfish craftiness of the Indian. He was denied all intercourse with his fellows except that which the officials had. His food was coarse, his water not plenty, his sunlight barred out, and his pure air made pestilential because of the filth with which they delighted to surround him.

Physical deprivations, however, made no way to subdue the lofty pride and the Christian heroism and fortitude of his kingly character. His head was yet borne splendidly erect, and in the day or the night-time, in a room that was like a dungeon, or in the vestibule where the naked and unwashed animals of sentinels slept, he was the same patient, kindly, courteous gentleman—true to his name, his lineage, and his manhood.

The half-breed butchers, however, who were soon to try him and to sit with sandaled feet about the table where military justice was to declare itself, tried first, in Indian fashion, to degrade the victim they meant to torture alive. A proclamation, purporting to have been written by Maximilian, was printed in every newspaper in the Empire. It bore no date. It was abject, cowardly, plausible if a Mexican had written it, a paltry forgery when ascribed to a Hapsburg, and it was as follows:

"The Archduke Ferdinand Maximilian, of Hapsburg, ex-Emperor of Mexico, to all of its inhabitants:

"COMPATRIOTS:

"After the valor and patriotism of the Republican armies have brought about the end of my reign in this city, the obstinate defense of which was indispensable to save the honor of my cause and of my race; after this bloody siege, in which have rivaled in abnegation and bravery the soldiers of the Empire with those of the Republic, I am going to explain myself to you.

"Compatriots: I came to Mexico animated not only with a firm hope of making you, and everyone of you, individually happy, but also protected and called to the throne of Montezuma and Iturbide by the Emperor of France, Napoleon III. He has abandoned us outwardly and infamously, through the fear of the United States, placing in ridicule France itself, and making it spend uselessly its treasures, and shedding the blood of its sons and your own. When the news of my fall and death will reach Europe, all its monarchs, and the land of Charlemange, will ask an account of my blood, and that of the Germans, Belgians and French shed in Mexico, from the Napoleon dynasty. Then will be the end.

"The whole world will soon see Napoleon covered with shame from head to foot.

"Now the world sees his Majesty, the Emperor of Austria, my august brother, supplicating for my life before the United States, and me a prisoner of war at the disposition of the Republican government, with my crown and heart torn to pieces.

"Compatriots: My last words to you are these: I ardently desire that my blood may regenerate Mexico; and that as a warning to all ambitious and incautious persons, you may know how, with prudence and true patriotism, to take advantage of your triumph, and through your virtues ennoble the political cause, the banner of which you sustain. May Providence save you, and make me worthy of myself.

"MAXIMILIAN."

The vile forgery went everywhere. The soldiers on guard that could read, read it aloud and laughed long and derisively in the hearing of the Emperor. A copy was brought to him. He wrote upon the back, in pencil:

"I authorize Colonel and Aide-de-Camp Prince Salm Salm to deny in my name this last effort to disgrace me before posterity. This proclamation is not mine, its sentiments are not mine, its declarations are not true, and these, therefore, certainly can not be mine. Should Colonel and Aide-de-

Camp Prince Salm Salm escape the fate certainly in store for me, he will publish in Europe this my earnest declaration."

Salm Salm did survive him, and history has given the lie fully to the black plot worthy of the nation that concocted it.

The trial was a farce. Since the work of the traitor Lopez, there had been no hope for Maximilian.

On Tuesday morning, May 28, 1867, the friends of the Emperor began to bestir themselves in his behalf. Mr. Bansen, the Hamburg Consul, resident at San Luis Potosi, the wife of Prince Salm Salm, Baron Magnus, the Prussian Minister, and Frederick Hall, an American lawyer, concentrated themselves at Queretaro and laid plans for the acquittal of his Majesty.

Maximilian talked much before his trial—the broken and unconnected talk of one who felt without seeing it the shadow of approaching death. He declared that he came to Mexico with the sincere belief that he was called to the government by the great masses of the people. After his reception at Vera Cruz he had remarked to the Empress: "Surely the deputation were right when they said a majority of the Mexicans were in favor of our coming to be their ruler. I never in all Europe saw a sovereign received with such enthusiasm as greeted us."[1]

He put upon Bazaine the responsibility of the decree of October 3, 1865, that decree which required the execution of all Liberals caught with arms in their hands. Bazaine, he said, appeared before the Council of State and declared that decree to be a military necessity. Juarez was in Texas, although Juarez had always denied having been driven out of the country. On this point he was exceedingly sensitive, and because of the statement made by the Emperor that Juarez was no longer in the territory he professed to rule over as President, he, the Emperor, was clearly of the opinion that Juarez most heartily despised him.

Maximilian might have gone further and said to his hatred there had been added ferocity.

The Emperor held the Americans in high estimation. He said: "The Americans are a great people for improvements, and are great lovers of justice. They pay such respect to the laws that I admire them. And if God should spare my life, I intend to visit the United States and travel through them. You can always rely on the word of an American gentleman."

Efforts were made to bring the trial before the Mexican Congress, but it failed. The cruel Indian, Juarez, dared not trust any tribunal other than the court martial, one organized to convict, and one that would, therefore, be deaf, blind and unsparing.

On the morning of the June 4th, Maximilian remarked gayly to one of his counsellors:

"We must hurry with business. I have been talking with Miramon. He has counted up the time and says that he thinks they will shoot us on Friday morning."

This was on Tuesday that he spoke so, and while under the impression that the lawyers he had sent for to the City of Mexico would not be permitted to come through the lines and defend him.

Still the lawyers did not come, and the Princess Salm Salm determined to go alone to look for them. She had a carriage but no horses, and an application was made to a Liberal General to furnish just two animals to take her to the nearest state station. The General replied that if he had a thousand to spare, he would not let one go for any such purpose. This kind of spirit prevailed, with here and there an exception, throughout the entire army. In such spirit was the Court Martial selected, and in such spirit did Escobedo declare to Juarez that unless Maximilian was shot he could not hold his troops together.

In these early days of June some thoughts of escape presented themselves to the Emperor's mind, and a plan to save him had been agreed upon. A slippery Italian rascal, one Henry B. del Borgo, a Captain in the Liberal army, had received two thousand dollars from Maximilian to purchase six horses, saddles, equipments and pistols. Of this amount the Italian spend six hundred dollars in horses and accoutrements, which were to be ready at a designated spot on a certain night. The three prisoners were furthermore to be let out at the proper time, when a quick rush was to take place, and a desperate gallop for the mountains. Mejia knew all the country, the plan was a most feasible one, but to the surprise of every one, the Italian, after divulging all the particulars of the plot, including his own actions, was permitted to retire upon the balance of the money and take with him the compliments of Escobedo for the patriotism and ability he had manifested in thus finding out and exposing the schemes of the traitors.

After this betrayal on the part of the miserable little Italian, all the foreigners were ordered to leave Queretaro. Escobedo would make no exceptions. Maximilian's American counsel had to go with the rest, and all of the Austrian and Belgian officers and soldiers who were not to be tried for their lives immediately.

The Government of Mexico recognized Maximilian only as the Archduke of Austria, and his Generals, Miramon and Mejia, only as so-called Generals. As such the court martial proceeded to try them—a court composed as follows: Lieutenant-Colonel Platon Sanchez, President; Captains Jose Vincente Ramirez, Emilio Lojero, Ignacio Jurado, Juan Rueday Auza, Jose Verastigui, and Lucas Villagran. It held its first session on the 27th of May, 1867, and on the 14th of June, of the same year, at

midnight, the three prisoners, Maximilian, Mejia, and Miramon, were sentenced to death. On the 16th, Escobedo telegraphed to Juarez as follows:
"CITIZEN PRESIDENT:

"The sentence which the Council of War pronounced on the 14th instant, has been confirmed at these headquarters, and to-day, at ten o'clock of the morning the prisoners were notified thereof, and at three o'clock this afternoon they will be shot.

"ESCOBEDO."

A petition, asking for Maximilian's life, signed by his Mexican lawyers, Messrs. Mariane Riva Palacio and Rafael Martinez de la Torre, was peremptorily denied. Again they sought the President, and begged at his hands a brief respite. Five days were granted, and an order was sent by telegraph to Escobedo to stay the execution until the 19th.

Juarez had his headquarters during the trial at San Luis Potosi. Hither came Baron Von A. V. Magnus, the Prussian Minister to the Imperial Government of Mexico. He came to intercede in behalf of Maximilian, and to do all that was possible to be done in his behalf. He, too, visited Juarez, represented to him the uselessness of the sacrifice, pointed out the impossibility of any further foreign intervention in the future, and in the name of mercy, and for the sake of Christian charity and forgiveness, asked the life of Maximilian at the hands of the President of the Republic.

It was of no avail. As cold as the snow upon the summit of Popocatapetl was the heart of Juarez.

Baron Magnus abandoned the effort and went from San Luis Potosi to Queretaro. On the 15th news came that the Empress Carlota was dead.[2] General Mejia was chosen to convey this information to the Emperor, which he did gently and delicately. Maximilian wept a little, went away alone for a few brief moments, and came back a king again. In his last hours he meant to be strong to every fate.

In the afternoon he wrote to Baron Largo, a member of his personal staff, and one who had been banished by General Escobedo on the 14th of March:

"I have just learned that my poor wife has died, and though the news affects my heart, yet, on the other hand and under the present circumstances, it is a consolation. I have but one wish on earth, and that is that my body may be buried next to that of my poor wife. I entrust you with this, as the representative of Austria. I ask you that my legal heirs will take the same care of those who surrounded me and my servants, as though the Empress and I had lived."

On the 18th Baron Magus arrived in Queretaro, and immediately visited the Emperor. Still hoping against hope, he again put himself in communication with Juarez. Maximilian was to be shot on the 19th, and at midnight on the 18th Baron Magnus sent the following message:

"HIS EXCELLENCY SENOR LERDO DE TEJADA:

"Having reached Queretaro to-day, I am sure that the three persons condemned on the 14th died morally last Sunday, and that the world so estimates it, as they had made every disposition to die, and expected every instant, for an hour, to be carried to the place where they were to receive death, before it was possible to communicate to them the order suspending the act.

"The humane customs of our epoch do not permit that, after having suffered that horrible punishment, they should be made to die the second time to-morrow.

"In the name, then, of humanity and heaven, I conjure you to order their lives not to be taken; and I repeat to you again that I am sure that my Sovereign, his Majesty the King of Prussia, and all the monarchs of Europe united by the ties of blood with the imprisoned Prince, namely, his brother, the Emperor of Austria; his cousin, the Queen of the British Empire; his brother-in-law, the King of the Belgians; and his cousins, the Queen of Spain and the Kings of Italy and Sweden, will easily understand how to give His Excellency Senor Don Benito Juarez all the requisite securities that none of the three prisoners will ever return to walk on Mexican Territory.

"A. V. MAGNUS."

To this appeal the present President of the Republic, then Juarez's Secretary of State, sent the following reply:

"SENOR BARON A. V. MAGNUS:

"I am pained to tell you, in answer to the telegram which you have been pleased to send to me to-night, that, as I declared to you day before yesterday, in this city, the President of the Republic does not believe it possible to grant the pardon of the Archduke Maximilian, through the gravest considerations of justice, and of the necessity of assuring peace to the Republic.

"SEBASTIAN LERDO DE TEJADA."

No hope. Maximilian knew and felt it from the first, and so he had long ago made up his mind to die. He made one more effort, however, to save the lives of his companions. On the 18th, the day before his execution, he sent the following dispatch to the President:

"SENOR BENITO JUAREZ:

"I desire that you may preserve the lives of Don Miguel Miramon and Don Tomas Mejia, who day before yesterday suffered all the tortures and bitterness of death; and, as I manifested on being taken prisoner, I should be the only victim.

"MAXIMILIAN."

To this touching appeal there never came an answer. The sullen and savage Indian was losing caste in this contrast with the chivalrous and Christian European, and to escape further humiliation, he added to his cruelty the natural national characteristic of stoicism.[3]

At about half past eleven o'clock on the night of the 18th, Escobedo visited Maximilian. The interview was very brief. He asked the Emperor for his photograph, which was given him, shook hands with him at parting, and strode away a guilty, swarthy, conscienceless murderer, not daring to look back upon the young, dauntless face, so fair and so fresh in its nobleness and beauty.

The Emperor next prepared himself for death. He took from his finger his marriage ring, and gave it to his physician, Dr. Samuel Basch, requesting him to carry it to the Archduchess, his mother. He still supposed his wife to be dead, and God in His mercy let him die so.

There were yet some letters to write. The first was to Baron Largo:

"I have nothing to look for in this world; and my last wishes are limited to my mortal remains, which soon will be free from suffering and under the favor of those who outlive me. My physician, Dr. Basch, will have my body transported to Vera Cruz. Two servants, Gull and Tudas, will be the only ones who will accompany him. I have given orders that my body be carried to Vera Cruz without any pomp, and no extraordinary ceremony be made on board. I await death calmly, and I equally wish to enjoy calmness in the coffin. So arrange it, dear Baron, that Dr. Basch and my two servants be transported to Europe in one of the two war vessels.

"I wish to be buried by the side of my poor wife. If the report of the death of my poor wife has no foundation, my body should be deposited in some place until the Empress may meet me through death.

"Have the goodness to transmit the necessary orders to the Captain of the ship de Groeller. Have likewise the goodness to do all you can to have the widow of my faithful companion in arms, Miramon, got to Europe in one of the two war vessels. I rely the more upon this wish being complied with, inasmuch as I have recommended her to place herself under my mother at Vienna.

"Yours,

"MAXIMILIAN."

Queretaro, in the Prison of the Capuchinas, 18th of June, 1867.

The second letter was again to Juarez:

"QUERETARO, June 19, 1867.

"SENOR BENITO JUAREZ:

"About to receive death in consequence of having wished to prove whether new political institutions could succeed in putting an end to the bloody civil war which has devastated for so many years this unfortunate country, I shall lose my life with pleasure if its sacrifice can contribute to the peace and prosperity of my new country. Fully persuaded that nothing solid can be founded on a soil drenched in blood and agitated by violent commotions, I conjure you, in the most solemn manner and with the true sincerity of the moments in which I find myself, that my blood may be the last to be spilt; that the same perseverance, which I was pleased to recognize and esteem in the midst of prosperity—that with which you have defended the cause which has just triumphed, may consecrate that blood to the most noble task of reconciling the minds of the people, and in founding in a stable and durable manner the peace and tranquillity of this unfortunate country.

"MAXIMILIAN."

This was all. The morning broke fair and white in the sky, and at half past six three carriages drew up in front of the main gate of the Convent of the Capuchinas. The bells rang in all the steeples, there were soldiers everywhere, and long lines of glittering steel that rose and fell in yet the soft, sweet hush of the morning.

Into the first carriage got Maximilian and Father Soria, a priest. The Emperor's dress was very plain. He wore a single-breasted black frock coat, with all the buttons buttoned except the last one, a black vest, neck-tie and pantaloons, plain cavalry boots and a wide-brimmed hat, or *sombrero.*

In the second carriage there came Miramon and his priest; in the third, Mejia and his. Then the solemn cortege started. In the extreme advance five cavalry rode, the one behind the other, with an interval between of twenty paces, and yet further in front of the five there rode a solitary Corporal. A company of infantry, eighty rank and file, came after the cavalry. Then followed the carriages, escorted by a battalion of sharpshooters, one-half of whom flanked each side of the road, marching parallel with the vehicles. A rear guard of 250 mounted men closed the mournful procession.

The sun arose and poured its unclouded rays over the city. All the people were in the streets. On the faces of the multitude there were evidences of genuine and unaffected sorrow. Some among the crowd lifted their hats as the victims passed along, some turned away their heads and wept, and some, even amid the soldiers and amid the hostile ranks of the Liberals, fell upon their knees and wept.

The place of surrender was to be the place of execution. Northwest of the city a mile or more, the Hill of the Bells, El Cerro de las Campanas, upreared itself. It was enclosed on three sides by six thousand soldiers of all arms, leaving the rear or uncovered side resting upon a wall.

It was half past 7 o'clock when the carriages halted at the place of execution. Maximilian was the first to alight. He stepped proudly down, took a handkerchief from his pocket and his hat from his head, and beckoned for one of his Mexican servants to approach.

The man came.

"Take these," the Emperor said. "They are all I have to give."

The faithful Indian took them, kissed them, cried over them, fell upon his knees a few moments in prayer to the good God for the good master, and arose a hero.

In front of the dead wall three crosses had been firmly embedded in the ground. On each side was a placard bearing the name of the victims to be immolated there. That upon the right was where the Emperor was to be shot, that in the center was Miramon, that upon the left for the grim old stoic and fighter, Mejia.

Maximilian stroked down the luxuriant growth of his long yellow beard, as it was his constant habit to do, and walked firmly to his place.

The three men embraced each other three times. To Mejia he said:

"We will meet in heaven."

Mejia bowed, smiled, and laid his hand upon his heart.

To Miramon he said:

"Brave men are respected by sovereigns—permit me to give you the place of honor."

As he said this he took Miramon gently by the arm and led him to the center cross, embracing him as he left him for the last time.

Escobedo was not on the ground. An aide-de-camp, however, brought permission for each of the victims to deliver a farewell address. The Emperor spoke briefly:

"Persons of my rank and birth are brought into the world either to insure the welfare of the people, or to die as martyrs. I did not come to Mexico from motives of ambition. I came at the earnest entreaty of those who desired the welfare of our country. Mexicans, I pray that my blood may be the last to be shed for our unhappy country, and may it insure the happiness of the nation. Mexicans! Long live Mexico!"

Mejia drew himself up as a soldier on duty, looked up once at the unclouded sky, and around upon all the fragrant and green-growing things, and bowed his head without speaking.

Miramon drew from his pocket a small piece of paper and read as follows:

"Mexicans! behold me, condemned by a Council of War, and condemned to death as a traitor. In these moments which do not belong to me, in which my life is already that of the Supreme Being, before the entire world I proclaim that I have never been a traitor to my country. I have defended my opinions, but my children will never be ashamed of their father. I have not the stain of treason, neither will it pass to my children. Mexicans! Long live Mexico! Long live the Emperor!"

When Miramon ceased reading, Maximilian placed his hand on his breast, threw up his head, and cried out in a singularly calm and penetrating voice, "Fire!"

Eighteen muskets were discharged as one musket. Mejia and Miramon died instantly. Four bullets struck the emperor, three in the left and one in the right breast. Three of these bullets passed entirely through his body, coming out high up on the left shoulder, the other remained embedded in the right lung. The Emperor fell a little sideways and upon his right side, exclaiming almost gently and sadly:

"Oh! *Hombre! Hombre!* Oh! man! Oh! man!"

He was not yet dead. A soldier went up close to him and fired into his stomach. The emperor moved slightly as if still sensible to pain. Another came out from the firing party, and, putting the muzzle of his musket up close to his breast, shot him fairly through the heart.

The tragedy was ended; Mexican vengeance was satisfied; the soul of the unfortunate prince was with its God, and until the judgment day the blood of one who was too young and too gentle to die, will cry out from the ground, even as the blood of Abel. Too generous to desert his comrades, too pure in heart to rule as he should have ruled, too confiding to keep a crown bestowed by a race bred to revolution, and too merciful in all the ways and walks of life to maintain fast hold upon a throne carved out from conquest and military power, he died as he had lived, imperial in manhood and heroic in the discharge of every duty.

THE END.

NOTES

Introduction

1. Conard, *Encyclopedia of the History of Missouri,* vol. 2, 355–56.
2. Shoemaker, *Missouri Day by Day,* vol. 1, 8.
3. Saults, "Let Us Discuss a Man," 8.
4. Ibid., 3.
5. Edwards, *Shelby and His Men,* 80.
6. O'Flaherty, *General Jo Shelby,* 28.
7. Edwards, *Life, Writings, and Tributes,* 15.
8. O'Flaherty, *General Jo Shelby,* viii.
9. Edwards, *Shelby and His Men,* 237.
10. Oates, *Confederate Cavalry West of the River,* 139.
11. Edwards, *Shelby and His Men,* 451.
12. Edwards, *Life, Writings, and Tributes,* 15.
13. Edwards, *Shelby and His Men,* 523–24.
14. Ibid., 524.
15. Bird, "Jo Shelby and His Shadow," 26.
16. Kerby, *Kirby Smith's Confederacy,* 428.
17. O'Flaherty, *General Jo Shelby,* 355–56.
18. Edwards, *Shelby's Expedition to Mexico,* 263.
19. Davis, *Fallen Guidon,* 69.
20. Ibid., 70.
21. Kerby, *Kirby Smith's Confederacy,* 428.
22. Creel, *A Rebel at Large,* 28.
23. Davis, *Fallen Guidon,* 81.
24. Ibid., 169–70.
25. O'Flaherty, *General Jo Shelby,* 313.
26. Ibid., 314.
27. Edwards, Letters to His Family (1865–1866).
28. Ibid.
29. Ibid.
30. Ibid.
31. O'Flaherty, *General Jo Shelby,* 323.
32. Nagle, *Missouri: A History,* 136–38.
33. As quoted in Bellows and Connelly, *God and General Longstreet,* 2.
34. Edwards, *Shelby and His Men,* 448–49.
35. Edwards, *Life, Writings, and Tributes,* 20–23.
36. Petrone, *Judgment at Gallatin,* 13.
37. Brant, *Jesse James,* 77.
38. Petrone, *Judgment at Gallatin,* 31.
39. Ibid., 35.
40. Edwards, *Life, Writings, and Tributes,* 38.

41. Ibid., 43.

42. Ibid., 26.

43. Ibid., 61.

44. Ibid., 189.

45. Edwards, *Shelby and His Men,* 393–94.

46. Bierce, "What I Saw of Shiloh," 22.

47. Wills, *Lincoln at Gettysburg,* 51.

48. Edwards, *Shelby and His Men,* 77–78.

Chapter I

1. Cincinnatus Hiner Miller (1839–1913) was a popular western poet who took the name "Joaquin" from the California bandit Joaquin Murietta. Throughout a long career as a versifier and journalist, Miller sought to celebrate the freedom and beauty of the American West on a heroic scale.

2. While in Texas, Shelby's numbers swelled to around a thousand, augmented by civilians and soldiers seeking asylum south of the Rio Grande. During the march into Mexico, the number shrank to around 500.

3. The "general" is Sterling Price (1809–1867), leader of the 1864 raid into Missouri, which ended in a debacle at the battle of Westport on Oct. 23, 1864.

4. This refers to the valiant rearguard action, fought by Shelby's Brigade on Oct. 25, 1864, that saved General Price's shattered army from annihilation.

5. This was the final attempt on October 28, 1864, by the Union Army of the Border under General Samuel R. Curtis to destroy Price's command.

6. James Gillpatrick Blunt (1826–1881) was Union commander of the District of South Kansas; his troops wreaked havoc on Price's army at the battles of Westport, Mine Creek, and Newtonia.

7. The "dethroned king" that Edwards alludes to is the Trans-Mississippi Department of the Confederacy, which, despite its capacity for continued resistance, was surrendered virtually intact to Union forces in June of 1865.

8. Edmund Kirby-Smith (1824–1893) was the civilian and military ruler of the Trans-Mississippi Department (Texas, Arkansas, Louisiana, Indian Territory)—nicknamed "Kirby Smithdom"—from January 1863 to June 1865.

9. John Bankhead Magruder (1810–1871) was a Confederate general whose impeccable manners and courtly bearing earned him the sobriquet "Prince John." Maximilian would appoint him chief of the land office of colonization in Mexico.

10. Simon Bolivar Buckner (1823–1914), a Confederate general, is perhaps best known for having surrendered Fort Donelson to Ulysses S. Grant in February of 1862. Buckner was a bitter disappointment to both Edwards and Shelby, who expected him to exercise more aggressive leadership following Kirby-Smith's resignation as commander of the Trans-Mississippi Department in June of 1865.

11. Thomas Caute Reynolds (1822–1887) was Confederate governor of Missouri following the death of Claiborne Fox Jackson in 1862. A graduate of the University of Virginia (1842), Reynolds was a skilled diplomat, fluent in three languages, French, Spanish, and German.

12. There were actually two conferences held in Marshall, Texas, on or around May 13,

1865. The first was a gathering of governors from the Trans-Mississippi states (Arkansas, Louisiana, Missouri, Texas); they strongly urged Kirby-Smith to surrender all military units to Federal authorities. A later session held nearby, consisting of a number of younger officers, including Shelby, decided that they would not be bound by such action.

13. Red Jacket (c. 1750–1830), a Seneca Indian, was an orator and a political leader.

14. Benito Juarez (1806–1872) was a full-blood Indian, a native of Oaxaca, who was elected president of the Republic of Mexico in 1861. Juarez inherited a depleted treasury that prompted Mexico's European creditors to land troops on its soil, thus opening the way for a French occupation force in 1862.

15. William Preston (1816–1887) was appointed Confederate emissary to Prince Maximilian in 1864.

16. Achille Francois Bazaine (1811–1888) was commander of the French Army in Mexico; after Maximilian, he was the most important French leader in Mexico.

Chapter II

1. Achille Murat (1801–1847), born Paris, France, was a member of the Bonaparte family. In 1823 he immigrated to America, where he settled in Florida. Described as having "a high order of mind," he wrote three books about America in the manner of de Tocqueville.

2. Edwards has this wrong. The battle of Gravelines, a conflict in the Franco-Spanish Wars, was fought on July 13, 1558. Sidney died 28 years later at the battle of Zutphen on September 22, 1586, during the Dutch struggle to gain independence from their Spanish overlords.

3. After serving in the Mexican-American War and teaching at West Point, Buckner resigned his commission in 1855 to enter the real-estate business in Chicago.

4. This refers to Reynolds and Shelby.

5. These officers commanded the various brigades, battalions, and regiments of Shelby's cavalry division, nearly all of whom Shelby (with Edwards wielding the pen) praised effusively in his wartime reports. For example, in his account of Sterling Price's Missouri raid, written December 1864, he says, "Elliott, Gordon, Slayback, Hooper, Smith, Blackwell, Williams, and a host of other officers seemed to rise higher and higher as the danger increased, and were always where the tide of battle rolled deepest and darkest." U.S. War Department, *War of the Rebellion: Official Records of Union and Confederate Armies,* 128 volumes (Washington, D.C., 1880–1901), ser. 1, vol. 41, pt. 1, p. 660.

6. This is a likely reference to Governor Thomas C. Reynolds, who accompanied Shelby into Mexico. Conversant in both French and Spanish, he served as the unit's official translator.

Chapter III

1. This is typical of Edwards's tendency to exaggerate the odds to make Shelby's men sound more besieged and beleaguered than they actually were.

2. Maurice M. Langhorne (1834–1898) commanded Company E of Col. David Shanks's 12th Missouri Cavalry, which served during the war as Shelby's escort company.

3. Pendleton Murrah (c. 1820–1865) was elected governor of Texas in 1863.

4. A picayune is a small coin, such as a nickel.

5. Trusten Polk (1811–1876) was a former governor (1856) and senator (1857–1861) from Missouri.

6. The most important of these people, if not already mentioned, will be identified further as they play more prominent roles in Edwards's narrative.

7. The issue of retribution weighed heavily on the minds of these former Confederate leaders. Abraham Lincoln had intended to treat them leniently in the wake of Appomattox, but with his death on April 15, 1865, a mood of vengeance swept through the victorious North, compelling many ex-Confederates, especially those of rank and prestige, to seek asylum in other countries.

8. Mesquites are spiny, deep-rooted trees.

9. Edwards persistently misspells this as *chapparal;* it has been corrected throughout to *chaparral* (a dense thicket of stiff, thorny shrubs).

Chapter IV

1. Known today as the Historic Menger Hotel, it was first built in 1859 by William Menger, an immigrant from Germany who arrived in San Antonio in 1847. Edwards and his cohorts called it by the nickname "Mingo's."

2. James Walker Fannin (1804–1836) was executed along with the remnants of his command by Mexican General Santa Anna on March 27, 1836, at the Goliad presidio during the Texas rebellion against Mexico. At Thermopylae in 480 B.C., a Greek army under King Leonidas made a valiant stand against a numerically superior Persian army under Xerxes.

3. *Prestamo* is a form of extortion.

4. Thomas Hindman (1828–1868) was former military commander of the Trans-Mississippi Department. His harsh enforcement of conscription and martial law resulted in his removal in 1862.

5. Semiramis was a mythical Assyrian queen, famed for her voluptuous beauty. Medea was a powerful enchantress of classical mythology.

6. A *parterre* is a garden or lawn.

7. Edwards appears to be referring to the battle of Cannae (216 B.C.), in which Carthaginians led by Hannibal demolished a Roman army by enveloping both its flanks. Capua most likely refers to the site of the defeat of the Bourbon armies of Naples by Garibaldi and Victor Emmanuel II during the struggle for Italian unification in 1860.

8. Victor Emmanuel II was one of the leaders of the Italian *risorgimento* (unification) in the 1850s and 1860s. Mario presumably refers to a popular opera star of the time.

9. This is a mix of biblical allusions. The "one ark" still floating from the Confederacy is Shelby's Brigade. When that brigade finally came to rest in Mexico ("Ararat"), Maximilian rejected its services, forcing it to disband.

10. Benjamin Winslow Dudley (1785–1870) was a practitioner and teacher of early surgical techniques.

11. Edwards has this wrong; at the time of the Confederate diaspora to Mexico, Magruder was 55 years old.

Chapter V

1. Rob Roy was a Scottish outlaw, comparable to England's Robin Hood, title character of a novel (1817) by Sir Walter Scott.

Chapter VI

1. To debouch is to march out into the open from a confined place.
2. Francis Preston Blair (1821–1875), a cousin of Shelby, was the scion of a famous political family and a staunch Unionist.
3. Col. Pierre Jean Joseph Jeanningros (1816–1902), a corpulent, bushy-faced veteran of the Crimea War and the China campaign, was commander of French troops in north Mexico.
4. *Bueana* is an expression of acceptance.
5. The *tiendas* are stores.
6. A *lusus naturae* is a natural curiosity or a freak of nature.
7. Before advancing into Mexico, Shelby and his men sank their headquarters flag into the Rio Grande in a scene that is described in the introduction. Jarrett Todd, a member of Company B, 4th Missouri Cavalry, later returned to reclaim the flag. The story goes that he kept the flag in the family until sometime before his death in 1938, when he gave it to the Oklahoma Historical Society. Regrettably, there is no proof or contemporary evidence to support Todd's story. According to historical society authorities, the silk flag shows no evidence of having been buried or submerged, leading them to discount that the flag ever belonged to Shelby's command.

Chapter VII

1. The Lipan Apaches were a branch of the once populous and widespread Plains Apaches, who after 1836 retreated from Texas into northern Mexico.
2. Desertions were a serious problem for French units fighting against the Juaristas in north Mexico. The proximity of the Rio Grande and a new life in the United States proved irresistible to many enlistees.

Chapter VIII

1. These *canaille* are the lowest class of people, riffraff.
2. Bloody ambushes such as the one at Lampasas convinced Shelby's men that the Juaristas were not to be trusted.
3. A *haciendaro* is a ranch owner.
4. A *fandango* is a dance.
5. "They will love/your spirit/and my heart."
6. *Catalan* is a fiery liquor; it comes from a French metallurgic term meaning forge or furnace.
7. A *rebosa* is a shawl.
8. The correct expression is *Morituri te salutamus:* "We who are about to die salute thee."

Chapter IX

1. Gravelotte was a battle between the French and Prussians, on August 18, 1870, during which the Third Zouaves were so badly decimated they ceased to exist as a unit. The fact that Edwards alludes to the battle in this context indicates that, while he first composed the manuscript of *Shelby's Expedition to Mexico* sometime between 1865 and 1867, he tinkered with it subsequently after returning to Missouri in 1867.

2. Old Guard was a storied unit of Napoleon's army, composed of veterans on whom he could count to give their all. The unit's last-ditch charge against British lines at Waterloo (1815) ended in failure.

3. Col. Francois Achille Dupin was also known as Charles-Louis Dupin, Jean-Charles Dupin, and Achille Dupon.

4. Warren Hastings was an English statesman and the first governor-general of India. His impeachment trial (1788–1795) on charges of corruption and misconduct inspired his famous remark.

5. *Toilers of the Sea* (1866), a novel by Victor Hugo, tells the epic story of simple fishermen struggling against nature. By extension, Edwards describes Dupin, with all his savage excesses, as an object of sheer malevolence, minus the nobility that Hugo's mariners achieve.

6. "That other Ney" refers to Michel Ney (1769–1815), who was Napoleon's battlefield commander at Waterloo. Jean-Baptiste Drouet Erlon commanded a French corps in the battle.

7. Mosby Munroe Parsons (1822–1865) was a former attorney general of Missouri and a veteran of the battles of Lexington, Wilson's Creek, and Elkhorn Tavern.

8. Aaron H. Conrow (1824–1865), a colonel in the Missouri State Guards, followed Parsons to Mexico in 1865.

Chapter X

1. William McKendree Gwin (1805–1885) was involved in a scheme to seize four northern Mexican states—Sonora, Durango, Chihuahua, Sinaloa—and colonize them with disgruntled ex-Confederates to serve as a buffer against the Yankee nation to the north.

2. John Bullock Clark (1802–1885) was one of the leaders of the Missouri secessionist movement.

3. Eugene Rouher was minister of justice under Napoleon III; Count Marie Edmé Patrice de MacMahon was a marshal of the French army.

4. Chapultepec Palace: Maximilian and Carlota made this vine-covered hilltop fortress near Mexico City their official Mexican residence and decorated it with French tapestries, chandeliers, ottoman rugs, gilded chairs and tables. Edwards spelled this *Chepultepec;* it has been corrected to *Chapultepec* throughout the text.

5. Buena Vista was a battle during the Mexican-American War, fought on February 22, 1846. A force of some 4,500 men under General Zachary Taylor was attacked by 18,000 Mexicans under General Santa Anna. Despite repeated assaults, Santa Anna failed to dislodge Taylor's troops. Though technically a draw, Santa Anna withdrew his men the following day, leaving the field to Taylor.

Chapter XI

1. David Smith Terry (1823–1889), a hot-headed California states-rights activist, killed Senator David C. Broderick (1820–1859) in a highly publicized duel on September 13, 1859.

2. Honoré-Gabriel Riqueti, comte de Mirabeau (1749–1791), was a statesman and orator of the French Revolution.

3. *Chasseurs* means light cavalry.

Chapter XII

1. *Quien sabe* means "Who knows?"

2. *Rancheros* are small ranchers.

Chapter XIII

1. *Per Dios* means "By God!"

Chapter XIV

1. "Scylla . . . Charybdis": These are a rock and a whirlpool, respectively, in the Straits of Messina, personified in Greek mythology as female monsters. This is an example of Edwards's stilted dialogue; it is hard to believe such an exchange would take place between two Missouri farm boys in the midst of a blazing firefight.

2. A *point d'appui* is a point of support, a prop, fulcrum, base.

3. Shelby's pincer movement against the Juarista besiegers at Matehuala was executed with such panache and skill that it convinced Marshal Bazaine that "he would have no Confederate units in the Imperial Army because of the excuse it would give for United States intervention" (O'Flaherty, *General Jo Shelby*, 283). Consistently throughout the march, Shelby's command exhibited remarkable discipline and flair in a variety of difficult situations. The fight at Matehuala marked the last time the brigade went into battle as a unit.

Chapter XV

1. A *chassepot* is a type of breech-loading rifle, accurate up to 1,600 yards.

2. Flodden, a battle fought on September 9, 1513, ended in a resounding English victory over a Scottish army led by James IV, who was slain. Louis XII and his queen, Anne of Brittany, appealed to James for help in their war against England. Anne sent James a turquoise ring to wear as her champion.

3. The *lazzaroni* are the outcast, the despised.

4. Gen. Felix Charles Douay (1818–1879), an ambitious Imperialist general and a division commander, sought to ingratiate himself with Maximilian by criticizing his superior officers, especially Marshal Bazaine.

5. *Vomito* is yellow fever, a terrible scourge, rampant in the lowlands around Vera Cruz,

that took a staggering toll of French military personnel. The first sign was constipation, followed by a headache, then neck cramps that spread through the body. After that came vomiting, with death usually following within six to twelve hours.

6. An Augustan age refers to the Golden Age of Roman literature during the reign of Augustus Caesar (27 B.C. to A.D. 14).

Chapter XVI

1. Commodore Matthew Fontaine Maury (1806–1873), Virginia oceanographer and naval astronomer, traveled to Europe during the war to help outfit ships and blockade runners for the Confederacy. The South's most distinguished scientist, he later became a trusted counselor to Maximilian and the Imperial commissioner of immigration.

2. A basilisk is a fabulous legendary serpent, lizard, or dragon whose breath, or even look, is fatal.

3. A *real* is a small coin, such as a dime.

Chapter XVII

1. A *baton* is a ceremonial stick indicative of high rank. Bazaine was living proof of Napoleon Bonaparte's belief that even a lowly private could rise through the ranks to the exalted title of marshal.

2. Edouard Curieres Henri Pierre Jean-Abdon, Count Francois de Castelnau, sometimes spelled "Castelneau" by Edwards, Napoleon III's personal aide-de-camp, was sent to Mexico to work out plans for the withdrawal of French troops and to persuade Maximilian to abdicate.

3. Phrenology is the study of the contours of the skull as indicative of the mental faculties.

4. William Henry Seward (1801–1872) was secretary of state under Abraham Lincoln. In late 1861 Charles Wilkes, a U.S. Navy captain, boarded the British ship *Trent* and removed two Confederate agents, James Mason and John Slidell, and carried them back to Boston. The British government lodged a strenuous protest. President Lincoln feared the incident might prompt Britain to declare war on the Union.

5. To get some idea of how the deck was stacked against Mexico in this matter of payment, consider that the claims against her included England's $69,311,657, Spain's $9,461,986, and France's $2,860,762 (excluding the so-called Jecker loan). Against all these claims, greatly inflated as they were, the annual income of the Mexican government totaled only 12,000,000 pesos—hardly enough to pay the interest, let alone reduce the principal.

Chapter XVIII

1. Pueblo, the spelling that Edwards used, has been corrected in the text to Puebla, a town southeast of the City of Mexico.

2. A soldier writing home to his mother described Gen. Elie Frédéric Forey (1804–1872) as he entered the capital: "What a man, what a peacock! He strutted around

for at least six hours. That's perfectly all right for a pretty gurl [*sic*] to do . . . but it is grotesquely ridiculous to see a fat old general of 63 doing the same thing. The entry into Mexico City looked like the promenade of the Boeuf Gras during carnival time" (as quoted in Burchell, *Imperial Masquerade,* 297).

3. Baron Alfons de Pont, an Austrian diplomat, was a longtime confidant and aide to Maximilian.

Chapter XIX

1. Viscount Palmerston (1784–1865). British foreign secretary and prime minister who helped maintain British neutrality during the American Civil War.

2. The Sandwich Islands are today the Hawaiian Islands.

Chapter XX

1. What actually happened was quite different from what Edwards so glowingly describes. Maximilian was interested in extending his empire to Central America, and in the fall of 1865 he sent Carlota on a two-week tour of the Yucatan Peninsula. She returned bitterly disillusioned, convinced that "the masses here are outrageously dull and ignorant" (as quoted in O'Connor, *The Cactus Throne,* 198–99) and that Mexico in its present state was ungovernable.

2. Carl Schurz (1829–1906) was a German-born soldier, journalist, senator, diplomat, and secretary of the interior. As senator from Missouri in the late 1860s, he helped defeat President Ulysses S. Grant's plan to annex Santo Domingo (Dominican Republic)—additional evidence that Edwards most likely revised the manuscript of *Shelby's Expedition to Mexico* upon his return to Missouri.

3. *Quien vive* means "Who goes there?"

4. Porfirio—not Porfino—Diaz (1830–1915), a mestizo general from Oaxaca, helped restore Juarez to the presidency. Later, he served as president of Mexico for seven terms (1884–1910); his dictatorial rule precipitated the Mexican Revolution.

5. *Ladrones* are thieves, robbers.

6. Langlais was a French financial adviser sent to Maximilian by Napoleon III to untangle the chaotic economy of the new monarchy.

7. Edwards most likely means *paseo*—walk, stroll, drive.

8. The *demi-monde* is the world of social outcasts—pimps, whores, gamblers, and thieves.

9. Isham Green Harris (1818–1897) was a former governor of Tennessee.

10. William Gannaway Brownlow (1805–1877), minister, newspaper editor, and staunch Unionist, was a Radical Republican candidate for governor of Tennessee in 1865.

11. Oliver Cromwell (1599–1658) was Lord Protector of England, Scotland, and Ireland; he was also known as "Ironside," for his fervent Protestant beliefs.

12. John Perkins Jr. (1819–1885) was a former Confederate congressman from Louisiana.

13. *Vertu* is a variation of *virtu,* a love of curios and *objets d'art.*

14. The *Shenandoah,* a Confederate cruiser purchased in England in September 1864, had a spectacular career, capturing or destroying 36 vessels valued at $1,400,000 in less than a year.

15. Again, Edwards succumbs to his insatiable urge to romanticize female figures. What actually happened was that on the trip from Mexico City to Veracruz, Carlota displayed disturbing signs of the erratic behavior that would eventually lead to a complete mental breakdown. When her carriage became mired in the road, she raged that "they" were plotting against her and that she was being detained so that the steamer for Europe would sail without her. Later, when a guerrilla band descended on the party, cutting off the caravan, the empress's escort stood by without firing a shot while the attackers drove off the horses and mules.

16. This refers to the famous British charge of 673 light cavalrymen at Balaclava during the Crimea War (1854) against a rank of Russian cannon lodged at the head of a narrow valley. The charge, which ended in pointless slaughter, was led by General Lord Cardigan.

17. *Mescal* is a potent liquor brewed from the maguey plant.

18. A *meson* is an inn, tavern, hostelry.

Chapter XXI

1. A gourmand delights in luxurious food.

2. Captain John Pelham (1838–1863) was an artillerist with the Army of Northern Virginia. Blond, blue eyed, and handsome—a beau ideal of the Confederacy—he was also a first-rate innovator and tactician.

3. Princess Iturbide was a member of an aristocratic Mexican family that attempted to establish an empire forty years before Maximilian. Considering the fact that after eight years of marriage Carlota and Maximilian were childless, it was suggested that the couple adopt as crown-prince designate one of the grandsons of former emperor Agustin de Iturbide.

4. *Muy bonita Americano* means "most beautiful American."

5. Gen. Tomas Mejia, the ablest and most dedicated of all the Mexican imperialist generals, was executed alongside Maximilian on June 19, 1867.

6. Mariano Escobedo was a Juarista general.

7. Baron Enrique Sauvage was granted the tract on condition that he would settle 300 families within one year's time.

8. Tuspan, the spelling that Edwards used, has been regularized in the text to Tuxpan, a town and river in eastern Mexico.

9. No information about Major McMurty, this seemingly important yet shadowy figure, seems to have survived. See O'Flaherty, *General Jo Shelby,* 300.

10. The Tolucas were indigenous people displaced by Confederate colonists.

11. A French *sabretache* is a small dress sword.

12. Henry Watkins Allen (1820–1866), under whom Edwards served as assistant editor, died in Mexico City on April 22, 1866.

13. Carlota was the stricken woman; Miramar was the beautiful castle she and Maximilian shared outside Trieste.

14. Col. Robert C. Wood served during the Civil War as an aide-de-camp to Sterling Price and, later, as commander of the 14th Missouri Cavalry Battalion.

Chapter XXII

1. Jubal Anderson Early (1816–1894), Confederate general in the Army of Northern Virginia, fled to Cuba after the war, then Mexico, then Canada, where he remained until 1869. Tacitus (A.D. c. 55–c. 118) was a controversial and outspoken Roman historian. Early stirred his own controversy in several books written after the war, in which he emerged as perhaps the most vocal of the Lost Cause apologists.

2. Saul was the first King of Israel, eleventh century B.C.

3. Miguel Miramon, conservative politician and general, was supported by the privileged classes, the landowners, the Catholic hierarchy, and most of the mestizos. Gen. Leonardo Marquez, an unpopular Imperialist general, virtually kidnapped men into his ranks and imposed heavy taxes on residents for their protection.

4. *Qui vive* means alert.

Chapter XXIII

1. History records something quite different from what Edwards indicates here. "With an escort of French and Mexican imperial troops they clip-clopped through silent streets and plazas. Not a Veracruzano could be glimpsed; the whole population stayed indoors, as though mourning its lost freedoms. The only welcoming sound came from the *zopilotes,* the huge black vultures waddling officiously everywhere in their function as the Veracruz Sanitation Department" (O'Connor, *The Cactus Throne,* 119).

2. This was evidently a rumor, though it was treated initially by Edwards, perhaps for dramatic effect, as fact. Carlota finally succumbed on January 16, 1927, in her native Belgium, at the age of 86.

3. This is Edwards at his stereotypical worst, ignoring the political and propaganda reasons underlying Juarez's decision to execute Maximilian. The death by firing squad of the European pretender sent a clear signal to the world of the fate awaiting any future usurpers of Mexican power.

BIBLIOGRAPHY

Primary

Blasio, Jose Luis. *Maximilian, Emperor of Mexico: Memoirs of His Private Secretary.* Trans. and ed. Robert Hammond Murray. New Haven: Yale University Press, 1934.

Britton, Wiley. *Memoirs of the Rebellion on the Border, 1863.* Lincoln: University of Nebraska Press, 1993.

Caskie, Jacquelin Ambler. *Life and Letters of Matthew Fontaine Maury.* Richmond, 1928.

Corti, Egnon Caesar, Count. *Maximilian and Charlotte of Mexico.* 2 vols. Trans. Catherine Alison Phillips. New York: Alfred A. Knopf, 1928.

DeForest, John W. *A Volunteer's Adventures.* Hamden, Conn.: Archon Books, 1970.

Dorsey, Sarah Anne. *Recollections of Henry Watkins Allen.* New York, 1866.

Edwards, John N. *Life, Writings, and Tributes.* Kansas City: Jennie Edwards, 1889.

———. *Shelby's Expedition to Mexico.* In *Life, Writings, and Tributes,* by John N. Edwards. Kansas City: Jennie Edwards, 1889.

———. *Noted Guerrillas; or the Warfare of the Border.* Dayton, Ohio: Press of the Morningside Bookshop, 1976.

———. *Shelby and His Men; or the War in the West.* Waverly, Mo.: General Joseph Shelby Memorial Fund, 1993.

McCorkle, John. *Three Years with Quantrill.* Norman: University of Oklahoma Press, 1992.

Pitner, Ernest. *Maximilian's Lieutenant: A Personal History of the Mexican Campaign, 1864–1867.* Trans. and ed. Gordon Etherington-Smith. Albuquerque: University of New Mexico Press, 1993.

Ruiz, Ramon Eduardo, ed. *An American in Maximilian's Mexico, 1865–1866: The Diaries of William Marshall Anderson.* San Marino, Calif.: Huntington Library, 1959.

Russel, Tom J. "Adventures of a Cordova Colonist," Parts I and II. *Southern Magazine* 11 (July, August 1872), 90–102, 155–66.

Salm-Salm, Agnes. *Ten Years of My Life.* London, 1876.

Salm-Salm, Felix. *My Diary in Mexico in 1867, Including the Last Days of the Emperor Maximilian; with Leaves from the Diary of the Princess Salm-Salm.* London, 1868.

Terrell, Alexander Watkins. *From Texas to Mexico and the Court of Maximilian in 1865.* Dallas: Texas Book Club, 1933.

Secondary

Bellows, Barbara L., and Thomas L. Connelly. *God and General Longstreet: The Lost Cause and the Southern Mind.* Baton Rouge: Louisiana State University Press, 1982.

Bierce, Ambrose. "What I Saw of Shiloh." In *Ambrose Bierce's Civil War,* ed. William McCann. New York: Wing Books, 1996.

Brant, Marley. *Jesse James: The Man and the Myth*. New York: Berkley Books, 1996.

Breihan, Carl W. *Ride the Razor's Edge: The Younger Brothers Story*. Gretna, La.: Pelican Publishing Company, 1992.

Brooksher, William R., and David K. Snider. *Glory at a Gallop: Tales of the Confederate Cavalry*. Washington, D.C.: Brassey's, 1993.

Brownlee, Richard S. *Gray Ghosts of the Confederacy: Guerrilla Warfare in the West, 1861–1865*. Baton Rouge: Louisiana State University Press, 1958.

Burchell, S. C. *Imperial Masquerade: The Paris of Napoleon III*. New York: Atheneum, 1971.

Castel, Albert. *General Sterling Price and the Civil War in the West*. Baton Rouge: Louisiana State University Press, 1968.

Castel, Albert, and Thomas Goodrich. *Bloody Bill Anderson: The Short, Savage Life of a Civil War Guerrilla*. Mechanicsburg, Penn.: Stackpole Books, 1998.

Conard, Howard L., ed. *Encyclopedia of the History of Missouri*. St. Louis: Southern History Co., 1901.

Creel, George. *A Rebel at Large: Recollections of Fifty Crowded Years*. New York: G. P. Putnam, 1947.

Croy, Homer. *Cole Younger: Last of the Great Outlaws*. Lincoln: University of Nebraska Press, 1999.

Davis, Burke. *The Long Surrender*. New York: Vintage Books, 1989.

Davis, Edwin Adams. *Fallen Guidon: The Saga of Confederate General Jo Shelby's March to Mexico*. College Station: Texas A&M University Press, 1995.

Fellman, Michael. *Inside War: The Guerrilla Conflict in Missouri during the American Civil War*. Oxford and New York: Oxford University Press, 1989.

Goodrich, Thomas. *Bloody Dawn: The Story of the Lawrence Massacre*. Kent, Ohio: Kent State University Press, 1991.

———. *Black Flag: Guerrilla Warfare on the Western Border, 1861–1865*. Bloomington: Indiana University Press, 1995.

Hanna, Alfred J., and Kathryn A. Hanna. *Napoleon III and Mexico*. Chapel Hill: University of North Carolina Press, 1971.

Harter, Eugene C. *The Lost Colony of the Confederacy*. Jackson: University Press of Mississippi, 1985.

Haslip, Joan. *The Crown of Mexico*. New York: Holt, Rinehart and Winston, 1971.

Horan, James D. *Confederate Agent: A Discovery in History*. New York: Crown Publishers, 1954.

Hynes, Samuel. *The Soldier's Tale: Bearing Witness to Modern War*. New York: Penguin Books, 1997.

Josephy, Alvin M., Jr. *The Civil War in the American West*. New York: Alfred A. Knopf, 1991.

Kerby, Robert L. *Kirby Smith's Confederacy: The Trans-Mississippi South, 1863–1865*. Tuscaloosa: University of Alabama Press, 1972.

Leslie, Edward E. *The Devil Knows How to Ride: The True Story of William Clarke Quantrill and His Confederate Raiders*. New York: Da Capo Press, 1998.

May, Robert E. *The Southern Dream of a Caribbean Empire, 1854–1861*. Baton Rouge: Louisiana State University Press, 1973.

Monaghan, Jay. *Civil War on the Western Border, 1854–1865*. New York: Little Brown and Company, 1955.

Monnett, Howard N. *Action before Westport: 1864.* Kansas City: Lowell Press, 1964.

Nagle, Paul C. *Missouri: A History.* New York: W. W. Norton, 1977.

Niles, Blair. *Passengers to Mexico: The Last Invasion of the Americas.* New York: Farrar & Rinehart, 1943.

Oates, Stephen B. *Confederate Cavalry West of the River.* Austin: University of Texas Press, 1961.

O'Connor, Richard. *The Cactus Throne: The Tragedy of Maximilian and Carlota.* New York: Putnam, 1971.

O'Flaherty, Daniel. *General Jo Shelby: Undefeated Rebel.* Chapel Hill: University of North Carolina Press, 2000.

Parks, Joseph H. *General Edmund Kirby Smith C.S.A.* Baton Rouge: Louisiana State University Press, 1992.

Petrone, Gerard S. *Judgment at Gallatin: The Trial of Frank James.* Lubbock: Texas Tech University Press, 1998.

Porch, Douglas. *The French Foreign Legion: A Complete History of the Legendary Fighting Force.* New York: HarperCollins Publishers, 1991.

Rea, Ralph. *Sterling Price: The Lee of the West.* Little Rock: Pioneer Press, 1959.

Ridley, Jasper. *Maximilian and Juarez.* New York: Ticknor and Fields, 1992.

Rolle, Andrew F. *The Lost Cause: The Confederate Exodus to Mexico.* Norman: University of Oklahoma Press, 1965.

Ryan, James W. *Camerone: The French Foreign Legion's Greatest Battle.* Westport, Conn.: Praeger, 1996.

Schultz, Duane. *Quantrill's War: The Life and Times of William Clarke Quantrill, 1837–1865.* New York: St. Martin's Press, 1996.

Scott, Mark E. *The Fifth Season: General Jo Shelby and the Great Raid of 1863.* Independence, Mo.: Two Trails Publishing, 2001.

Settle, William A., Jr. *Jesse James Was His Name; or, Fact and Fiction Concerning the Careers of the Notorious James Brothers of Missouri.* Columbia: University of Missouri Press, 1966.

Shoemaker, Floyd, ed. *Missouri Day by Day.* 2 vols. Columbia, Mo.: State Historical Society of Missouri, 1942.

Tolstoy, Leo. *Sebastopol Sketches.* Trans. David McDuff. New York: Penguin Books, 1986.

Wellman, Paul I. *Angel with Spurs.* New York: J. B. Lippincott Co., 1942.

Wills, Garry. *Lincoln at Gettysburg: The Words That Remade America.* New York: Simon & Schuster, 1992.

Wilson, Edmund. *Patriotic Gore: Studies in the Literature of the American Civil War.* New York: Oxford University Press, 1966.

Wilson-Bareau, Juliet. *Manet: The Execution of Maximilian: Paintings, Politics, and Censorship.* London: National Gallery Publications, 1992.

Newspapers, Periodicals, Booklets

Bird, Roy. "Jo Shelby and His Shadow." *America's Civil War,* March 1995.

Ganther, Ken. "Eagle Pass and the Graveyard of the Confederacy Incident." Manuscript.

Hanna, Alfred J. "A Confederate Newspaper in Mexico." *Journal of Southern History* 12 (February 1946).

Hanna, George D. "Confederate Migrations to Mexico." *Hispanic American Historical Review* 17 (November 1937): 458–86.

Joseph, Robert. "Tramp General." *Old West* (winter 1966).

Kinsall, Al. *Graveyard of the Confederacy.* Eagle Pass, Tex.: Fort Duncan Restoration Association, 1996.

————."Shelby's Iron Brigade Flag May Still Be Around." *Eagle Pass (Texas) News Guide,* August 1, 1996.

Obituary for Jarrett Todd. *Magnum (Oklahoma) Daily Star,* November 21, 1937.

Pingenot, Ben E. "General Shelby's Dream." *Texas Parade,* February 1963.

Rice, Herbert F. "The Editor, the Governor, and the Outlaw." *Kansas City Times,* March 13, 1962.

Worrell, Dorothy Ostrom. "Last Confederate Flag Lowered in Rio Grande Here; Gen. Jo Shelby Buried Battle Standard on July 4, 1865." *Eagle Pass (Texas) News Guide,* June 30, 1949.

Manuscript Materials

Edwards, John N. Letters to His Family (1865–1866). Western Historical Manuscript Collection, 23 Ellis Library, University of Missouri-Columbia.

————. Letters to Frank James (1882–1885). Western Historical Manuscript Collection, 23 Ellis Library, University of Missouri-Columbia.

Lavery, Ray. "John N. Edwards: Author, Editor, Soldier." Manuscript in the William A. Settle Jr. Papers, Western Historical Manuscript Collection, 23 Ellis Library, University of Missouri-Columbia.

Saults, Dan. "Let Us Discuss a Man." A talk on John Edwards, delivered before the Kingdom of Callaway Historical Society, Fulton, Missouri, February 19, 1962. Western Historical Manuscript Collection, 23 Ellis Library, University of Missouri-Columbia.

Westlake, Thomas. 1865 Confederate Trooper Thomas Westlake's Journal. Western Historical Manuscript Collection, 23 Ellis Library University of Missouri-Columbia.

INDEX

Note: Where spelling varies between the introduction and body of the text, the spelling in the text is
used. Page numbers in the form 202n. 1.3 indicate that the reference is on page 202 and note 3 of
chapter 1.

bankruptcy of Mexico, 147, 154, 178
Banks, Nathaniel, xvii–xviii
Bansen (friend of Maximilian), 193
Barbusse, Henri, xxxiv
Basch, Samuel, 190, 197
basilisk, 119, 208n. 16.2
baton, 107, 208n. 17.1
battles. *See specific place name*
Bazaine, Achille Francois: advice to
  Maximilian, 178; approach to Church
  party, 143; authority of, 126; black
  flag order and, 165–66, 193; character
  of, 122; as commander of French
  army in Mexico, 203n. 1.16; death of
  troops of in marshes, 106; Douay's
  criticism of, 207n. 15.4; Dupin and,
  62; evacuation orders and, 155–56;
  final conference with Maximilian,
  179; generosity toward Expedition,
  138–39; gift of arms to Shelby,
  170–71; Allen and, 173; Jeanningros
  on, 60; Maximilian and, 70; meeting
  of Shelby and Maximilian and,
  133–35; meeting with General
  Preston, 8; order for Shelby's progress
  to Mexico City, xxiv, 78, 82, 107,
  115; reaction to financial problems,
  147; relationship with Magruder, 115;
  relationship with Maximilian, 72,
  132–33; rise to power, 208n. 17.1;
  rumor of visitor from Napoleon, 154;
  Salm Salm and, 148; use of firing
  squad, 132; work of in 1865, 145
Bee, Hamilton P., 18, 30, 142
Belgian troops, 132, 134
belles-lettres tradition of literature,
  xxxiv–xxxv
Berry, Dick, 31, 35–39, 76–77, 87–90
Berry, Ike: attack on Parras road and,
  76–77; branded horse incident and,
  35–39; capture of near Dolores
  Hidalgo, 101–2; at Encarnacion
  hacienda, 87–90; at Thrailkill-West
  duel, 117–20
betrayal, 183, 184–86, 194
"better man" concept, xxvii
Bierce, Ambrose, xxxiii–xxxiv

Biesca, Andres: branded horse incident
  and, 38–39; interview with Shelby,
  32–34; offer to Shelby, xx–xxi; purchase of artillery, xxiii, 34–35, 39–40,
  50
Bingham, George Caleb, xxxiv
Bird, Roy, xx
black flag order, 165, 193
Blackwell, Yandell: ceremony with
  Confederate flag, xxii–xxiii; defense of
  stores at Tyler, Texas, 14–15;
  Encarnacion and, 83–90; in Price's
  raid on Missouri, 203n. 2.5; at war
  council, 10; watch on road to Mexico
  City, 82–85
Blair, Francis Preston, xv, xix, 32, 205n.
  6.2
blankets of Dolores Hidalgo, 99
Blasio, Jose, 185, 190
Blunt, James Gillpatrick, 2, 202n. 1.5
Borgo, Henry B. del, 194
Boswell, Thomas, 54–55, 87–90, 157–64
Boucher, Cam., 27–28
Bragg, Braxton, 73
brands, 35
Bravo, Leonardo, 82
Bravo, Nicholas, 82
Brazos march, 7–8
Broadwell, William M., 18
Broderick, David C., 77–78, 207n. 11.1
Brown, B. Gratz, xv
Brownlow, William Gannaway, 152,
  209n. 20.10
Buckner, Simon Bolivar: career of, 203n.
  2.3; under Kirby Smith, 3; at Marshall
  conference, 4–5; physical features of,
  7–8; surrender of, 8–9, 202n. 1.10
bueana, 34, 205n. 6.4
Buena Vista battle field camp, 73–74,
  206n. 10.5
burial instructions, 195, 197
Burwell, W. M., 166–67

Camden battle, xviii
canaille, 50, 205n. 8.1
Cannae battle (216 B.C.), 22, 204n. 4.7
Cape Girardeau raid, xvii

71–73; lieutenant of Foreign Legion and, 60–61; on Maximilian, 59–60; military command of, xxiv; reaction to artillery sale, 50, 58; reception of Shelby, 59–60; succor to Mejia at Matamoras and, 169; view of future, 108; warning to Americans going to Camargo, 65

Jecker bank bonds, 128

Jeffries, Albert, 14–15

Jenero (Captain of Imperial army), 186

Jenkins' Ferry battle, xviii

Johnson, Joe, xix, 87–90

Johnson (Colonel of federal troops), 28–29, 68

Johnston, Albert Sidney, 152

Jones, Charley, 76–77

Jones, Sandy, 157, 161–64

Joseph II, Emperor of Austria, 124

Juarez, Benito: annulment of Paris treaty, 127–28; Bazaine and, 122–23; black flag order and, 165, 193; confiscation of church lands near Cordova, 140; control exerted by in 1965, 145–46; Porfirio Diaz's help, 209n. 20.4; execution of Maximilian, 195, 197–98, 211n. 23.3; exile of, xxi; as leader of Liberals, 127; letter from Maximilian, 131; Maximilian's approach to, 108; as President of Republic of Mexico, 203n. 1.14; recruiting tactics of, 173–74; takeover of French held territory, 179; treaty with European troops, 129; United States support of, xix, 32

Juaristas, 31–32, 42–45, 65–66, 123, 205n. 8.2. *See also* Escobedo, General Mariano; guerillas; Juarez, Benito; Liberal party

Jurado, Ignacio, 194–95

Kansas City Times: Edwards as editor of, xxix; Edward's freedom at, xxx–xxxi; launching of, xxvii; "Poor Carlota" published in, xxv; *Shelby's Expedition to Mexico* publication and, xxxv

Karnak (Lieutenant under Maximilian), 134–35

Kerby, Robert L., xx, xxii

Kirby-Smith, Edmund. *See* Smith, Edmund Kirby

Kirby Smith's Confederacy (Kerby), xx

Kirtley, James B.: branded horse incident and, 35–39; character of, 158; defense of stores in Tyler, Texas, 14–15; at Encarnacion *hacienda,* 87–90; federal troops and, 28; Parras road duty, 75–77; rescue of Depreuil and, 157–64; rescue of wounded at Sumapetla, 109–12; Salinas River crossing, 45–46; scout patrol at Matehuala, 91

Kossuth (leader of Republic of Hungary), 124

Kritzer, John: branded horse incident and, 35–39; defense of stores in Waxahatchie, Texas, 15; horse thieves and, 19–20; Parras road attack and, 76–77

Kritzer, Martin: branded horse incident and, 35–39; defense of stores in Waxahatchie, Texas, 15; horse thieves and, 18–20; Parras road attack and, 76–77

ludrones, 146, 209n. 20.5

Lampasas, Mexico, 53–57, 205n. 8.2

Landberg (Austrian General), 166–67

Langdon, Patrick, 64–67

Langhorne, Maurice M.: branded horse incident and, 35–39; command of, 203n. 3.2; crossing of Rio Grande, 30; defense of stores in Waxahatchie, Texas, 15; on French reception of Shelby's Expedition, 115; horse thieves and, 19–20; Matehuala scout patrol, 97; Parras road attack and, 76–77; Salinas River crossing, 45–46; at war council, 10

Langlais, M., 143, 147, 209n. 20.6

Lanier, Sidney, xxxiv

Largo (Maximilian's staff member), 195, 197

Carlota's death and, 195; command of field troops in Queretaro, 180–84; Confederate emissary to, 203n. 1.15; conferences at Orizava, 178–79; confirmation of decree of confiscation, 140; dream of, 112; John Edwards's devotion to, xxv; evacuation of French and, 165; execution of, 136, 166, 182, 198–99, 210n. 21.5, 211n. 23.3; flight to Cuernavaca, 166, 178; *hacienda* of Santa Anna and, 151; imprisonment of, 190–98; Iron Brigade's decision to support, 33–34; Jeanningros on, 59–60; June 18th interview with Escobedo, 197; lack of heir, 210n. 21.3; letter to Juarez, 131; meeting with Shelby, 133–35; Napoleon's order for abdication to, 208n. 17.2; offer of the crown, 130–31; palace of, 206n. 10.4; plans for extension of empire, 209n. 20.1; plea for help from Americans, 175–76; preparation for execution, 196–98; Preston's trip to negotiate with, 8, 71; Queretaro takeover and, 185–90; reception in Vera Cruz, 132, 193; refusal of Dupin, 62; refusal of Gwin's patent, 70; refusal of Shelby's offer, xxiv, 134–36, 204n. 4.9; relationship with Bazaine, 71, 132–33; religious beliefs of, 143; retrenchment of, 154; return to Mexico City, 179; rule of, xxi, 131–32, 145; threats of excommunication against, 143, 147; trial of, 193–95

Maximilian I, Emperor of Austria, 123

McCausland, John, 142

McClurg, Joseph, xxix

McDougall, John, 35–39, 45–46, 76–77, 87–90

McKee, William, 73

McKinney, Rainy, 59

McMahon, Marshal, 71, 124–25

McMurty (Major in American Expedition), 142, 170, 210n. 21.9

McNeil, John, xvii

Meadow, James, 13–14, 75–77

Medea, 22, 204n. 4.5

Medomark (Major of Foreign Legation), 149–51

Mejia, Tomas: conviction of, 194–95; escape from Matamoras, 168–69; escape plan and, 194; execution of, 198–200, 210n. 21.5; news of Carlota's death and, 195; Queretaro takeover and, 187; at takeover of Queretaro, 188–90

Mendez, Juan N.: black flag order and, 165, 166; death of, 189; at Queretaro, 183, 187; relief at silver mine from, 175; retreat of, 180

mescal, 159, 210n. 20.17

Mesillon (Captain under Douay), 160–64

meson, 159, 210n. 20.18

mesquite, 204n. 3.8

Mexia, José Antonia, 82

Mexican infiltration, 29–30

Mexican Revolution, 82, 209n. 20.4

Mexican soldiers, 132, 177

Mexican Times, xxv, 173

Mexican warriors. *See* guerillas; Juaristas

Mexico: bankruptcy of, 147, 154, 178; conditions in 1865, 142–43; crossing plains of, xxiii; debts of, 208n. 17.5; foreign take over of, 127–29; government of, 126–27, 130, 132; view of American troops, xix–xx. *See also* Juarez, Benito; Maximilian, Emperor of Mexico; *specific town or event*

Mexico City: disbanding in, xxiv–xxv, 137–38, 140, 141; under Maximilian, xxv; offer to emperor in, xxiv; surrender of, 130, 181

Miller, Cincinnatus Hiner "Joaquin," 1, 202n. 1.1

Mina, Xavier, 82

Mine Creek battle, xviii, 2, 202n. 1.6

Mingo (hotel manager), 21

Mingo's Hotel, 21, 22–23, 204n. 4.1

Mirabeau, Honoré Gabriel Riqueti, comte de, 207n. 11.2

35–39; Encarnacion and, 83–90; mule thieves and, 28; rescue of Depreuil and, 161–64; Salinas River crossing, 45–46

Wyatt, Conquest, xiii

Yablonski (adjutant to Lopez), 185

Yell, Archibald, 73

yellow fever: Carlota's ministry, 145; death of Henry Watkins Allen and, 173; French soldiers and, 106; Mexican term for, 207n. 15.5; at Vera Cruz, 145, 155, 173

Yerby, Thomas J., xiii

Yowell (American soldier), 35–39

Yucatan Peninsula tour, 145

Zerman, Thomas, 125

zopilotes, 211n. 23.1

Zouaves: Americans as, 141–42; battles of, 58, 104; battle with Negrete, 146; Kirtley as, 157; outposts of, 32; provisions of, 147; at Puebla, 130; succor to Mejia at Matamoras and, 169; yellow fever and, 106. *See also* French troops